Conservation in Time of War

Praise for *Conservation in Time of War*

Conservation in Time of War is a truly remarkable book about a remarkable and courageous woman. LoraKim writes of her passion for conservation and the repeated dangers into which this led her. She shares how she overcame depression and now battles with renewed commitment to saving wildlife. It is a story of love (for parrots), determination and the indomitable human spirit. All who read it will surely be inspired to make their own contributions to help our endangered wildlife. LoraKim I salute you, and I thank you. For I too love parrots.

– Jane Goodall PhD, DBE,
Founder of the Jane Goodall Institute
and UN Messenger of Peace.

Conservation in Time of War

A transformational journey through beauty and tragedy

LoraKim Joyner

Published by One Earth Conservation in the United States
Hollis Hills, NY
www.oneearthconservation.org

ISBN: 978-0-992070-0-0
Library of Congress Control Number: 2017911771
First Edition First Printing

"Conservation in Time of War" is a conversation and a community project. Accordingly we invite your comments, questions, suggestions, and edits for future publications and for the work of One Earth Conservation (info@oneearthconservation.org). All proceeds from this book go to the 501 (c)(3) nonprofit organization, One Earth Conservation, which dedicates these funds to the people and parrots of Latin America.

Author's Note to the Reader and Characters

I wrote this book as a witness to the lives of parrots and people in Central America, using my journey as a means to show how wondrous the conservationists, people, and parrots of this region are, and also to depict the challenges they face. My goal was to portray people in a way that reflected my personal experiences and thoughts of the time. I was a white suburban gal from North America fumbling through life, and in these early years I was not the most kind and aware that I could have been towards others, or myself. For this reason, sharing this memoir lays open my vulnerability, and I hope the readers will forgive me my youth and inexperience, and theirs as well in the process. The conversations in the book all come from my recollections, and they do not represent word-for-word transcripts. Rather, I have retold them in a way that describes the events, feelings, and meanings of each encounter, striving to keep the essence of the dialogue as accurate as possible. In nearly all instances, especially before 2010, I have changed the names of the people so as to respect their privacy and minimize any harm or discomfort. For the same reason I have changed the names of most of the identifying landmarks. As I wrote of others, I held each individual in my heart with the deepest regard, gratitude, and compassion, and I hope that comes through in the written word. May those I wrote about know how beautiful they are, and how much I wish the best for them. Without them, I would not be able to care for the parrots and people of this region today. Thank you.

To the parrots and people of Latin America,
who continue to rend and mend me

CONTENTS

Region where majority of memoir takes place

Other locations in the memoir where I have worked: North America (Alaska, California, North Carolina, Texas, Florida, New York), Philippines, Puerto Rico, Dominican Republic, Mexico, Belize, Guatemala, Honduras, Guatemala, Nicaragua, Costa Rica, Panama, Guyana, Paraguay

They who bind to themselves a joy
Do the winged life destroy
But they who kiss the joy as it flies
Live in eternities sunrise
  --William Blake (Adapted)

PROLOGUE
COVER ME, I'M GOING IN
South Coast Guatemala, early 1993

"Cover me, I'm going in!" I spanglished to my armed guard Ramon, both of us belly down in the dirt and ash from the recently harvested sugar cane. He nodded, smiled at my *machisma,* and drew his gun. Ramon was head of security for the *finca*-- (In Guatemala's southeast coast, *finca* is a farm, ranch or property that varies in terms of size and use, typically for agriculture and livestock)-- where one of the first parrot conservation projects in Central America was taking root. On a lark, he had decided to come with me and Eric, a visiting college student assigned to me for the evening to learn how to do conservation in Latin America. Ramon was curious about why all the *gringos* were on his *finca.* That night we were counting yellow-naped amazon parrots. A slight breeze softened the day's heat, and the sun bent in the hazy, smoke-filled horizon of the dry season. The light was perfect for reflecting the parrot's emerald-green feathers. On the rise we could see the fields, forest, and volcanoes that surrounded us. As we began the count, Ramon rationalized his time away from other duties by explaining that our hiding place on the edge of the *finca* near the forest wasn't a safe place to count birds because of guerilla and military violence in the area.

Belly down is not the way to conduct parrot counts, but a truckload of armed men had driven into the field. We were desperately short of cover because the cane had been burned, cut, and hauled away, leaving only black ash between us and possible danger. We edged backwards into the sparse grass along a creek that doubled as an irrigation ditch. We weren't spotted only because the invaders were more intent on disappearing into the forest. We wondered out loud what they were doing. Were they guerillas training? A patrol? A paramilitary or private assassin squad searching for us? Did they have hostages and bring them here to murder them? Were they hunters or poachers stealing wildlife from the *finca's* forest? Was the answer a combination of all those crimes? Whatever they were there for, they had interrupted our parrot count, and instead we were scanning the area for assailants. We settled into a hyper-vigilant bimodal survey – eyes up, eyes down, head up, head down.

A man with a rifle climbed a tree, making us even more visible, and we knew they were hunters. There was no way I was going to allow that on my watch. I had to get closer. My goal wasn't to confront them but to count the guns and men, and note the make of the truck and the license plate number. As I prepared to crawl closer to the invaders, I told Eric, "Pack up in case we have to run. If we do, stick with Ramon and stay low." Eric's mouth dropped open. I didn't translate what else Ramon had said, that Ramon had only one pistol and probably wouldn't be able to protect me if the situation escalated.

I crawled on my belly across the field, pausing every 10 seconds to slap my binoculars on the guy in the tree. *"Mierda*-- Shit,*"* I thought, angry that I couldn't watch for parrots. Even if the parrots called I wasn't sure I could hear them over my heart racing, not from fear but from excitement. I had always wanted to say, "Cover me," and risk my life for others. I was having a great time. What could go wrong?

I slid close enough to read the license plate, about half a soccer field away. I may not have gotten a count of the parrots, but I had vital information. Memorizing the intel, I backed away and slithered up the hill to Eric and Ramon. *"Vamos,"* I said, *"Hay bastante peligro y tengo la información*-- "Let's go. It's very dangerous and I have the information." Eric was ready to run, but Ramon balked. Unbelievably, he took the safety off his pistol, stood up, and started walking towards the forest. The guy in the tree spotted him, climbed down, and started walking towards us. They were like actors in a spaghetti western: two armed men slowly walking towards each other over a dusty road, hoping to scare the other off, or improve their chances of a mortal wound.

At least that's how the plot played out in my head as they approached each other, and all the events that led to that moment flashed through my mind.

Chapter 1
THE CALL OF THE WILD
Newhall, California and Guatemala, April 1987

Oh noooo, I don't have time for this, I thought when Evan, director of the Aviculture Breeding Facility in Southern California, intercepted me outside the clinic. Usually he rushed by on his way to the parrot breeding barns, and if he did pause I couldn't always follow what he was saying because he was often in soliloquy mode, always referring to "nesting this" and "nesting that." His eyes this time focused intensely on me. I steeled myself to pay attention because I desperately wanted to follow his train of thought. "Kim, your chance has come! I just got a call that will change your life." I understood that, but then caught only a few words, like "parrots dying" and "Guatemala," and "what you've always wanted." He then spun and rushed away, stepping high in his Birkenstocks and leaving me standing there, staring in my tennis shoes and lab coat. "I'll meet you in 30 minutes. I have to check on some nesting birds," he shouted over this shoulder.

I had birds to check on, too, and made my rounds in the nursery and clinic before heading to Evan's office. He shared the office with other staff of the large bird and breeding facility where I was the senior veterinarian. It was not a peaceful setting, not so much because of the taxed air conditioner that hung in the corner battling the valley heat of this mountain desert region that usually hovered over 105 F this time of year. The cause of the worst racket was a golden conure, Queenie, whose shrill call battled the din of phones ringing from customers who wanted to buy baby parrots. We worked for a wealthy investor who collected and bred parrots for the pet trade. Mine was a coveted job, one of only a few full-time jobs for avian veterinarians in the nation, but I

3

wasn't happy. Evan was right; I wanted to get out of there and into the wild.

At his office he had slowed down enough to share a story that caused my heart to race. He'd had a call from the San Diego Zoo director, who had received a call from a Guatemalan woman who urgently needed an avian veterinarian. A batch of 200 yellow-naped amazon chicks had been confiscated from poachers and were dying, and only a few were still alive. She also had a small collection of parrots and wanted to set up breeding pairs. She needed someone who could surgically sex the birds and offer general consultation in aviculture and avian medicine. Dale thought that our boss, the big honcho, would let me go since we had two veterinarians. "Kim," he said, "you've wanted to see a wild parrot fly free since you were child. Now get to it!"

1987

Guatemala became the ninth country to accept the compulsory jurisdiction of the Inter-American Court of Human Rights. President Vincio Cerezo granted a meeting with native groups who were lodging complaints of missing persons, but police forces met them at the Palace and denied them entry. When they refused to leave, the 200 men, women, and children were severely beaten and had to seek refuge in the Metropolitan Cathedral.

By the end of the day I had permission to leave for two weeks and had spoken with the woman in Guatemala, Anita. I had a week to get my passport renewed, obtain a visa, and train in surgical sexing with injectable anesthetics. I was just learning how to do this surgery using general anesthesia, but after performing a handful of procedures I thought I had the hang of it, more or less. Not knowing what I would need, I filled two large suitcases with every surgical, diagnostic, and treatment item I could imagine. And then I was on my way. I barely slept on the red-eye leaving from Los Angeles, awed by the volcanoes that we slipped between as we approached the narrow runway in the pre-dawn. Not understanding a word the flight attendants said, I simply followed others down a hallway where passengers stood in a single line that led to immigration. There were no bathrooms, exit doors, chairs, or English speakers. There was just a slow line of people who disappeared behind a mysterious door. My turn at last came and the world opened up around me as if I had entered a gladiator arena. On the floor above me, looking down through glass walls were hundreds of people, and on my level, a single conveyer belt loaded with our luggage. Mine cycled through, but I wasn't sure what to do next because a chaotic swirl of people surrounded me. There was no clear exit, only hundreds of unavoidable stares, until a man tapped me on my shoulder and gestured for me to follow him. He was a customs agent, an associate of Anita, whom she had asked to help me navigate the customs process. The agent began arguing with other customs agents who were pawing through my suitcases of syringes, medications, and surgery equipment. I don't know why they were carrying guns, perhaps passengers sometimes tried to make a run for it or posed a danger. Those watching us from above must have been waiting for some kind of show. Hundreds of eyes tracked every item in my suitcase, and it was nice to know that my underwear could provide high entertainment in more than one country. At last, the dour agents zipped my suitcases, and I followed the agent to the barricaded hall leading to yet another mysterious door.

Through the next door I ran a gauntlet through crowds looking for returning friends and family. Out of the masses emerged Anita, a woman of my short height, her husband Sebastián, and a third man, their armed bodyguard. "I was expecting someone taller and older," she said as she kissed my cheek. She led us to their waiting car and settled into the backseat with me. The drive to their city house was short, but dozens of armed people lined the road, along with military vehicles loaded with soldiers. "Why all the guns?" I asked. Anita said there had been some kidnappings, "But don't worry about it. It has calmed down and the car windows are bulletproof."

We stopped by a high wall topped with barbed wire and broken glass. We climbed stairs to their posh colonial home where another armed guard slid open a metal window in the double doors and checked us out before he opened the doors. I was shown their youngest son's room where I would stay for two weeks, and I was offered breakfast. Anita went back to bed. I was too excited to sleep and ate with Sebastián. Afterwards I said, "I could use a run. Is there anywhere I can jog?" "Sure," he said in beautifully accented English, "just stay on the avenue and you will be fine." As I ran I saw that every house had some kind of barricade around it, and armed guards on roofs seemed common place. What was going on?

We didn't start work until after lunch. I soon learned that Anita never appeared until lunch because evening socializing ran late in their home. I was mostly on my own in the mornings that first week, learning to use the room-to-room phone system to ask for *cafe con leche*-- coffee with milk. Each morning I drank the best coffee I'd ever had, ran, and waited. I had hours to tend to the surviving parrot chicks and oversee the management of the older homed parrots and birds. We worked until dinner, around 9:00 on a good night.

I was invited to join larger family gatherings, where conversation was about an engagement party for a niece I didn't know to be held at Anita's mother's house next door. Fortunately, Anita and I were both of the same size, because my best dress wasn't formal enough. I primped nightly for these gatherings and tried to be clever with that prominent Guatemalan family. Anita mercifully did most of the talking for me, and I eventually picked up that she was using me as her shield and javelin to promote avian conservation. Conservation, I was learning, was new to Guatemala, and it helped the effort to have an outside expert generate energy to focus others on our cause. They listened raptly when I spoke, and I felt I like a celebrity when everyone hung on every word I muttered.

For the big bash engagement party, I was seated at the table with the younger kids. Anita elected to sit with me and not the old fogies she found boring. The tables were set, the champagne served, nameless servants puttered around us, and I at last felt comfortable. I just laughed whenever I saw others laughing so I could fit in. Hint to those traveling and wishing to appear sophisticated: When you don't speak the language, don't laugh when others do. It's a sure sign you haven't a clue what people are saying. One particular joke made them all laugh, and when it was translated in English, I belly laughed, rocking back in my antique chair. Another hint: Do not ever move rapidly while sitting on furniture of unknown age or stability. The chair went down, my legs went up, and I flipped backwards. The fifty wealthy, aristocratic Guatemalans hushed, stared at my hosed, slippered feet, and elegantly reminded each other and assured me that at most parties at least one person commits a gaffe that the family talks about for years.

Besides working on my social skills, I treated sick birds and taught assistants to do the same. I also performed sexing procedures by surgically slipping an endoscope into a small incision in the abdomen of a bird to view its internal gonads. Males and females look alike in most parrot species, and before DNA sexing became available, surgery was required to tell a bird's sex. My surgery table in Guatemala City was a child's Tea Set table, where I sat in a miniature chair. I tried to not kill Anita's birds while she paraded through with family members and politicians who were important conservation-wise. And all the while her schnauzer, Alonso, would bark, if not bite. Anita did most of the translating and helped out with handling the birds, so her absence was felt when she had social events. I learned that no matter who was my Spanish speaking assistant, slamming the table, turning red, and sucking air until my eyes bulged was a universal way of saying, "I just about fucking killed the bird when it moved! Give it more anesthesia! Pay attention!" I don't know how, but we never lost a single bird of the hundreds that underwent surgery. It helped that Elizabet, a medical technologist with excellent English came to work with me when she could.

At the end of my first week, I was scheduled to speak at the National History Museum. It was a black-tie affair, and once again I wore one of Anita's dresses. I was the guest of honor and was constantly offered water and food, both of which I accepted, and neither which was a good idea due to the risk of food and water born illness in this country. I was quite impressed with myself to be honored and to address the upper echelons of Guatemalan society and the scientific community so soon after leaving veterinary school.

The next day we flew to one of Anita's country *fincas*, Tecanal. Our destination was a zoo owned by Sebastián and located in the center of the finca. There I would surgically sex their parrots and conduct health exams. We were traveling in Sebastián's 4-seater airplane that he piloted. We flew over a volcano chain that separates the highlands from the Pacific lowlands, where we were headed. I could see only the peaks of the volcanoes that were cloaked in acrid smoke from wood burning stoves and landscapes burned to clear fields for farming. We flew so close to the volcanoes that I felt I could touch them. Anita said Sebastián's brother had died in a helicopter crash coming through this pass, "But don't worry, planes are much safer than helicopters."

That wasn't much consolation as we dropped a mile through air whipped up from the Pacific coast's heat to the cool air of the highlands. Safely landed we motored along the *finca's* grassy air strip, breathing in what felt like steam coming off a jacuzzi. But gone were the cement and car exhaust of crowded Guatemala City. Green was everywhere, as if urged on by the force of creation it was asserting its rightful claim and meant to crowd out invading masters.

House servants carried our luggage into the main house, *La Casa Patronal*. We were met by Elizabet and her husband who had driven down. We drank fresh coconut juice served by Chema, a man of indigenous heritage even shorter than I am. Anita invited Elizabet and me for a drive to look for parrots. Anita had left behind her city persona and was now a cigarette smoking naturalist, familiar with the land and rough terrain. She piloted the *finca's* four-wheel-drive Jeep like an old ranch hand as we worked our way to the Montaña, one of the few forest tracts left in the region. We were driving toward the zoo, bouncing and banging our way through thick smoke. It was not parrots that I saw that first foray, but a burning forest. "Anita, what's happening?" I asked. "My husband had to clear over half the forest because government regulations demand that we decrease the amount of land that lies unused. Guatemala has such crazy regulations and this latest attempt won't achieve anything but the loss of the forest." Later that night she added that it all had something to do with the national debt and pressure from international banks that force increased production from Guatemalans.

As we drove further towards the relatively untouched forest, all around us were burning stumps of old trees that had housed up to three parrot nests in each. The large scarlet macaws no longer flew over these lands; they had been poached out 25 years ago. But amazon parrots and parakeets still flew free and fought for survival. I felt righteous and indignant at witnessing such devastation, with my camera snapping away to show the bird community back home. The sun was setting, and the haze was so thick that we could look directly into the sun that burned into my heart.

We ended up having even more time to look for parrots than we expected when the Jeep got stuck in mud. Lucky for us, a crew was chopping trunks with *machetes* and stopped to rock the Jeep free. The land was soon swallowed by a deep shadow so we weren't able to enter the *Montaña*. Instead Anita veered into the zoo, but the gates were locked. We tried to find our way home, while Elizabet screamed at every bump and dip. About the time we knew that Anita, however picturesque she was as a Marlboro woman, was lost, the radio sputtered to life. It was Sebastián, worried about his wife. He sent Samuel, the administrator of the ranch, to guide us home in the dark, without seeing a single parrot.

Dinner felt regal with an AC unit, though it hummed as loud as the singing insects. Many of us gathered together, though most of us were dead. Every inch of wall and floor space was occupied by Sebastián's father's hunting successes. A hundred conquered eyes watched our every move as we ate hand-patted tortillas, black bean soup, freshly made white cheese, and drank lime water. We talked so late into the night that we didn't work again until morning.

We drove to the zoo to set up an area for surgical sexing. Our operating room was the administrator's office. So many sexing procedures were planned that I was nervous. I would direct not only Elizabet and Anita, both of whom had helped me sex birds in the city, but also a bunch of gun toting finca guards who anticipated Sebastián's every command. I had just finished placing sterile drapes on the make-shift surgery table when I turned to help someone about to lose a finger to the first macaw. In the commotion, a guard placed his rifle across the sterile drapes. In one fell swoop, sterility and innocence were broken. This was now my reality: land owners carried guns to keep the non-owners from poaching, hunting, and kidnapping.

The day allowed no inner stillness. My goal was no bird should lose her or his life that day or any other day. A pattern was quickly set; I injected anesthetic into one bird, and while waiting for the bird to sleep I ran to check on other birds recovering from surgery in cardboard boxes, and then returned to sterilize my hands and instruments for the next surgery. Of course, there was no air-conditioning, just one squeaky fan blowing microbes all over the place.

Sexing surgery is not complicated. It entails a small skin and muscle incision in the flank, placement of a small-diameter endoscope into the body cavity, and then a glorious peak at the inner miracle of a breathing bird. I have traveled all over the USA and beheld grand vistas that sparkle in my memory like precious stones, yet nothing has ever compared to the awe I feel each time I view the internal world of a living being. The heart in its glistening sac beats red life down through the pulsing arteries, feeding the multitude of organs that dance almost in sync with my own. For one brief instant in time I am connected to the bird as I discover all of its intimate details. The bird inhales, expanding its body and rocking my endoscope. To minimize possible trauma, I breathe with the bird. Air rushes through the small opening that connects perfect pink lungs to air sacs that expand, gleam, and cuddle up to the kidneys, intestines, heart, liver, spleen, and, of course, the object of my quest, the internal gonads. Angling the endoscope in a circular fashion I behold it all. I examine the bird for respiratory infections, a diseased liver, and the status of the gonads. Is the bird mature? Male? Female? During this procedure the ordinary becomes a treasure, but when I withdraw the endoscope, the abdominal muscles seal shut the point of my penetration and I return to the world of mere mortals. Once again the bird becomes an object to band, tattoo, fret over during its recovery, and join the ranks of those held captive for a lifetime.

After the last surgery when I was certain all the birds would survive, Anita took me on rounds so I could take samples of caged birds in the zoo and offer advice for treatment. Away from the swirling fan, the thick air closed around us with the multitude of feathered captives that watched as I hauled my red suitcase full of medical supplies. Externally I was not the professional image one sees on the Discovery Channel, with trendy tropical clothes and medical packs, but all day my inner chatter was piping, *how cool am I?*

We planned to sex more birds the next day and again look for wild parrots, but during the night I was hit with my first attack of amoebic dysentery. I think the first is always the worst and then you become acclimated to the little buggers. But this first bout left me drained of all energy and fluids. Such a marvel it was to be spurting rejected fluids from two orifices at one time. My only consolation was a bidet next to the toilet, both of which I used liberally through the night. Anita found me in the morning on the floor and apologized profusely for my state. I spent all day sleeping and wishing to leave this land.

Late in the afternoon Anita suggested one last tour of the *finca* to try to see parrots that she insisted she saw all the time, except when I was with her. On a barely settled stomach I could not imagine bouncing around in a smoke-filled Jeep, but the call to see a wild parrot was too great. This time we stuck to a levy road, called the *Muro* road because it was a human-built rise to keep the floods out. The air was sick with human pollutants, and my eyes stung and watered until I wondered if I'd be able to see a parrot even if it flew right past me. Anita apologized and said the smog was unusual. The rains were late and a major inversion layer had settled in, trapping the smoke from kitchen fires and garbage burning – and forest clearing I wanted to add. I was beginning to think that all the wild parrots were extinct in this area when I heard my first yellow-naped amazon call, a raucous ear splitting attention gatherer. A pair of silhouetted forms high in a tree bugled, crazily squawking over the hum of the Jeep's motor. I'd seen them, and now I could die, which seemed a real possibility. Whatever else in the world there was left to conquer, I had managed to fill the center square in the bingo card that represented my life's winning hopes.

Because I was so ill we left soon afterwards for Guatemala City in Sebastián's plane. Imagine a stomach, empty but revolting against every breath, a fluid-filled colon, and a brain trying to regain control of the body's sphincters. Eyes turned inward to find a hiding place, anything to avoid the torture of bodily functions gone haywire. A shout from the front of the airplane surely heralded another nauseating plummet. Looking up, I saw volcano peaks dance with the falling orange sun, and clouds part like ladies in waiting. The lights of Guatemala City below meant I would soon have a chance to get some rest in a stable bed at Anita's house, but my stomach jumped and spun as much off the plane as on it.

Most of the next week was spent avoiding seeing, smelling, and thinking of food. I only got worse and went to see Anita's brother-in-law, a doctor. Poked and prodded, gas-filled belly harrumphed at; I was diagnosed as having amoebas, two kinds. Medicine galore helped so I was soon well enough for Anita to continue to introduce me to government officials who might aid her in saving the birds of Guatemala, and to finish the medical work.

The day finally came to return to L.A. Leaving Guatemala felt like a gift from heaven. In the past I had resented living in the Southern California Valley where the bird ranch was located. A group of us from the ranch had together seen a film where a woman jumped off a skyscraper and shattered a car, and a colleague whispered, "Someone must have told her she had to move to Newhall." That summed up my feelings about the smog and people-choked byways, but on that day I kissed the cement at LAX, vowing to never return to Central America where I was only trading one overpopulated, smoke-filled wasteland for another.

Chapter 2
DOMESTIC DUTY CALLS
*Newhall, California;, Guatemala; Loxahatchee, Florida; Alaska; Davis, California;
Philippines, mid 1987-1990*

1987

*U.S. Senate and House panels release reports charging
President Ronald Reagan with "ultimate responsibility" for the Iran-
Contra Affair. Senior administration officials hoped to sell illegal guns
to Iran, secure the release of several U.S. hostages there, and to fund
the Contras in Nicaragua, which had been prohibited by Congress. The
Contras were backed by the USA because they fought the left-leaning
government not favored by the USA.*

It took about a month to recover from that first dysentery case. I figured I
was fully recovered if I could once again consume salad, pizza, and beer, but
comfortably eating all three together took several more months. I didn't have
time to be sick between being Senior Veterinarian at the Aviculture Breeding
Facility (ABF), a volunteer wildlife veterinarian at Topeka Canyon Nature
Center, and a traveling avian veterinarian lecturer. I had just broken up with a
boyfriend, though I lived in his motor home in his back yard on the edge of the
Los Angeles National Forest. He knew I longed for the wilderness and so

11

agreed that I could stay. It was cramped with the dashboard for my desk, my parrot Exodor in a cage on the kitchen counter, and the bedroom up a ladder into the added-on loft under a sky light. What mattered was that it was out of the urban area and close to the bird ranch.

The bird ranch was tanking. Soon after I returned from Guatemala the owner decided to sell the farm. Our family flock was to be divvied up to the highest bidders and sold piece meal all over the US. To see a bird you had known for years be netted, boxed, and carted away to the airport was a constant sadness in those last days at ABF. We were losing friends, and the birds seem to pick up on our sorrow with diminished vocalizations and activity. The promise that I had made to care for them was broken. As 1987 progressed, the barns became emptier and emptier, until there was just a handful of staff and feathered ones left.

One of the staff was a veterinary technician who lived with her family up the canyon road from me. After her last day of work, I drove up to visit her and to say goodbye. Out came the tequila as we watched the sun set over the brown tarnished mountains rimming our valley. We told stories of lost birds and lost friends, and soon the tequila was gone. Her husband asked if we should go buy more tequila. We all know that the answer to that should always, always be no. I answered, "Sure, who should drive?" Again, we all know that the answer to that is always, always "No one." So we all took turns driving down to the country store and back and were soon perched on their porch with twinkling stars parading around us and eyes glistening from repeated goodbyes. The time came for the last goodbye and they asked me, "Can we drive you home?" "It's only a mile on a single road, I'll be fine." I wasn't. It was a very dark and curvy road, which presented no problem, but I couldn't find my dirt road to my motor home.

I knew I was close when suddenly the car stopped with a grinding noise underneath. I figured I had run over some bush or tree trunk so I backed up and heard a crunch. No go. So I went forward and heard a double crunch. After a few minutes of forward and backward rocking with no progress, I abandoned the car, spied my motor home, and climbed up to and fell into my bed at the same time.

Not too many hours later I had to get up and get to work. As the coffee was percolating it dawned on me that I didn't know where my car was. Carefully cradling my coffee and my head, I, with the greatest caution, navigated the two steps down to my yard, and there was my car, in the middle of my neighbor's garden. It was still early so no one had seen what I had done. Heck, I hadn't either come to think of it. Peering under the car I saw the reason the car had stalled out; it had drug a railroad tie bordering my neighbor's garden through the yard until it had maneuvered itself at an angle, both blocking one rear tire from going forward and one front time from going backyards.

Clutching my coffee as an anchor to hope that the headache and nausea would soon dissipate, I got out the jack, raised the car, and pulled out the tie, every moment not knowing if I would either pass out from pain or throw up. I still hadn't tasted any coffee, but it was a beacon inviting me to return to normal functioning (social functioning?) I could not let go.

At the bird ranch, I couldn't even turn to say hi to anyone because moving my head even a fraction to either side was too painful. That's why it hurt so much when the phone rang, the screech suggesting that I wouldn't like what the caller had to say. The wildlife rehabber from the Topeka Nature Center was on the line. "Hey, Dr. Joyner, we have a swan with a broken wing that just came in. Can you take a look at her?" I had to go when I only wanted my bed. The wild swan was quite aggressive so we had to anesthetize her to examine her wing, which had an open, infected, smelly, and maggot swarming wound. Extracting maggots with the mother of all hangovers really, really, made me never want to drink tequila again.

The summer of 1987 was to be my 30th birthday. It was time to accomplish a goal I had always wanted, to climb Mt. Whitney, the tallest mountain in the lower 48. With no one left to go with but my ex-boyfriend, we left in the dark of night so we could get to the mountain's base as the park opened. We hiked eleven miles with full packs that day, all straight up. I thought I was in good shape, but people literally were running past us on the increasingly narrow trail. We didn't make it the whole way, just to the relatively crowded base camp at the foot of the last long and steep climb. Just as we got there the weather turned cold and it began to rain. Huddled into a tent hastily thrown up, we took out our drinking cups to dig a ditch around the tent so the water could be channeled out and around the tent. As we dug, human feces were uncovered and joined the deluge filling up the camp. When the rain stopped and a sewage smell hung in the air, we hung our wet sleeping bags over rocks, wondering how we'd sleep that night, cold, wet, and just two of many attempting this most popular mountain climb in the Americas.

The next morning we took off early, and it was ice cold, in the middle of July. At the first pass, a huddle of people was deciding what to do. Many of them had spent the night in the unexpected cold without tents and sleeping bags, and some even wore shorts. One woman was about to be med-evacuated out. We paused and rested with them, but then thought what the heck; we have to make it to the summit no matter what. So the two of us alone continued on through the increasing snow fall until we reached the peak. The weather had scared off everyone else, with puddles of recent rain water almost frozen and diminished visibility because of the raging snow and wind. Though signs warned us otherwise, we entered the emergency hut at the top to get out of the wind. There wasn't much to do there but huddle, and one thing led to another, and not only did we spend my 30th birthday higher than anyone else in the lower 48th, but also we were the highest people having sex, and given our position I was highest.

Summer moved into fall, and while ABF was winding down, Anita called one afternoon and suggested another trip. I was eager to play the role of a rejuvenated savior. She added a carrot, this time we would get out of the house to see the countryside. Our first trip was north of Guatemala to stay at Sebastián's hunting cabin on *Rio Pasion*-- Passion River. We would spend an entire day on the river hunting fish that were as long as Anita and I were tall (really, I can show you the pictures, this is no fishing tale). During the long day of motoring up and down this river that was nearly as wide as a lake, we saw incredible views. Silhouetted scarlet macaws in the distance flew over tree tops to out-shout the howler monkeys that were incessantly bellowing their mournful cries. They sounded like they knew something I didn't and had experienced something I couldn't even imagine. Keel-billed toucans whistled and cackled along the shore, incredibly defying gravity as they balanced a body with as much beak forward as body and tail behind. That night was another long one, with frequent bathroom runs and insufficient toilet paper to make it to the morning's light. But I buckled up, determined to have a great time, and suggested we go on to Tikal, the Maya ruins, as planned.

After touchdown, we were joined by a local tourist guide who showed us the ruins, and my stomach kept getting worse. Dreaded amoebas had once again embedded themselves in my intestinal wall. Within the ruins is the Central Plaza, where one of the many temples is located, surely to tempt nauseated, height-fearful tourists into climbing. Crumbling narrow steps shoot up towards the pagan sun, with a small chain leading the way for timid souls migrating to the gods. Not knowing if I would ever visit again, up the temple stairs I went, trembling at each grasp of hands on the anchored chain. At the top I was shaking, nearly puking, and wondered how I'd ever get back down. It wasn't any help to see a crowd at the top gathered around a pale-faced woman and encouraging her that she really could take the first step down the temple. I gently edged against sturdy ancient walls, eavesdropping on their psychological support before heading down myself. If I fell I'd be just one more sacrifice on the temple stairs. That night I dreamt of Mayan royalty and awoke with wonder, and slightly less nausea.

After returning from Tikal and recovering from my latest reunion with Montezuma, life again settled into the tedium of Guatemala City. We returned to the zoo and finished sexing the birds there. I was becoming part of the family and hung out with them during the day. Anita did arrange for a drive out to the Sierra de la Minas, a range of mountains that extend so high they pierce clouds. Accompanying us was a famous Central American wildlife artist who knew of some good birding areas in the mountains. It was nearly noon before we were in the long line of cars dropping down out of the highlands, our progress hampered by the two-lane highway and slow trucks. The lower we dropped, the hotter and drier it became, and more desolate. In fact, the area on the northeast side of the city is a desert.

After hours of driving we finally turned left on a dirt road and started to climb. This road took us by thatched homes, guarded on all sides by cacti and desert. People and wildlife were scarce. The vista changed as the road led us through dry pine forests, humid mixed forests, and, finally, a world of misty unknowns. We left the car at the end of a logging trail and blundered through the forest, banging our shins as we slipped on moist trunks and roots. Not an inch of ground was uncovered and hardly a single patch of tree trunk or branch surface was unadorned with orchids or bromeliads. Brightly and broad breasted trogans whipped by us, their wing tips grazing our faces as they thundered by, and barred parakeets chattered in the distance.

We weren't able to stay too long as dark was on its way. My two fearless leaders weren't sure which way the car was, but finally Anita and I decided on a direction completely opposite from our guide because we were panicking as we circled and circled. I'm not sure we would have ever found our car if we had trusted his instincts. By the time we got in the car, the comfort of sunlight had left us and we crawled down the mountainside to keep tires from slipping off the narrow tract. I had to get out and lead the car as point person to help us out of narrow stretches and once over a log bridge, which collapsed after our passing. We regained our confidence when we hit hard dirt roads. I withdrew into the silence of the back seat because their Spanish was incomprehensible and their subject, God, unknowable. Perhaps out of pique for getting us lost, our driver drove like a bull in rutting season to get us home. On that long drive back, we nearly had two accidents, one from him recklessly passing a truck, another from a robbery attempt, at least that was what Anita told me. All I knew was that the car swerved, tires squealed, and I ended up in the front seat after brakes were applied. After this I shut my eyes and prayed to get home alive and without injury.

In the city we planned one last event, to go to the National Museum where I had spoken during my first trip to Guatemala. This time I was to hear Anna LaBastille, the avian conservationist and author of *Mama Poc.* It was thrilling to see her in person and hear her stories of how she tried to save the flightless Atitlan grebe, a duck like sea bird that went extinct despite her efforts. I imagined I could be her one day, but I wouldn't be announcing extinction, but sharing how we had saved parrots from disappearing. I would also never give up and leave Guatemala or have an affair with a married Guatemalan that wouldn't last, as she had done.

After this trip, it was time for me to leave Southern California. I was the only medical staff left. I was open to where I went next, except it would never be southern Florida because it was too much like California. I wanted peace and beauty, not touristy urban sprawl. Karma caught me and I took a job as the first staff veterinarian at the Avicultural Center of Southern Florida. I packed my belongings from the motor home into a moving truck, and also most of the medical clinic equipment and supplies from ABF that were purchased by my new boss. I sold my car and got on a plane to a place I swore I would not go, but it turns out I will go anywhere to be with birds. The night I arrived was dark, cool, and rainy, and there was no welcome at the airport, except for a driver who took me to my three-bedroom house on 40 acres. He handed me the keys to my very own golf cart and promptly left. There wasn't much to unpack, and I wasn't even sure if I should because the owner that night was undergoing a liver transplant. If his health deteriorated, this whole adventure would end prematurely.

The owner did well and soon came home, though the health of his avian collection was another thing. During my year-and-a-half there the birds survived an outbreak of Psittacine Beak and Feather Disease, Papilloma virus, sarcocystis, trauma and death caused by cockatoo male aggression, chicks failing to thrive, and burned crops, which happens when too hot liquid feeding formula is fed to parrot chicks. All in all, it was fairly typical of bird collections in this area, but the challenge for was that were so many parrots. We were the largest collection of parrots in the USA at that time, and we were growing.

Our growth led the owner one day to say, "We have got to start selling the chicks. We've run out of room, and we've got to make some money." I couldn't imagine subjecting the birds to the risk of disease, being raised without their parents, and ending up who knows where. I was also uncomfortable with the social ecology of the farm. There was a fair amount of dysfunction, probably both within me and around, making me crazy most of the time. I lasted as long as I did because the natural isolated beauty of the farm was in itself soothing. I had the back 20 acres to myself. I also had Finnie, my friend Linda's German shepherd-lab mix, who shared my home while his human companions were touring the world. Finnie would jump into my golf cart and go with me to work, sleep on the floor near my desk in the clinic, and accompany us to the rows of cages for checkups and treatment. At lunch he would join me in the cart when I rode to the small muddy pond where I swam for exercise. He was uncertain about this activity as he watched from the cart, whimpering as I went into the water. Even with some Labrador in him, he didn't like to swim, or so I'd been told. I took off swimming, hoping he'd settle down, and he did quit whimpering at last because he was now swimming up behind me, and then with me. From that day forward he would swim laps with me. I was glad for his company because I had heard there was a large snapping turtle in the pond and one never knew when a gator would take up residence.

Finnie also took up bodysurfing with me in the ocean, another new for him. When his parents came to get him after their trip around the world, they didn't recognize Finnie the swimmer. It was a sad day to see him go back to California. Other friends then became my company in the pond, including a man who enjoyed riding in the golf cart to the pond at night and sipping champagne while floating and looking up at the stars. The next morning there was a price to pay with the hangovers and the detritus left on the beach, hoping that I could clean it all up before the ranch guards wrote in their log book that lights and giggling had gone on for hours on the back 20 acres.

I also got away from the dysfunction at the ranch by speaking once a month at some parrot conference or another. I continued consulting with Anita's conservation efforts in Guatemala. Her goal was to build an aviary in the lowlands, away from the hustle and bustle of her home, where very few birds would breed. Her husband had set aside a tract of land on the edge of the zoo and she needed someone to help her build the cages and hospital. Our group of collaborators increased. Elizabet continued to work with us, and we added a veterinarian friend, Tom, as well as a string of Americans to care for the growing numbers of birds at the zoo – Carmela, Vincent, and, the last, Perry.

1988

The USA, under President Regan, because of human rights violations finally placed economic sanctions on Paraguay's regime led by Alfinnieo Stroessner, whom they had backed for 34 years, despite decades of abuse and repression. The USA backed Stroessner because of his anti-communist stance.

While in Florida, I managed one trip to Guatemala. Tom, a colleague of mine wished to dabble in conservation, so I invited him along, in part for fun, and in part to fulfill my salvific mission of building bridges between distant worlds. Tom got to see my fiefdom in Florida and my benefactor in Guatemala. We had a good time jacuzziing with Elizabet and Anita amongst the frogs and wall spiders, swimming with fallen mangos and drowning bats, and quenching our suburban boredom as we dashed to open cattle gates in pouring rain and flashing light.

One morning on that trip, Vincent guided us on an early morning sojourn up the water tank of Tecanal. Vincent said it was a cool place to watch parrots. He promised to knock on our doors early so we could climb the water tank.

The pounding wakeup call came with Vincent shouting, "We're heading up the tank now!" I ran into Tom in the hall of the *Casa Patronal*, both of us busily slinging binoculars and cameras over our shoulders as we raced after Vincent and the five others who had come to pay homage to the Doctors from the North. Tom and I were the last ones to get to the tower. The ladder leading up the five stories was just barely visible in the dawn. There was enough light, however, for Tom and I to lock eyes that said, "You've got to be kidding." The ladder snaked up between mango limbs and disappeared. "Come on, Tom, Vincent says it's flat on top and we'll be safe up there." I took to the ladder before Tom, the first firmly grasped rungs easily suggesting my challenge to manhood. About 10 feet up, however, each gained rung was at the cost of sweating, swearing, and shaking of limbs. The only thing that kept me going was Tom behind me. Later Tom told me that the only thing that kept him going was having me in front of him.

I finally reached the top, and it wasn't flat. The surface was slanted and crowded with bodies, and the tank was swaying in the wind. Eager hands pulled Tom and me up; eight of us atop the world, watching the sun give birth to tropical mysteries. To the north, the plumes of the Pacaya and Fuego volcanoes flagged our attention. No other clouds marred the scene as we looked far to the northwest to peer, as millions had before us, at the line of volcanoes reaching up into Mexico. Turning and looking southeast, quieted volcanoes stretched to El Salvador. Below us awoke the world in a symphony of sounds; hands slapping *tortillas*, parakeets chattering in the mango trees, and horses calling their last shouts of freedom before heading out with the cowboys to work in the pastures. Each new moment, the artistic sun painted another stroke of the panorama of life. Palm trees now could be individually distinguished from the mass of green that provided the backdrop for the flying white sheets of egrets as they moved from roost trees to foraging grounds. Swaying metal contraptions and complex sounds left behind, we headed down the ladder to the day's work.

By now our surgical sexing area had moved from the zoo to one of the two houses next to the airfield. Our entourage had grown so much that Tom and I barely had to work. A party atmosphere prevailed as we sweated through the 100 degree heat and occasional surgical surprises.

After this visit, Anita visited me in Florida. Her husband had a polo tournament in West Palm Beach, to which I was invited. After giving Anita the tour of the forty-acre bird ranch in my golf cart, we quickly showered and drove to the festival of the elite. It was an exhausting time, as I was working 80 hours a week, my parents were visiting, and it was the breeding season. I think Anita was impressed by what a collection of birds could look like, just as I was losing hope in what a collection of birds could be for. It fed ego and the hope to gain money and prestige, and I'd had enough. It was time to leave, but I was at a loss as how to work with birds without contributing to their unjust imprisonment in captivity.

1989

The Exxon Valdez oil spill occurred in Prince William Sound, Alaska on Good Friday, March 24, 1989. It spilled 11-38 million USA gallons of crude oil, making it one of the most devastating human-caused environmental disasters. Deaths included 300 harbor seals, as many as 250,000 seabirds, at least 2,800 sea otters, approximately 12 river otters, 247 bald eagles, 22 orcas, and an unknown number of salmon and herring.

I finally came up with a plan – it was time to go to Alaska. I applied for a post-DVM degree in Preventative Medicine, which was basically an epidemiology degree, and was accepted to start in August of 1989 at the University of California, Davis. I would end up there after driving across the country in my Chevy van and then north to Alaska. Part way across I traveled with my brother, dropping him off in Las Vegas after burning out the brakes on western mountains. I picked up my dear friend Avery from the foothills of the Sierra Nevada and north we drove, camping along the way and sleeping on the deck of the ferries. Our goal was to meet up with other friends, an ex-boyfriend of mine and his pregnant spouse who had moved to Alaska the year before. All summer I used their homestead outside of Wasilla to come and go, hosting alternatively Avery, the same ex-boyfriend who had lent me his motor home, and my sister. Sharing the closed space of a Chevy van wasn't conducive to relationships, but with all of the outdoors beyond the van doors, no one went home unhappy.

The motor home ex-boyfriend did get a little grumpy one time. We were sitting around the fire in our friend's cabin, while the rain poured down outside, having a beer or two in the late morning. Someone mentioned fishing, and soon we were packing our gear to hook some salmon in the rain. We drove down a long gravel road to the river, and hauled our gear to the bank, the nine-month pregnant spouse with waist high rubber boots leading the way. A line of closely packed fisher people were in place along the bend in the river, so we took up the end of the line in stiller waters. We weren't getting many hits, while those at the river's bend were. After 30 minutes, I took my pole and managed to find a space in the crowd at the river bend where I wouldn't foul anyone's line. Immediately I started getting hits, which propelled my friends to squeeze in as well. After a couple of hours, we counted up the salmon to see who had the most and the biggest, and I won on both accounts. Seeing the glare of my guy friend, someone told him, "Well, your fish is bigger if you stretch out her tail." He began to smile again and offered to cook the salmon for dinner as he was, after all, the big winner for the day.

I grew tired of salmon that summer in Alaska. We had so much of it that I began to think of it as a trash fish. We stocked our refrigerator and pantry when we accompanied Alaska Fish and Game to a stream where they harvested female salmon for their eggs. By harvesting I mean killing them at the stream and slitting them open to remove their eggs for the hatchery. The females were soon to die anyway after laying their eggs naturally, so I didn't feel too bad about what we were doing. It also didn't bother me the night we went out to a stream to hook king salmon. I don't remember which laws we were breaking, but it had something to do with the season and it being night time. Saying it was night though is to misspeak. The sun never really set at that time of year, but instead skirted around the horizon going from east to west. The river was near mountains, so as the sun wove in and out of each mountain peak, I saw ten sunrises and sunsets on that long night.

On another rainy day, Avery and I met an old homesteader who had two wives. Of course, it was raining when we went to visit in the rustic cabin that had a white bucket for a toilet. Tale after tale came from the man who was an avid hunter, and most of them were about bears he had nearly escaped or had to shoot. Bear tales were the fruit of the vine for Alaskans. Men went to the porch to talk about bullet calibers, and women went to the kitchen to share bear tales. So much talk happened in those cramped quarters that soon movement spontaneously erupted to go out and look for bears. It wasn't bear season so we couldn't hunt them, but nothing said you couldn't follow their spoor, and if you happened across one and it charged, you were allowed to shoot the bear for protection. The hunter outfitted us with rifles and off we went through the tall grass by a river. We couldn't see ten feet in front of us, and we were following the trail of a bear. Most times in Alaska places where bears had been seen are avoided, and one always, always made noise when walking so as not to surprise a bear, because you never want to surprise a bear.

We were lucky and didn't get surprised with a bear and I never did see a bear in Alaska at a close distance. Once when camping at a homesteader's cabin that we reached by horse, we saw signs of bears everywhere and we and the horses were skittish on the trails. After my last night there running through the forest naked down to the frigid lake, I rode out to get back home. My pregnant friend and her sister went riding in the other direction and took a bathroom break. With pants around their ankles, and the guns left in the saddles, a bear caught wind of them and started to charge. There was nothing to do but out-bravado the bear, so the sister jumped towards the bear, banging together pans they had brought to make tea. The bear broke her charge. This bear story ended well, while others tell of maulings and humans eaten.

For this reason, my friend took the life of a bear soon after the birth of her first daughter. One night she heard snuffling and a racket in her back yard. She got out of bed and looked out the window to see a bear eating the dog food from the back of her truck. She knew it wasn't the bear's fault, for she had accidentally left the food that lured the bear in, and she knew it was not bear season, but she could not have a bear returning to her home with a small child in her care. She grabbed her hunting vest, and with that as her only clothes, stepped outside into the moon light and shot the bear.

Many things died that summer around me in Alaska – fine body grayling fish almost too pretty to snag, salmon, bear, halibut, clams, and sometimes birds. My sister and I had just spent a long day at Kennecott Copper Mines. We got there in narrow metal chairs suspended from steel wire that spanned high above the length of a river. With gloves on, we pulled ourselves and the chair slowly across the river, both coming and going. Then we drove on a gravel road that played hell with my tires. We were down to zero spares, so I stuck close to a truck in front of me in case we got another flat. It meant eating a lot of dust, but worth it as we were far from any houses or people. Suddenly a large partridge-type bird ran across the road, and the truck ahead hit it. She went spiraling up into the air as both of us slammed on our breaks. A man and a woman got out of the truck, and met me by the still bird on the road. I told them to stay back if they didn't want to see a dying bird or any gore. They stared at me as I quickly examined the bird and saw so much wrong. I was about to explain to them that I would need to break the bird's neck to end her suffering, when she died. I turned to them to express remorse and ease their pain for having hit the bird, when the woman said, "Can we have the bird now? You aren't going to keep it, are you? I mean we did hit it, so we get to eat it, right?"

Leaving behind the bird and longing to return to work where one tried to save life instead of killing it, I packed up the van in August and alone headed south down the 3000 mile road, most of it dirt and gravel until I got to Seattle where I visited my sister and attended the Association of Avian Veterinarians Annual Meeting. I was a bit unanchored while there because I was not an employed avian veterinarian but still was part of the in-clique as Secretary of the Board. Dreams of the Avicultural Center of Southern Florida's birds I had left behind haunted me every night. I had left my charges and was adrift without a way of saving the world of parrots and being part of their family. I was also lost without my work in Guatemala. Without a home collection to call my own or supplies and support, I didn't know how I could keep helping Anita. Tom was in a much better position than I, so left it to him to organize the next surgical sexing trip while I was in Davis for one very stressful year with almost no money. I worked incredibly long hours with consulting, a house call practice, and studies.

In the midst of that trying time, Tom made sure I came with him on a Guatemalan surgical sexing trip in a real hospital, newly finished on the day we arrived. It even came with an air conditioning so there would be no risk of our sweat dripping into the surgical field. The night before we were to sex birds, we helped clean up the construction debris and set up the instruments on an honest-to-goodness surgery table. The next morning Vincent, Anita's aviary manager, had all the birds ready to go. We were to sex some forty birds that day and all of us were anxious to get going. I was just about to place the endoscope into the depths of the first bird when Anita came crashing in, yelling at us to stop. Fearing at the very least a revolution, we looked up to see a priest blessing the new building, holy water splashing here and there. A few drops even landed on the surgery drapes.

It was during this trip, while I was living in California, that Anita and I shared our dreams. Her birds had moved to the zoo, the first babies were being raised by Vincent, and she had hopes and dreams for more. So did I. Together we plotted how to save the birds of Guatemala. One way was my long-term goal of sampling wild parrots to understand what species of bacteria were in their intestinal and respiratory tracts, a microflora study on wild parrots. Within avian medicine circles, there was always a debate about what bacteria were "normal" in a bird, and which bacteria should be treated with antibiotics. The overuse of antibiotics always irritated me, poor birds getting stuck, prodded, and wiped out from treatment. If I could prove that wild parrots survived quite well with supposedly pathogenic species of bacteria, then perhaps birds would be treated better in captivity. Anita said she would help me with the ground work and in-country support, all I had to do was find the money.

I knew just the place to look. I applied for a research grant through the Association of Avian Veterinarians. They usually funded just three grants a year, and my grant was listed fourth. I was still the Secretary of the Board but was no part of the grant decision, and I had not been lobbying anyone to change the outcome. I had simply not made the cut, and my dreams for working with wild parrots would have to wait for another time. Then the unexpected happened. Members of the board tweaked the recommendation and moved my grant to the number three slot because of redundancy in two of the higher ranked grants. There still wasn't enough money to cover all three grants, for I needed a lot of resources to work with the wild parrots in the rugged and remote countryside of Guatemala. It looked like I still wouldn't get the money when members of the board and committee chairs volunteered to cut their budget and swing it my way so I could be funded. The time came to vote my grant up or down, and I was excused from the room. Reentering I was met with applause; the vote had gone in my direction and my life in another.

1990

Two gunmen in the Philippines kill two US Air Force airman on the eve of talks between the Philippines and the USA regarding the future of American military bases in the Philippines.

After the end of the meeting I called my new-found colleague, Susan, at the University of California Davis, from the conference hotel to tell her I had gotten the grant. I had met Susan a few months back and we had plotted together. She was interested in establishing a Latin American conservation base for the Psittacine Research Project at U.C. Davis. If I got the grant I'd need help since I'd never done wild parrot research. We agreed that she'd organize a group of biologists to help me with the work if I could help her meet the contacts she needed in Guatemala so we could work together on an even larger project. I was nearly shaking as I told her the news - we were going to Guatemala in January, 1991 to begin. The trick now was how to actually do the work for the amount of money I asked for, and how could I spend time away from paid work while also finishing my Master's. I was living in a converted garage at U.C.D. and was planning to move to Alaska after completing my Master's. The lure north there was just too great. My ex-husband was there, an ex-boyfriend, and now a future boyfriend with whom I would live for a short while. My only income was from consulting at an even larger captive breeding facility in the Philippines. That year I averaged $180 a month net income as I bounced between Alaska, the Philippines, and Guatemala. I had no guaranteed employment in Alaska, but the call of the wild was too great. I had had enough of domestic concerns.

LORAKIM JOYNER

Chapter 3
INTO THE WILDERNESS
Alaska and Guatemala, 1990-1991

The big move to Alaska came in October of 1990. My friend Avery was game for another drive up from Northern California, some 3,000 miles from our destination of Anchorage. Our plan was to camp out along the way, which didn't really work out very well since we hit a blizzard the second day. Soon my van was sliding off into ditches and getting flats along the snowy road. We were lucky that some other travelers were still out in the weather to offer winches or advice. At one gas and repair stop, a traveling Norwegian told me, "Lady, every time I pass you are in a ditch or fixing a flat. Get snow tires." I was a little miffed about being told what to do and laughed with Avery when we discovered that he too had a flat on the road. There was some advice I did want, and that was what the road was like ahead of us. Travelers coming the other way said it was bad. In fact, they had seen a van just like ours flipped over. We didn't know what to do but thought we could go slow, put on tire chains if needed, and once in White Horse, Canada, we would consider getting snow tires or at least hole up until the worst had passed.

Creeping up a hill soon after the last gas station, the car hit black ice and went into a slide. We swerved across the road and almost went into the ditch on the left side of the road. I knew not to brake, but still pumped them a bit, madly turning the wheel, no time to think if I should steer into the direction of the skid or away from it. At the last minute the van sailed back onto the road and spun towards the other ditch. Beyond cognition, I acted on instinct, both Avery and I gasping as the car just barely missed careening off the road, and instead came to a standstill in the wrong lane, headed the wrong direction, but there weren't many fools on the road. So on went the tire chains, which didn't do much for my confidence. By the time we made White Horse, I was a nervous wreck and my hands hurt from gripping the wheel.

We spent a couple of nights there and bought snow tires I couldn't afford. While waiting for the tires to be put on the van, I went to a restaurant where everyone was telling "coming through the blizzard and spin out stories." I shared my story and asked if I handled the spin correctly with breaking and turning the wheel, first left, then right, then repeated that twice more. Someone said, "Lady, if you didn't end up in the ditch, you did it right." We continued to do it right and steered clear of any serious mishaps the rest of the way, though the drama didn't end. Entering Alaska we hit a fog so thick we couldn't see in front of us, the windows were iced, and the windshield wipers froze. I got out of the van, set my morning coffee in the back of the van, and found windshield wiper fluid to help me chip ice off the front window and for Avery to throw on the window as we drove. By the time I got back to my coffee it had frozen solid.

Getting to Anchorage was no relief, for the roads were even worse there. My anxiety went up even more notches when a friend said, "If you aren't in a ditch two or three times a winter, you just aren't getting out enough." I hoped that I had used up my ditch quotas for the year, and wondered how I could survive in this harsh environment. Then I remembered, now that my amygdala had calmed down, a scene along that blizzard road a week earlier, right after we left Liard Hot springs (and after one ditch and one flat). We were the only ones on the snow-packed road and had not seen any humans for hundreds of miles. We couldn't hear the car move over the soft snow. I happened to glimpse in the rearview mirror and there was a coyote following us on the road. I saw a fox cross the road in front of us through the snow mist just before we came to a slight curve and rise in the road. At the top, the snow fall suddenly lightened, allowing us a broad view over the Yukon Territory we were entering. Caribou stood still in the mist, as did we, the coyote, and the fox, canids, cervids, and hominids on the road together. Then the snow smothered the view and we all disappeared from one another.

There wasn't too much to do in Alaska in those short days. I cross country skied almost every day or evening, as Anchorage has trails lit by street lights in city parks. The lights gave just enough advantage to avoid barreling into the herds of moose, or, if lucky, enough to see your boot straps as you frantically undid them so you could run away from a charging bull. During working hours, I was organizing for my first field work in Guatemala, as well as trying to earn money from consulting as an avian veterinarian in the Philippines. Consulting was just about my only income, which in 1991 netted me $189 a month. Mostly I worked off-site analyzing and making recommendations, and then made two on-site extensive trips to the world's largest bird breeding facility in the world,

Birds International. While there I handled the much endangered Spix macaw, had a prostitute sit on my lap, and traced a scar on a man's neck made by a Philippine monkey-eating eagle that nearly killed him. I thought the work was interesting enough, but my thoughts were really with the wild parrots in Guatemala.

Finally, I began research on wild birds when Susan, John, and I arrived in Guatemala in January, 1991. John was a famous parrot biologist, having literally written the book, and decided to advise us on our project. We spent a few days in Guatemala City with Anita, working on a bigger grant than the one I had received. Anita took us up to Tikal, the Maya ruins in the northern forest of Petén. We spent days sweating, bird watching, and climbing temples, but what we really wanted to do was to get to our field site. Finally we were off, chauffeured to Tecanal through the volcano passes.

On our first morning, Susan and I got up early, we thought, to tour the *finca* but John was nowhere to be seen. We figured he was off looking for parrots, leaving Susan and I to meet the guide Anita had assigned to us, Daniel. Daniel came to the door of the Casa Patronal, and there was enough light to see Daniel's form. John later told us that if there was enough light to see this, we weren't leaving early enough. Daniel was just an inch or so taller than me, which isn't saying much, although the ever-present sombrero gave him added stature. His skin, coffee colored to be sure, was barely covered by a rag-tagged shirt and pants with a broken zipper. He was very Guatemalan, and his poverty embarrassed me. Daniel was indistinguishable from all the other service workers I'd met.

The *machete* he carried in his left hand while he extended his right, thumbless hand to greet us and smiled. The contact brought me suddenly into his world, even more awkward than I had been seconds before. I felt a sense of vertigo and decentering, for his intelligence, presence, and command were unexpected. With Susan doing most of the talking, as I was only capable of a few words in Spanish, we followed him down the *Muro* Road. Soon we veered off to cross into the *fincas* bordering the local river, *Micaela Linda*-- Beautiful Micaela. Daniel stretched the barbed wired fence so Susan and I could squeeze through when bees flew into my face and Susan started yelling. We quickly turned around and I took off, trying to outrun the little stingers, with Susan and Daniel trying to keep up. Daniel was shouting something I couldn't understand, and finally I heard Susan say, "Stop. Stop running." Daniel caught up to me and twirled me around. Gently in words that I didn't understand, but in a tone that bespoke confidence and care, he willed me to hold still while he and Susan worked the bees out of my hair and shirt. We had stumbled into a "face bees" nest, whose target is, well, you guessed right, the face. Daniel's world looked very scary, with real danger and real humans. No longer a faceless peasant, he was a miraculous being whose beauty was completely unexpected. Suddenly, there were more than birds worth living for, worth dying for.

We didn't see many parrots that day, but we did get to know the *finca* better. Daniel showed us a depression in a pasture near the landing strip where a military parachutist had died when his chute failed to open. He told us that military maneuvers were not uncommon on our *finca* because of the air field. At lunch, the new aviary manager, Perry, confirmed what Daniel had told us. "The military covets this *finca* , as do the guerillas." "What guerillas?" I asked. "The guerillas are very thick here. In fact, just last week the *finca* was overrun by them." I laid the spoon down, giving Susan my "What have we gotten ourselves into, we can never do conservation here, my veterinary reputation is ruined, and we are all going to die" look.

"I thought I was going to die," Perry continued. "I was at the aviary one day when suddenly Sebastián sped by in his truck on the inner *finca* road. I got a call from Chema, Daniel's brother at the *Casa Patronal* that guerillas were at the front gate taking guns away from the guards. I jumped in my truck, following Sebastián, but before I could catch up, he was already taking off in his airplane. I ran into my house, you know, the one at the end of the airfield next to where you used to sex the birds, and curled up in the bathroom, waiting for the worst. It was hours. Finally, Chema came and said the guerillas had gone. They had taken over the office, stolen the guns, and had made the usual threats." "What threats are those?" Susan asked. "The ones where they leave a note, with or without a body or body part, saying that you have to start paying your workers better or else." "Has that ever happened here before?" I asked. "Oh yes, one time before there was a dead person tied up to the zoo gate entrance one morning with a note. That's why I don't come out of the gate by myself or in the dark." "What are you still doing here?" Susan exhaled, and I thought "What are we doing here?" "Saving birds. If it gets worse maybe I will need to leave. I'll keep you posted if I hear anything more," Perry stated rather more blandly than I cared for.

After lunch, we drove through that zoo gate, which now seemed sinister with its rusting metal and chains. Perry was giving Susan a tour of the aviary and the Safari park, while I was distracted, wondering what in the heck had happened to John. There was no sign of him all day, or early evening. Returning to the *Casa Patronal*-way before dark, we sat waiting for him, the dinner growing cold, 6:30 p.m., 7:30 p.m., and then the phone ring. The *finca's* security guards had spotted a lone man, dressed suspiciously like a member of any number of potentially dangerous political agencies. Breathing a sigh of relief, we told the guards to let the man pass, he was with us, well sort of. John trooped into the *Casa Patronal* wordless, showered, and came to dinner without mentioning his long day alone. He did say he trekked across the *finca* in the dark to spend the day in *la montaña*-- the forest, looking for parrot nests, and had found one which he proceeded to sit by for the next 12 hours, observing behavior. Waiting until activity finished at oh-dark-thirty, he headed home. Walking under the stars he had a general idea of which way to head, but not the specific routes. He kept hitting up against fences and finally had to climb a few. Just as he was about to swing a tired leg over a fence, he heard a roar from only meters away. He had wondered into the Safari Park and was about to become a plaything for the bored lions. I kept silent though I wanted to criticize him for his foolishness and the worry he had caused us. He did not know the terrain before placing himself in the power of the landscape and could have been killed. I did tell him what we had learned of the guerillas in the area and he agreed to take someone with him in the future.

We buddied up for the rest of our days. To encourage my use of Spanish, Daniel and I were paired to look for parrots on the northern part of the *finca* on the other side of the paved road. We were hiding behind a burned-out log in the middle of the field. I think only a blind and deaf parrot wouldn't have seen us or heard our laughing attempts at communication. At one point I desperately had to go pee and I did not know how to say this in Spanish. My idea was to have Daniel walk away so I could use the log as cover. We struggled through many attempts, drawing pictures, and finally I mimicked unbuckling my pants. God only knows if he thought I was propositioning him. Finally, he understood when I said, "Pee."

That obstacle finished with, we settled into parrot observation mode: comfortably hugging the earth, smelling the open fields, and watching the multitudes of bird and reptile species play around us. Toward dusk, parrots called frequently, so we returned the next afternoon. We split up for a broader view of where the birds might be. Sitting anxiously alone where guerillas had so recently trod, I spied a pair of birds fly into a tree, and only one leave. This pattern is typical in nesting season when the male escorts the female to the nest, and then he leaves to perch nearby. Custom dictates that those who find a nest can name it, so I named it for the field we were in, *Campo Santo 4*-- Sacred Field 4. Its name came from being an ancient cemetery. "Who were the people buried here?" I asked. "I don't know. I only know that the place is *malo*-- evil. That spooked me as we hiked home in the dark, quietly, without lights, not wanting to attract attention as we carefully approached the dark, paved road from Guatemala City to El Salvador.

Despite my fear, the world shone. To the north, in the far distance, the volcano Pacaya spewed a fire streak down her side. In the day, it appeared to be a furrowed scar, but at night the lava was like an arrow pointing to the skies, which sparkled with the flock of stars that flew over us. To the west were the parents of the newly discovered parrot nest, new to us, but not to others with decades of parrot experiences. To the south was the military that had bivouacked on the *finca* a few days before. In response to the recent guerilla activity, the military camped around the landing strip as a warning. Young, nervous guys with automatic weapons were not what I had envisioned when I considered the romance of parrot conservation. To the east were the murderous wastelands of El Salvador. And all around were the sacred fields full of parrots and promise, shiny with blood, star dust, pink skinned parrot chicks, and political conniving. My spirit fell in love for the first time.

It was with a soaring heart that I accompanied Susan and John back to Guatemala City. They would return to the USA, and I would stay on for another couple of months. They were worried about leaving me, given the political situation, but when we asked Anita if there was any real danger, she said no. After dropping them off at the airport, Anita told me to get out of my field clothes because we were going to the presidential palace. She had been named as some sort of environmental advisor by the newly elected president, Jose Elias Serrano. On the way to the palace, she told me that Serrano was a family friend and friendly to conservation. If we played our cards right, we could get some pro-environment legislation passed, and we might be able to enforce the anti-poaching laws. "Why do you need me?" I asked. "You are, how do you say it, my ace in the hole. You can bring the science and authority to what is happening here and help me convince the president to support our cause." At the palace, we were searched by guards, and then shown into one of the many rooms that were brimming with fountains and flowers. We didn't have to wait long, for in strode the most powerful man in Guatemala. We all did the standard kissy cheek greeting, I wore my placid pretending-to-understand-Spanish face, and Anita and President Serrano wove themselves deeper into a world that lost its shininess in this political dark room. It was hard to fathom how I was of any use there, but I liked the sound of it, advisor to the advisor to the president of any country.

The next morning, I was anxious to return to what I had fallen in love with. I finally left the city in the late afternoon, nervously because it was unwise to drive at night. At the *Casa Patronal* I was met by Chema, Daniel, Perry, and a host of aviary workers who met me at the door with a bottle of rum, coke, and cold beer. They knew it was the first anniversary of my father's death, and it was the local custom to have a *novena* mass--9 successive days of prayers-- and celebration after a year had passed. We skipped the church part and took the libations directly out to the pool, where they asked about my father. My Spanish was still too poor to describe much, so Perry helped me out. I wondered what I could say in a few words that would honor the man, expose my grief, and also hold true to the mess our relationship had been. I stared into the pool where I was told to never swim at night because drowned bats floated like fallen mangos or clumps of leaves. A few more sips of rum and I had an idea that could possibly translate. I told them my father had given me the best advice of my life. I had just graduated with a B.S. in Avian Sciences from U.C. Davis and was about to take off in an old Pinto with a young man to tour every one of the lower 48 states, living off of $10 a day. In that momentous moment as we hugged goodbye, he said, "Don't do anything stupid"-- "*No hagas nada estupido.*" My father lives on in me with these words, I explained, and I hoped now he did so with them as well. "*Vaya con Dios, no con estupidez*"-- "Go with God, not with stupidity"--, we told one another as we slipped off into the night.

1990

The USA, under President Bush, invades Panama, disposing and capturing General Manuel Noriega. Noriega had worked for the CIA for decades, serving as one the primary conduits for illicit weapons, military equipment, and cash destined for USA backed forces throughout Central and South America. The USA Intelligence community knew he was a major drug trafficker but allowed it because of his usefulness for their covert military operations in Latin America.

The Gulf War, a war waged by coalition forces from 34 nations and led by the USA against Iraq, begins in response to Iraq's invasion of Kuwait.

LORAKIM JOYNER

Chapter 4
TRYING NOT TO DO ANYTHING STUPID
Guatemala 1991

The barrier to socializing with "the help" had now been broken, and so not too long afterwards, Daniel, Perry, and Chema came for me so we could go up to the local *tienda*-- store-- for *Gallo* beer. Shortly thereafter I was sitting at the Las Rosas *tienda* kicking at chicken shit in sandaled feet and watching the scavenging pigs through a *Gallo* beer haze. Suddenly a sharp image of my future flashed into my mind; one of loneliness brought on by rejecting a status quo life that increasingly seemed to be no more than delusions. Also, I sensed a great deal of sacrifice and life-long commitment, but toward what end I was not sure. I now felt that there was a greater reason to live, although any truth to this was elusive. I was literally crying in my beer, surrounded by caged and roving birds and children, all fated to die sooner than their counterparts in the USA.

Most days we worked, the days stretching long, hot, and boring. Even though no new active nests had been discovered, climbed, or protected, we monitored our study area as much as possible. Daniel and I headed out one morning before sunrise on a walking tour of the entire finca. There hadn't been much activity as the day lightened, and so to pass the time as the miles ground under our feet, we shared stories of our lives. Daniel began to speak of his love of Mary and Jesus. Born on the *finca* into the Catholic faith, I suspected that he did not have a very nuanced view of religion, and I was sure as he expanded and became more animated that he was aiming to save my soul. Far too many times I had been on the receiving end of a zealous Christian and did not savor the possible awkward situation arising. Coming from a man so different from

33

me, though, I gave him the benefit of the doubt and tried to understand his explanation of how much Mother Mary meant to him.

We were coming to the edge of one of the last large remaining tracks of forest on the Pacific slope, in a pasture of high grass that didn't completely cover the burned stumps, evidence of the forest burned during my visit to Guatemala in 1987. Just as Daniel was reaching the climax of his witnessing, the sun rose over the tree canopy and steam billowed up into the skies, along with a flock of chattering *loros*—parrots. I gasped and fell to my knees in the tall grass, crying, perhaps from joy, and perhaps also shock and embarrassment. What had just happened? All I knew as Daniel helped me to my feet was that when Daniel and others spoke of their Mary and Jesus, they were speaking of my trees and birds. There are just different words for the immense beauty, interconnection, and unity that hold each and every one of us.

A few days later I was headed back to the *finca* for lunch when I saw militia stopping public buses outside the house I just moved into.. They ordered everyone off the bus, and lined up the boys and men. This did not look good so I stomped on the brakes and swerved into the *finca* where armed guards could offer cover. The living fence of young growing trees strapped with barb wire was all that was between me and the infamous military that had killed thousands of civilians, raising cries of genocide. Spying through the fence, I saw the military pull out the youngest and fittest to join them – a forced draft right in front of my eyes. Eventually they left, the people reboarded the bus, and the military took off with their haul.

Despite this, I was antsy to see more of Guatemala. When the invitation came to visit La Azul, the *finca* of the director of the La Aurora Zoo in Guatemala City, Daniel, and I jumped at the chance to see how the parrots were faring. It felt risky to be taking the beaten down *La Paloma* that great of a distance into the volcanoes, so we left plenty early in case we had mechanical issues. We got there by midday, the smoking nearby volcano nearly completely shrouded in clouds. During lunch with the director, the rain poured down on us like grief unrelenting, but as we finished I imagined it was growing lighter. So anxious was I to discover the land that Daniel and I practically ran up the volcano slopes in the drizzle. We wound over the hilly trails through coffee and bean fields and eventually came to a rise that had the only large trees in the area. There weren't many, so it wasn't hard to figure out where to settle in for parrot watching. Our nest for the night allowed us to look across a ravine at the smoking volcano and look back at the tall trees. Misty fingers floated all around. Daniel and I were damp from the hike, and I was anxious to see and feel all I could.

While watching the sun set, we began to lose hope until we finally heard *loros* near the large trees. One pair was in some kind of Bolero tree, which looks like a Eucalyptus tree. They kept yelling and yelling near this tree that had a cavity for a parrot nest. Their calls were disturbing because they both were yelling very close to the cavity and no other parrot pairs were squawking in response. The kind of pair duetting that we were hearing was usually in response to some kind of visual threat in their territory. In the evenings these calls were often ritualized as pairs went to the edges of their territories to holler at their neighbors. It was too far for us to see what was going on, so we thought that this was a very vocal pair. They could also have been responding to people or predators near their nest.

When it was nearly dark we began to hear other strange parrot calls. These were coming from a great distance away, down the ravines that ran into streams, rivers, and finally to black volcanic beaches and the Atlantic Ocean. Wings rapidly beating, dark parrot-sized objects flew from below us up into the ravines. They had to be parrots, but their calls were so strange, so much more mournful than the calls we were used to. It was likely that the parrots in the highlands had different dialects than the parrots we knew in the lowlands. That's the science talking, but my heart said they were sad.

Once again we were walking in the dark, each refusing to turn on our flashlights and lose macho points. Eventually we had to because we were way lost, and yet so close to the *Casa Patronal*. We eventually found it, took a shower, and ate beans and tortillas to candlelight and cicada music. After dinner, we took a walk up the rock-lined road to candle lights we saw up on the hill. Roman, a *finca* worker and temporary guide, walked with us and introduced us to some of the locals who were gathered around the dark *tienda* and gulping beer. One boot clanking paunch-bellied cowboy, another Samuel, told of us how he and others poached parrots on the Director's *finca*. After some rapid discussion between him and the cowboy, Daniel turned to me, brown eyes glistening. "*Lo siento señorita, Kim--* I'm sorry--, but there is so much poaching competition here that no chicks ever hatch from wild nests, let alone fledge. You see, they are so anxious to claim a nest that they even take the eggs so that others won't get them. La *parte triste* -- the sad part-- is that very few of the eggs hatch, even though they place them under any ducks they have that are also incubating their own eggs. The breeding season starts later here, so that pair of birds that we heard this evening probably just had their eggs stolen, perhaps even while we were out this evening." "But, Daniel, that means if there are no chicks fledging here, the survival of this species can't be guaranteed." I didn't have enough Spanish to say my heart would be broken, but my eyes did. Daniel didn't preach any parrot gospel to this gathering because we were strangers in town and were surrounded by drinking *finca* workers. Even I knew that it would be stupid to say more.

My eyes opened up to a black morning by a gentle touch from Daniel. "Kim *Levantate,*"-- "Kim-Wake-up" (pronounced more like Kem). A quick café and *pan dulce*-- sweet bread-- later, we were walking by 5 a.m. and we weren't alone. Roosters crowed, Mayan hands sharpened machetes, and soft voices spoke as we headed up into the hills. It was a fairly uneventful sunrise, despite the always present anticipation of discovering a nest. But we knew our odds were slight given the confessions we'd heard the night before. Sure enough, no birds came to the suspected nest tree. After hiding near the tree until 7:30, we took off to see the layout of the land. The volcanic plume of Santiaguito was clearly visible as the winds pushed the volcanic spiral away from us. The sun beat down on us and the many workers we passed in a field.

When we came to a drop off, Daniel asked some of the workers what was at the bottom of the ravine, and one said, "*Un río Don* Daniel,"-- "a river Sir Daniel." Almost straight down we climbed, holding onto slippery roots and doing magnificent butt slides to the bottom, where a sparkling river babbled, and we heard a new parrot call. *Chocoyos*! -- green parakeets (conures)! These are small green parrots with relatively long tails that look much like a small macaw. Conures are my favorite kind of parrot and I'd never seen them in the wild. Doubly delightful was the presence of many birds nesting in the vine covered cliffs above us. We hiked to the river's gravel banks and lay flat so as to not disturb the birds. The sun filtered through vegetation, giving the whole primitive scene a surrealistic glow.

Not for long. The day was so hot, the river so inviting, and the birds so peacefully close, I had to get into the water. I stripped down to a t-shirt and underwear, and plunged into the tropical world. I rolled onto my back and beheld green flashes of perfection flying in and out of their cave-like nests. I floated, trying to ignore Daniel's silent watch over me. I was in God's arms, connected to this great land. Finally, the fact that I was enjoying myself so thoroughly, alone, in front of an audience much less, ended the rapture and brought me out of the cradling water. Dripping wet I ascended the ravine and was almost dry by the time we reached the *Casa Patronal.* We had to get back to our ranch before dark.

We drove out of coffee plantations and entered rolling fields of sugar cane, which eventually leveled out as we entered the coastal plain that stretches from the volcanic highlands to the Pacific along the southern border of Guatemala. As stark as the coffee plantations were, denuded of most natural foliage, sugar cane was even worse. This was my first time to see the bareness of this crop, as our home territory was still mostly cattle. Sugar cane fields were good for hiding people, from the lowliest woman needing a refuge to pee, to the highest Guerilla commander hiding with fear and rage.

We pulled off the road and I slipped into the sugar cane, much like the scene in <u>Fields of Dreams</u> where heaven-sent bodies return to their ethereal home by slowly disappearing into the corn field. When I returned, Daniel had spotted an odd looking building down a dirt road that divided the sugar cane. To investigate it, I guided the *La Paloma* slowly to a mausoleum. The sugar cane divided around the building, allowing enough space for graves. Some of these were relatively recent graves that were decorated with cheap, colorful plastic wreaths and flowers. It was a festival for the eyes, despite the poverty of materials.

Daniel and I were silently circling the cemetery when out flew four pairs of *chocoyas*—green parakeets-- from the open arch of the mausoleum. They perched in a nearby small tree and squawked raucously at us. Our curiosity peaked as we moved toward the darkened recess of the ancient building. A young boy appeared from nowhere. He eyed us with mistrust and told us we couldn't steal the parrot chicks in the nests the adult parakeet had just flow from. "What parrot chicks?" we asked? "The ones in the *chocoyo* nests." "*Donde?*"-- "Where?" The boy walked us into the building dating to the Spanish colonization of the area, centuries ago. He pointed up the curving wall to various holes had been formed by the crumbling mortar and rock. "No one takes these parrot chicks because there is a curse on any who tries. Not too many years ago a man came to steal the chicks. He climbed up the stones and was about to rob the nests, when out from one of the other holes came a revenging horde of bees. At this danger, he fell from the wall, only to come to his death at the floor as his head hit the corner of one of the crypts and his body was covered with bees. No one takes these babies, and I advise you to do likewise!" Harrumph, I thought. European settlers came to this land, murdered it and its peoples, and tamed what survived. Their living legacy abounds in the tortured land and in the guarded faces of the survivors, but their deaths also adorn the land, such as this mausoleum. When they lived, their hands wrought desolation, and in death their bones and bricks offer life and death. We inheritors are cursed – what our ancestors gave us can both save and destroy parrot life.

They needed saving, or at least to be left alone. It seems like every day we discovered one more nest of parrots poached. In that year we were studying mostly orange-fronted parakeets, also known as orange-fronted conures. We still hadn't found many yellow-naped amazon nests, or learned how to climb to them very well. Instead, we studied the more abundant and accessible small, long-tailed parrots that swoop and chatter all around the Pacific slope of Guatemala. They nest in arboreal termiteria, termite nests built in trees. Parents excavate an entrance hole and an inner cavity where they lay their eggs and raise their chicks. During the breeding season, both parents sleep in the nest. We couldn't get to the chicks deep into a termiteria, but we could capture the adults when they flew out in the skimpy light of the morning. While it was still dark, we approached the nest and placed a butterfly net at the end of a long aluminum pole over the entrance. This meant being in the field at 5 a.m. or earlier, while the stars still shone. Upon arriving, the "catcher" placed the net against the nest opening, while I organized the sampling gear on our portable surgery table, my rain *poncho*. Talking was forbidden so we wouldn't scare the birds into leaving before there was enough light to work with them. We spent long hours at the base of these nest trees because the parents often chose to sleep in, exiting at a more civilized hour.

As time went on, we grew relaxed about holding up our capture net with our arms; we wedged the bottom of the pole into the ground or leaned it into our shoulders. I had seen Daniel close his eyes while on pole holding duty. The rest of us could be more obvious about claiming much needed sleep because we didn't have pole holding duty. The *poncho* on the cool, wet grass was an inviting beacon, drawing supposedly energetic biologists into dreams where birds weren't poached and human babies didn't die of dysentery. This relaxing was always a bit risky because the parents could shoot out of the nest at any time and if the net pole was not firmly in hand or directly over the entrance, we could lose one or both parents.

This practice was also risky for other reasons. One morning, only Daniel and I were doing the conure catch. The targeted nest was along the main road near the entrance to Tecanal, el Porton. As the nest was high in the tree, Daniel had to climb the tree a ways before holding the net against the entrance. He soon settled himself in, as I did at the base of the tree. I laid out all the vet gear and sat in the ditch depression alongside the road. Truckers occasionally passed, roaring into our forced silences, but it did not keep either of us from falling asleep. I was forcibly awakened by breaking branches, a thud, and a cry of *"Dios Mio!"*-- "Oh my God!" Daniel hadn't fallen all the way to the ground, but was low enough for me to see his resentment that he didn't have as comfortable a bed as I did, and that I was blowing snot out of my nose I was laughing so hard. Silently he went back up the tree until we caught both of the parents in a single moment.

Once the birds were in the net, it was a mad scramble to get them out of the net as quickly as possible. The mesh of the net was quite fine and it could get as tangled as unbrushed hair. We eventually learned to just cut them out of the net because it was too time consuming to try to work the fine threads out from around feathers, nails, and snapping beaks. And they bite! If one got a hold of you, the plan was just to bear it, because worse than the little fiends bite was the angry look of the vet, that's me, as one of the possible samples flew away. We would begin by doing a thorough physical exam, which included measuring beaks, wings, and feet. Next on the list would be collecting any external parasites, which we would occasionally see scurrying around the face of the birds. One of the last things we would do was to take a blood sample from the bird's jugular vein.

This particular pair from the roadside termiteria where Daniel had fallen seemed normal enough, except that the female was a bit thin. Skinny parents were not an abnormal finding. Both parents were then banded, placed in a small sack and weighed, and then released together. I had also collected blood, cloacal, and choanal microflora samples. We worried that the parents would be so disturbed that they'd never return to their nests, so we placed an observer after a climb to monitor the parents' return, and they always did.

A few weeks after we sampled this nest, our crew of biologists and visiting ecotourists were driving along the road, returning from another conure capture. As we passed in front of el *porton*, Daniel and I went into panic mode when we saw a line of fence workers chopping back the annual growth from the live fences. We had repeatedly asked Samuel, the *finca* administrator, to give these temporary workers a short speech on anti-poaching, which we repeatedly suspected that he didn't do because we kept finding ruptured termiteria in the wake of their work. I suspected Samuel was not on the conservation side. Perhaps he had been insulted that I hadn't taken him up his offer to sleep with him, or whatever he was suggesting when he stuck out his tongue at me one night.

Fearing the worse for our beloved conure nest, we sent all our Spanish speakers along the long line of workers to tell them not to harm the termiteria or hunt any iguanas. Down the line I heard Daniel yelling for the others to join him when he saw a worker up in the tree hacking open the nest with his *machet*e. A few chicks were in his lunch pouch and the rest were being eaten alive by the swarming termites in the nest. Daniel quickly retrieved the chicks from the man's bag and the nest. Then we sat down and carefully but quickly removed the termites. The chicks ranged in age from barely having pin feathers all the way up to having green tips emerging from the sheathed feathers. From past experience, we knew that the youngest were most susceptible to the bites of the termites due to their size and lack of protective feathers. The youngest chick looked a bit shocky, but the rest appeared unaffected as we cleared the last of the termites. In the meantime, Susan had fetched Samuel in hopes he'd loudly fire the man on the spot. A Guatemalan stand-off ensued, resulting in Samuel once again promising to warn the fence workers to not poach birds. The fence worker, apparently stupefied about all the fuss over a few parakeets, was asked to leave. I am sure that taking nests of parrots was one of the benefits for these men that hacked in the hot sun all day at minimum wage (a little over $2 a day, or 12 *Quetzales*-- Guatemala's local currency).

Though it was a tough break for the conure family, this was the first time we could study conure chicks. There in the hot sun, next to the roaring vehicles blasting us with exhaust, we recorded as well as we knew how the parameters of the five chicks' perfection, weighing and sampling them with delight. They were returned to their nest once the termites had settled down in the termiteria. Daniel placed a dried cow patty atop the opening to shield them from rain, and even with all that disturbance, both parents returned and did so for several more days.

We eventually quit watching the nest and others, because I had to concentrate on processing the samples we'd collected at the aviaries, which we called *La Guacuera*-- the place of macaws. I was working with bacterial samples when Daniel's daughter Hilda came rushing into the room. Her long dark hair swept down her back in a permanent braid and her eyes were of such a dark hue that the pupils merged with the irises, making one fall constantly into her steady gaze. We were not yet friends, but I was enamored with this 11 year-old Maya descendent. She had visited here before when Daniel had sent her to me to learn science and medicine. She had delivered poop samples from members in her family to see if they had internal parasites, worms. I had urged Daniel to have his family tested after one of the younger nephews had coughed up a round worm into my hand. I was explaining to her the various species of worm eggs on the slide under the microscope when she suddenly bent over and placed her teeth against my waist. It all seemed to happen in slow motion, much like a bad porn movie as I watched her invade my personal space and make such an erotic gesture. Turns out she was only removing a loose thread that was dangling on my field pants and simply used the handiest cutting tool available. I was amazed at the grooming rite she performed and that I was trusted enough to become a grooming partner. I had seen similar behavior among the *campesinos*-- small farmers-- and it had often raised envious hairs on my white hide, watching people help each other clean up pimples, scabs, and knotted hair.

This day, however, Hilda came not to groom but to bring me a sick adult parakeet that she'd found near the school. The bird was nearly comatose and I was amazed that Hilda had been able to recover it before its final moments were ended by predators. As I performed a quick triage and began emergency treatment, I discovered that the bird had a band on its leg. It was one of our wild conures that we had captured and she was gravely ill. As I let the treatment of heat, oxygen, intravenous fluids and antibiotics settle into her, I drove home to get the nest records to find out who she was and to gather the background medical data that we had taken when she had been sampled.

It could not have been worse, for she was the mother of the five chicks that we had just sampled less than two weeks ago. I rushed back to the hospital only to stare as she staggered around her incubator, immune from further challenges in this world. I was wracked with guilt. Perhaps our manipulation of her, her mate, and her chicks had led to some stress-related disease. Her death later that day was not unexpected, although unwelcome. It did, however, give me the chance to perform an autopsy. A wound on her wing and the deep ascending tract of necrotic flesh from her damaged wing into her chest, as well as the septicemic look to her organs, indicated the possibility of an infected wound. A culture of the organs and wound showed that the bird was overcome with Pseudomonas, a common infection after a bite wound. It was also during

40

the necropsy that I was able to confirm that it was a she, for now I could behold her recrudescing ovaries and oviduct, the origins of the now motherless five chicks in the damaged termiteria.

Not knowing if the chicks had a father still attending them, we posted observers at the nest to ensure the chicks were fed. We climbed the tree to inspect their status and weigh them. All five chicks were doing fine, the oldest of which wasn't far from fledging. Looking back on captive data and the few damaged nests that we observed, five was probably the uppermost limit that could be successfully raised by a pair of conures. It seemed incredible that a single parent could forage enough food for themselves and for the large brood, but we'd never know if a single parent could do the deed. By the second day there was a second adult flying with the male and entering the nest. We couldn't figure out who this bird was because we were reluctant to attempt any further captures. All we knew was that all five chicks had full crops when we checked them, were gaining weight, and all successfully fledged. The family of seven was seen around the nest area as the rainy season began, and we could only wonder at the story buried deep within their avian brains. Had the mother been bitten by some predator, such as an iguana, a raccoon, or a *taquazin*-- opossum-- attempting to enter the termiteria? Did the father immediately recruit a new mate to help him with his family responsibilities? Had he a girlfriend waiting in his wings? To live well, were the parrots evolutionarily designed to have multiple mates? Why did all five chicks have such a high percentage of basophils (a rarer kind of white blood cell that could possibly be present in histamine releasing events, such as termite bites)? We did not have any answers, but were in awe that this family had survived intervening scientists, poachers, and predators, and were glad that we were able to save them from the termites.

1991

Poverty rate in Latin America 33%, in Guatemala over 50%.

The Cold War ends, but it's the 11th year of Civil War in El Salvador; Salvadoran rebels shoot down a USA Army helicopter and execute the 2 surviving crew members

21st year of Civil War in Guatemala; Jorge Serrano Elias is elected President making history as the first successful transition from one democratically elected civilian government to another; USAA suspends military aid to Guatemala 2 weeks earlier, but military training and "flight safety equipment" aid continues.

1st year after the Nicaragua Civil War ends (Contra anti-government forces supported by USA)

Mt. Pinatuba erupts in the Philippines, killing 700 and leaving 200,000 homeless. The Philippine senate rejects a treaty with the USA, ending almost a century of USA military presence.

An amateur video records the beating by police offers of Randy King in Los Angeles

Exxon agrees to pay $1 billion for the clean-up of the Exxon Valdez oil spill in Alaska

CHAPTER 5
PARADISE FOUND
Guatemala, early 1992

My dream of living in an Alaskan paradise was falling apart. I broke up with a boyfriend, moved in with my ex-husband, and lived in another motor home in the backyard of another ex-boyfriend. It didn't help that I was hardly ever in Alaska, but usually in the Philippines or Guatemala. I spent so much time in Guatemala in 1992 that I took up residence in a worker's home outside the guarded *finca*'s gates on the main road where I had seen young men forced into the military. I sparsely furnished it and found curtains to shut out prying eyes during the day, and especially during the long nights.

1992

Rigoberta Menchú Tum, a K'iche' political activist from Guatemala, receives the Nobel Peace Prize for her work promoting indigenous rights in the country after approximately 200,000 Mayans in Guatemala were murdered in the1960-1996 civil war. Most were killed in an organized and systematic slaughter, primarily during 1981-1983.

It felt good to move out of the Casa Patronal and into my own space in Tecanal, though I was often up in Guatemala City-- *Guate*-- to do errands and

43

work with Anita. The field work was cranking now with parrot counts, sampling parrot nestlings, conducting physical exams, and hospital work at the aviaries. My plan for this day was to quickly meet with Anita and return to Tecanal. Instead, Anita invited me to stay for the night. She and Sebastián were attending a function at the Presidential Palace to celebrate President Serrano's first year in office. Anita said all the cabinet members would be there and wanted me to meet them as I gave her my best you've-got-to-be-kidding look. Dressed in dusty jeans and a t-shirt I stammered that I needed to get back to work and, besides, I had nothing to wear. "No problem," she said, "I have just the dress for you." It sounded like a long, boring night, but then I could always say I had attended a state function.

Anita picked out a bright red and white dress, fashionable pumps, and sleek stockings. I was sent off to her daughter's closets to search for hair adornments and, when finished, was placed on her cosmetic throne where the final touches were added. This was awkward not only because I never wore make-up, but also because of a little eruption that had suddenly appeared on my upper lip. The spot had been sore all day, probably from the wind storm the last few days. The Northern Wind-- *El Viento Norte*—combined with the relentless sun chapped and fried our skin, and in this case my lips because I had been in the field all day, every day, the last week. Looking into the mirror, I realized this was no ordinary blemish. It reminded me of the herpes outbreaks on a friend's lips, and sure enough, at that moment it oozed as hers had.

Anita and I navigated carefully around my ulcer, which was largely hidden by cosmetics and bright red lipstick. Great, just great, I would go oozing to my first presidential affair. Despite my misgivings, I cut a rather nice Latina profile and thought I could get away with it. As I predicted, the evening began slowly. I knew very few people in the packed ballroom and was lost without Anita's introductions. Luckily those attending switched to English when I was introduced, and I attempted cocktail party small talk, which I had never been good at. Introduced as *la conservationista*-- the conservationist--, however, gave me some basis for conversation. Anita left me with a cabinet member as she went in search of others. No matter the dignitary she brought to me or to whom I was guided, I thought they were staring at my ulcer that was now probably as big as my nose. Its dull pain was growing sharp and felt like it was covering half my face.

Midnight was the dining hour for late night social gatherings. I kept looking at my watch, feeling hunger rumbling my stomach and disciplining myself to not lick the ulcer and smear lipstick everywhere. Whatever the outbreak represented, it brought with it a feverish aching throughout my body. I was more than ready to go home when finally Anita said the late evening cocktail party was over, but then we were invited to dine with the president and his family. Wow, now everyone would see my ulcer in the smaller, well-lit dining room.

I followed Anita and her husband to a nondescript door where a palace security knocking ritual commenced, and uniformed, armed soldiers escorted us into a long, underground hall. Our clacking heels echoed in the long corridor as a soldier led us through a maze. We walked under the city's streets to reach the president's living quarters that were centered within the protective eye of the palace. We were met with the president's and first lady's hugs and kisses, which made me wonder just how many people I had spread herpes to that night. We met Serrano's sisters, his five children, and another guest. While the awaiting cooks were given orders what to prepare, I took a tour of the palace and residential area, walking into meeting rooms in stocking feet, my high fashion borrowed pumps long discarded in favor of comfort.. In these cloistered areas there was no telling what deals had been arranged that sealed the fates of millions

Serrano himself guided me to his bird collection and we then discussed health problems of a few. I promised to phone his secretary to set up a treatment and a diagnostic schedule. We sat down to dinner at 2:00 a.m., and the conversation bounced between English and Spanish. They seemed like ordinary folks who enjoyed good food. I even had a good time because, in their gracious manner, I had been included in the conversation, and the ulcer that had surely now grown as big as my head was not commented on. Finally, the evening ended and an armed soldier walked us out of the palace to Sebastián's car. The streets around the palace at 4:00 a.m. were strangely quiet and dark except for the moon that dropped rays onto the soldier's rifle, as if symbolic of the honor I naively felt to now be the president's official avian veterinarian. Stepping into the guarded car, I was leaving Camelot. Silently I vowed to fight with all my might for what was right. With the backing of this king, the parrots would surely be saved.

But from the start of our fieldwork, the year wasn't looking good for the yellow-naped amazons. There weren't many nests on Tecanal, so we extended our conservation area to neighboring *fincas*. Daniel had arranged with the manager of a neighboring ranch, *Esperanza*--- Hope--, for a tour by one of the older hired hands who knew where all the parrot nests were. We arrived at 6:30 a.m., just as the ranch hands gathered at the office. Their horses were ponies and small mules. Their patched-together tackle and sullen faces told me this was not as happy as a *finca* as ours, and there weren't many workers or cattle. Many of the grazing fields near the *finca* roads, the paved CA-1 *carretera*-- highway-- to El Salvador and the dirt road to *Finca Arveja*, Puertas had been converted to *caña*-- sugar cane-- which was managed differently than cattle. Sugar cane needed fewer people and more machines, and it caused more pollutants.

Daniel shook everyone's hand and made them laugh. He had an

ingratiating way that was appreciated because he was one of them. Together we were an unstoppable pair – Daniel with the know-how and me as the symbol of authority and, I thought, hope. The administrator gave us permission to work on the *finca* whenever we wanted. I would later finalize this arrangement with the *finca* owner, whom I never met. He never came to the *finca*, but through Sebastián I was able to pass letters back and forth. Daniel told me that the real power lay with the administrator and we had to work with him, buy him beer, and take him out to lunch, just as we did Samuel from our own ranch.

Juanito was assigned to us for the day. He was toothless and grey-whiskered, in rubber boots and rope-tied zipperless pants. We headed down a dirt road that paralleled the Puertas Coaches road to Arveja. It seemed to go on forever, but we eventually came to a group of corrals where many fields fanned out. The road ended, and we drove across the fields. I hesitated because of mud from the rainy season, when rain fell nearly every afternoon. Juanito said don't worry, the *La Paloma*, our white pickup truck, wouldn't get stuck. It did within 50 feet.

We used *machetes* to cut mud away from the submerged wheels, while we dodged fire ants whose homes we disturbed. The cowboys caught up with us and gathered branches and palm-tree debris to wedge under the wheels that we tried to jack up. We bonded even though the gringa lost major macho points with this error of getting the vehicle stuck. During the loud spectacle of grunts, laughter, and muttered responses to muttered orders, Daniel heard a pair of yellow-naped amazons. Then another pair and another. We were astounded. Never had we observed three pairs of loros in the same field. We decided to return in the evening if we ever got out of the blasted field. Eventually we quit. Daniel climbed up behind a cowboy on his diminutive steed to go find the tractor we heard churning in a nearby field. This was a triple bonus for a *gringa* in Guatemalan face losing bingo: getting stuck, having others see you get stuck, and having a tractor pull you out.

The morning was a wash; our only success was connecting with the others. A little humility is a good thing when sucking up to the workers. We were learning that we needed them on our side because they apparently decided whose nests were poached and whose weren't. We returned in late afternoon, this time parking the *La Paloma* a good distance from the muddy fields and walking in. We set up our observation points for the evening on a drier aisle between two live barbed-wire fences, where we could look into several fields at once, although our overhead vision was restricted. Daniel settled about 40 meters away from me and we waited.

A few noisy pairs flew in early, and we watched to see if they entered cavities. Surrounded by trees, it was hard to pinpoint where the birds were calling from. In the field to the west were palm trees, a low sprawling *ceiba*, and a larger *ceiba* that reached at least 35 meters into the sky. *Ceibas*, long revered by

46

the Maya, are the national tree of Guatemala and engender awe and respect wherever they are, and this field was full of them. The field to the east was La Chinga Ceiba that stood over 40 meters high. The fields to the north had more *ceibas* and many more palm trees, and by the corrals were two ceibas and a *castaña*-chestnut tree. It was into this chestnut tree that the most vocal pair landed and stayed. We also heard pairs all around, easily three or four nests.

At dusk Daniel joined me to celebrate with hugs and excited chatter when suddenly a hum of wings passed over us. The nesting birds had settled in for the evening, so we had no clue what these birds were. We couldn't see in the failing light, but we caught glimpses of large groups of green messengers flying overhead. We couldn't fully absorb what we were witnessing, it was that miraculous. Birds amassed here in numbers perhaps only known before the time that humans destroyed earth's sacred garden. As we walked out of the dark field under branches laden with parrots, Daniel reached for my hand and I let him. I was certain I had found paradise.

The next morning we excitedly returned to *Esperanza* to see the glory repeated and count the birds. By the time we got to the corrals it was already light. Parrots with nests often fly at this time, but we heard no sound after I killed the engine. Maybe last night had been a dream, our fantasy that the world was a different place. Not thinking, we slammed our car doors and the sky exploded. Wings beat against roosting branches as raucous, green clouds of parrots lifted from the highest ceibas and flew east. We couldn't count the exodus, but we estimated at least seventy napes had been roosting in these trees. We couldn't believe our eyes or ears. How could such original beauty still exist in that disturbed land?

We had discovered a roost site, where parrots-- *loros*- communally spent the night. If we could keep track of how many birds or families of birds slept there, we could estimate the population and fledglings each year. *Loros* fly in pairs, and if they are flying in 3s, 4s, or 5s, they are parents with chicks from that year. Because of a roost site's importance to population monitoring, we regularly counted this site for the rest of the year. One night 250 birds flew in during the non-breeding season, June to December, when paired birds returned to roost trees after the nesting season, with or without rambunctious chicks in tow.

There are many theories about the necessity of roost sites for parrots, other than striking awe and dropping jaws of those who glimpse what the land looked like before a capitalist economy came to the New World. What Europe's hoards would pick at, the American pet bird industry would demolish. But that year we observed what parrot abundance looked like, and because we were so close to the birds from our counting positions, we felt like we were part of their culture. As the birds arrived in groups of two, in family groups of three to five, or in larger flocks of the younger, unpaired birds, they raised a hellacious chorus as they lit in the trees. The shadows at roosting time challenged us in determining the age of the birds, as loros younger than two years have hardly any yellow nape; their necks are green. It was easy to imagine that the birds tumbling in the air and dive bombing each other were the younger, energetic, hormone blasting youth nearly crazed with the excitement of the upcoming night.

They reminded me of a company picnic. The adults were all business, despite the holiday atmosphere, because they had seen it all before. They protected the fledglings, eyed the interactions of their mates with others, and looked to the next day's concerns. The babies of the year demanded attention, their chick cries easily heard by the spying biologists below. Then there were the youths, never still in the roost sites, squabbling and growling, occasionally shooting from the tree with loud squawks to chase each other around the highest *ceibas*. One can almost imagine them rolling up cigarettes into their shoulder feathers, baring their appendages so that their beautiful tattoos attract future mates.

It is an insane spectacle to observe, a powder keg of intelligent beings crammed into a relatively small space, much like the countryside of Guatemala. All it takes is one real or imagined threat to upset the appearance of calm. We knew all too well what these birds were capable of. Many times when night was coming and the count was nearly completed, something would startle the birds. One time a crane flew over the trees. Parrots know what a crane is. It doesn't look anything like a predator, although it has evolutionary links to vultures, but these parrots know all too well what vultures are. No big deal. But all it takes is one juvenile, one bored mate, or perhaps even an over-zealous sentinel bird to sound the alarm, and presto, instant confusion, like the Big Bang theory. Bang goes the universe and out swells chaos, exploding from the center roost trees. Then they slowly fly, revolving round and round, much like swirling galaxies, ready to bang again, but hopefully not until the morning so that tired biologists can call it a day. During these minutes of confusion, we tried to count how many birds left and how many birds returned. It was like a game of fruit basket upset on fast forward. In the game, each person sitting in a circle has a name of a fruit. The "it" in the center calls out two fruit names, and those players must exchange seats while the "it" tries to beat them to one of the empty seats. The "it" can also make everyone explode out of their chairs by calling, "Fruit basket upset!" I once played the game with a young boy, and he couldn't stand up because he laughed so hard. That's what it's like, I thought. The sight of so many birds at one time gives rise to the impulse to run, jump, and fall.

At the end of the breeding season in 1992, like most other days and like most other nearby humans, I rose with the sun, with nurturing deeply embedded in my goals for the day. Time crunched against a departing, mid-afternoon flight. I was hours from the airport, far into countryside only reachable by a dangerous winding road through the volcanoes, with an entire morning of nest surveys to complete. We didn't get farther than the first yellow-naped nest in a decrepit old *sauce*,--willow tree-- on the banks of a creek squeezed between cattle fields. We lay low in thorny brush, waiting for the parents to leave the nest, but they never did because they hadn't been at the nest that morning or for the last couple of days. "*Esta seguro de que no estan aqui?*"-- "Are you sure they are not here?"-- Daniel asked as we approached the tree. Climbing the tree, he chirped his surprise when the two chicks were still there. My dismay at their condition silenced any hope. The two chicks were thin, dehydrated, and starving.

We put them back in the nest, with misgivings. Would they survive without me to make critical decisions on their behalf? As I rushed home for my suitcase, I shouted, "If the parents don't come in tonight, you might need to rescue the chicks so they won't die." We agreed that bringing wild parrot chicks into human homes was not exactly rescuing. Daniel suggested we name the sick chicks Mary and Joseph, which with my newly acquired openness to things spiritual seemed reasonable.

Sadly considering the condition of these birds and their unknown future, I drove with a heavy foot to Guatemala City and the airplane that would take me home to Alaska. Rushing through check-in and immigration, I caught my breath after I plopped down in a window seat. As usual there was a delay, so in between looking out at the volcanoes beyond the tarmac I read veterinary journals and caught up on what I missed while immersed in the communication-dead zone of the Pacific Coast.

"Kim!" a voice called. I poked my head over the head rests, looking for someone I knew. No one was familiar, and I returned to my reading. "Kim!" my name was called. This time I stood and looked up and down the aisle, *nada*--nothing. Not even another paragraph into the article, again I heard, "Kim!" This time I walked back to the bathroom, looking at all the seats, opening the bathrooms, and searching to the cockpit's open door. No one I knew was on the plane.

In my seat, my muscles tensed for what I feared I'd hear, and I jumped when again my name was called. I thought, "Okay I'm listening. What do you want?" "Move to Guatemala." "I can't move to Guatemala. I don't have a paid job there." "Move to Guatemala," the voice repeated. "I can't move to Guatemala. There is little I can do there, and it will kill my veterinary career." "Move to Guatemala," the voice insisted. "Nope, that is not going to happen. It's too dangerous. My life will be over." "Move to Guatemala!" My thoughts were replaced by shallow sobs. "All right, I'll go." The voice stopped, and I was alone physically, but my heart was full of joy. I knew clearly that I had been given a gift far more valuable than a career or desire or plan. I was given love.

Fear, anxiety, and doubt slipped away and I knew the great calling of my life –
to live in love, to receive it, and to give it. Nothing else mattered.

Chapter 6
THE LONG HAUL
Guatemala, 1992

1992

Boris Yeltsin announced that Russia will stop targeting the USA with nuclear weapons.

A jury convicts former Panamanian dictator Manuel Noriega of assisting Columbia's drug cartels, sentencing him to 40 years in prison.

A jury acquits four LAPD police officers accused of excessive force for beating black motorist Rodney King, setting off riots that lead to 53 deaths and $1 billion in damage.

In the summer of 1992, I moved to Guatemala. Before leaving Alaska I had my broken teeth fixed with crowns, resigned all my commitments to professional organizations, and said goodbye to friends along the west coast. My port of departure was Los Angeles where I rendezvoused with my friend Linda and Andres in Los Angeles. Linda had been taking care of Exodor, my small parrot of 12 years, which she took home with her after visiting me in Alaska. I couldn't drive the 3,000-plus miles through the wilderness in a car that tended to break down with my fragile winged wonder. I met up with Exodor and all my supplies I had ordered and had delivered to Linda's house, where I proceeded to organize my life of 35 years into 17 packages to take to Guatemala. As I packed, I remembered the story of Anna LaBastille, the avian conservationist who left Guatemala and her love behind to return to the USA. I was determined to stay for the long haul. It seemed I'd be able to swing this as Anita offered me a salary as the aviary veterinarian and also because Susan and I had just been awarded a grant from US AID (Agency for International Development) for $150,000 for the reproductive seasons of 1993-1995. The preliminary work would begin in 1992. Our project was one of the first sizable parrot conservation efforts in Latin America and required a significant amount of equipment – hence the reason for all that luggage, including Exodor whom I promised I'd never leave again.

Anita contacted Aviateca so that the airline officials would be waiting for me at the airport. She also arranged for them to accept Exodor and allow me to carry him on board with me. The thought of letting him ride as baggage on a Central American airline caused me great anxiety, and I refused to take that risk. Also, Anita arranged for me not to pay for all the extra bags. Linda and I drove to the airport filled with anxiety about what Aviateca would do. We expected a Guatemalan standoff. I didn't know if I would even fly that night because if Exodor didn't stay with me, I wouldn't go. We arrived at LAX full of determination and last-minute burgers and fries. I couldn't leave the states without a last stop at In-and-Out Burger. Almost immediately after we stepped into the crowded and crazed international terminal and walked up to the Aviateca line we were met by a supervisor who asked, "Doctor Joyner?" "Yes," I replied, probably the last truth I'd utter for some time. "I see you have all your bags. Why don't you step up to the counter and we'll get you taken care of."

At the counter, the haggling began. It involved long stories of volunteering my time for the good of the country, various stamped and signed documents, and tossing around the names of my influential friends. I spewed my wizened arguments and burger breath. At last, dropping the name of the supervisor who approved my bird in the cabin satisfied them, Exodor's papers were stamped, my luggage was taken away with no extra charge, and I was saying goodbye to Linda.

Anita met me at the gate in Guatemala City by using her diplomatic passport. There she helped slip us through immigration and customs, warning me to "keep the damn bird quiet." I smiled as we drove to Anita's home. I was finally home and wouldn't have to leave any parrots or people behind again.

At Anita's house I was greeted with a bright and shiny nearly-new Toyota Land Cruiser, deluxe model. I now had reliable 4-wheel drive car for the field work and promptly named him *El Gavilan*-- the Hawk. Loaded up, I raced down to the lowlands, radio and AC blaring. There was no welcome party at my house, so Exodor and I settled in for the night. In the morning I headed off to the aviary in my Cruiser. It was the nonbreeding season, with fewer demands for working in the field. I could concentrate on work in the aviary, which ended by 4 p.m. every day. This left a lot of hours to fill in the late afternoon and evening, with electricity in my home on until 9 p.m., and nowhere safe to go. Many of my neighbors had no electricity at all. I wondered how they managed the tediousness of having so few options for diversion. Despite the boredom, I was still riding high come Sunday, everyone's day off.

I tried to sleep in, but the roosters started at 4 a.m., the *tortilla*-slapping hands at 5 a.m., and the sweating at 6 a.m. I eventually had to emerge from bed, if only to sweat somewhere else. I made a cup of decaffeinated coffee, caffeine long gone from my vocabulary with the constant threat of dehydration and bladder infections. Nothing like drinking hot liquids on a hot morning. To continue the outpouring of bodily fluids I set out for my morning run. But by 8 a.m. it was too hot for serious exercise. I had to either run along the Muro Road if I felt like dodging Santa Gertrudis cows or along *la carretera*, if I was up to the multiple honks and stares from passing motorists. I imagined in each passing car was a potential murderer and kidnapper, and there probably were more than a few.

Back from the run I took a cold shower, the only option in my home. At 9:00, the whole day spanned before me. I finished my unpacking, and it was only 10:00. I swam at the pool at the *Casa Patronal*. At noon I headed to Daniel's house where I was invited for Sunday dinner. Though the shower and pool had cooled me off, I stuck to the car seats in my shorts and tank top. Daniel's children, Hilda and Camila, ran to give me hugs. Chickens were scampering about, turkeys called to lost mates, and cousins and family swayed from hammocks dispersed under banana and avocado trees. Such an idyllic family scene, and I longed for it to be mine. But there was a difference between them and me, one that I could never eliminate—they weren't sweating.

Lunch was quietly served on the front porch by Alejandra, Daniel's wife. Alejandra humbly and hopefully laid out her morning's toils, and then retired to the kitchen while Daniel, the two children, and I sat on wobbly wooden chairs, scooping up rice, salad, and steaming chicken soup with our *tortillas*. I soon was dripping sweat but no one else was even glistening. I just didn't get it. Here it was nearly 100 degrees and we were eating hot soup. Outside no less!

After lunch began the long, hot wait for evening coolness. There wasn't much to do except to find a hammock or bed to nap the heat away. That day there was the usual Sunday afternoon soccer match, and Daniel and his family invited me to join them at the field that served as both cow pasture and soccer field. We sat under mango trees, me trying to be interested in watching 22 men run around a field, kicking a ball. My only engagement was wondering how they could stand the heat and humidity. I was wiped out, and I was only watching.

My after-work afternoons and Sundays went that way for the next couple of weeks. I grew irritated, angry, and bored with spending my afternoons and evenings alone, away from fun, frolicking, and family. One Sunday, brow bent and hell bound, I changed into athletic shorts and tank top, donned my running shoes, and motored down the dusty cow pasture to Daniel's house. Jumping from the car, I greeted the hammock occupants and announced my plan. They couldn't refuse me because I was a woman with a mission: today I would play soccer. I would enter their world, even if it meant kicking around a stupid ball on a field speckled with cow dung and swamped with afternoon rains.

Slowly and groggily Daniel and Hilda put on shoes and meandered over to the soccer field with me. We were stopped by a sudden rain storm. Temporarily defeated we withdrew onto their porch and once again the hammocks filled, and Alejandra eyed me, unbelieving that a grown woman could share a man's prerogative. But then I was a *gringa*, and probably nothing we did surprised her. Soon the rain let up and I shooed my reluctant volunteers to the field. Napping in the cool brought on by rain is a rare luxury in this tepid country, and Daniel was cranky at having his Sunday disturbed. But perhaps, like me, he and Hilda were also bored, and flat tired of the few options available in this rustic spot. They didn't own a soccer ball, so we used Camila's small plastic ball. Seeing her toy being taken, she followed us to the field.

Now when I say soccer field, I speak liberally. True, it measures somewhere close to regulation play, but it basically was just a rectangular space kept mostly fenced off from the cow pastures and mostly mowed down. It was fenced with barbed wire on three sides, much to the dismay of many who owned punctured soccer balls. The near end of the field wasn't wired, but opened onto the patio of Tito and Anabel, and Anne and Sofia their orphaned nieces. To get to the field, one had to cross through their yard, scattering ducks, chicks, turkeys, and children who congregated with their parents to buy food from the on-*finca tienda*. We tromped through puddles, a parade of yawning crusaders in the probing eyes of the *finca*. Whatever occurred on the field that day would be talked about over dinners throughout the *finca*.

We began with a few tentative kicks by Hilda, Daniel, and me. As we hurled the ball forward, mud and water spattered our ankles. We stayed away from the big patches of standing water, hoping to stay somewhat dry. With only three folks, our warm-up began to pale and I wondered what all the excitement was about with this sport. Camila soon got bored watching and joined our group so we could play a game.

We marked off a small playing field with the coconut shell debris discarded by those under the palm trees at one end of the field. It was Daniel and Camila against Hilda and me. The tempo suddenly picked up in earnest and after a few minutes I was panting, puffing, and wishing the game would end. I wanted to stop, out of boredom and gut upset due to the heat and exertion. Just when we were ready to quit, Alejandra walked to the field, demurely straightened her skirt, kicked off her sandals, and walked into our midst. No one met her eye, but the sideway glances of her family members reminded me of the stories Daniel had told me about her temper. We played for another few short minutes, until further rain and exhausted bodies called a halt. A strange silence accompanied us off the field as Sofia, Anne, and Anabel watched our muddied march back to Daniel's house. Whispered exclamations of *"Doña Alejandra"*-- "Madam Alejandra"-- followed at our backs. It was one thing for a *gringa* to kick up her heels, but another for the respected and matronly *Doña* Alejandra to be seen playing.

We returned the following evening for more of the same. This time Hilda went in advance to ask Sofia and Anne, both in their mid-teens, to join us. Alejandra kept saying no, she wouldn't go and Camila clung to her mother's traditions of women in skirts and kitchens. Daniel and I ran down the field, doing passing drills. Sure enough, Alejandra soon stepped on the field, her skirt gathered close around her wide hips. Again, we choose sides and began a game. This time Anne and Sofia came to watch the fun. Suddenly the clouds parted, and the sun shone on the muddy field. Like a cloud burst, laughs echoed across the deadened *finca* as we slipped in the mud and hacked at the spinning ball in deeper puddles. Soon covered from head to foot in mud, no longer caring who saw us or approved, something had changed for all of us. These were timid women, barefoot and in tent-like skirts, but soon Alejandra elbowed me into the fence, Anne pushed me into puddles, and Sofia beat me to the ball and sped away as I flopped down and slid on my butt across the field.

The rest of the rainy season we continued to meet on the soccer field after work. More and more women joined our play. The core group remained, however: Sofia, Alejandra, Hilda, Anne, and me. The married women were a bit harder to win over, although Antonia would occasionally come out with us. As the weeks went by, Daniel and I began to plot. Playing scrimmages with the women, children, and the occasional men was one thing, but what if we played a real game? We heard rumors that the women in the houses up the road, Las Rosas, had once played. Daniel joined me as we drove up to the Las Rosas *tienda*, also known as *Tienda de la Ceiba*, where I had my vision the year before. The owner of the *tienda* had two daughters, Mirsa and Micaela, and if anyone knew of the goings on in the area, it would be them. Andres's *tienda* was a major gathering point and hosted some of the largest *fiestas*.

Mirsa and Micaela confirmed that at one time some of the Las Rosas women had gathered to kick the ball around. We invited them to play against our Tecanal team. Their faces didn't communicate much, but they didn't turn us down either. If they had enough women to play a game, they'd get back to us. Negotiations went on for many days as the Tecanal women waited excitedly. Some women were showing up in shorts and a few borrowed tennis shoes from brothers, husbands, and fathers. Finally, an answer came back: Las Rosas would play us on a Monday evening in two weeks.

Given the new seriousness of our evening practices, Daniel and I began to organize the team. Time was spent in practice, money was sought to buy uniforms, and more women were entreated to join the team. Our best hope to gain more players was to appeal to Adam's family, my neighbors, eight people, including five daughters, ages eight to 18, living in the same size house as I, alone. Finally, consent was given, although sporadically, for the three oldest girls to practice. Perhaps it was a competition within the family, but these girls were fighters, and although without much skill, they could run you into the ground. We also asked a few husbands for permission for their wives to not only practice, but to play in the upcoming game. Some were allowed, and some were not.

On the weekend before the game, we put notices all over the area, inviting the public to the event. Tecanal women and girls practiced for two hours during the Saturday sun, Sunday was a day of rest, and then came Monday. Much preparation had gone into the game. Alejandra had saved up money to buy herself a pair of sneakers, and others wore shorts under skirts the entire day. Makeup was carefully applied before arriving in the windy *La Paloma*. It was going to be the greatest moment for many of these campesinos. Was I any different? Well, it took me several days to figure out which shorts to wear and I couldn't sleep the night before.

The game was at the Las Rosas field, a few blocks from Tienda de la Ceiba. The field was edged in by more *tiendas* on either side, sugar cane at one goal, and the main road on the other. The Tecanal people were the first to arrive. Those that couldn't fit in for our multiple car runs came on bike and foot. When we first arrived, there was no one. Slowly they trickled in, but not enough it appeared to play a game. We continued to warm up in the threatening weather, which was thundering and lightening over the distant cane fields. At last, Mirsa came carrying an armful of colorful jerseys, and like a magic act, women appeared out of nowhere to put on the uniforms and run to the field to warm up. Trickling in also were our fans from the community, and by the time the game began we had some 125 people were either watching or playing.

I started the game, playing forward with Hilda. Hilda and I forever bonded as we pushed relentlessly to the goal. On one advance I ran to meet a shot at the goal by Hilda and put it past their goalie, who came running out to secure the ball. I had no choice but to jump, tuck, and roll over her lowered head. The crowd went wild, jeering at our lack of success and hailing the goalie. The game went on for an hour of grueling slamming and sprinting; two thirty-minute halves, with a chaotic half-time to calm what surprised me–I had an inner soccer fury. Despite that, the second half didn't change the score and we ended in a tie with the approaching dark denying us any time for sudden death or penalty kicks. I was done anyway. There were young chicks at the aviary to feed after we drove our chattering team to our home *finca*. By the time I got home that night I realized my back was out, my knee had been sprained and was beginning to swell, and there was a tightness in my chest. The next morning I could barely move, and even breathing brought sharp pains. I had bruised my ribs, if not broken them, when I dove over the goalie.

After winning the next two games against Rosas, we looked for different teams to play. Argentina was the next *pueblo*-- town-- down the road towards Escuintla, and we scheduled a game with them. Their field was a grazing area for cows, rough and hidden in the depth of the *finca*. They too fell to our might twice. Bravo, the ram-shackled town between Argentina and Las Rosas, also organized a team. We now had four local teams and my boredom disappeared. There were always soccer stories and plans to share, and on the weekends when we weren't playing, we could always watch the other teams play each other.

For one game we joined with Rosas to play against La Morena, up in the hills outside of Chiquimuilia on All Saints Day, November 1st, 1992. For some reason we took *La Paloma,* perhaps because we thought it could carry more players. The white marvel slowly chugged up into the cloud-adorned, resting volcanic hills, drawing an excited crowd of women and children. Wherever there are women in the Guatemalan countryside, there are also children. I never thought that we would reach a town along that dirt and rock road, but there it was, and there were other vehicles that had made it as well, although not many. We searched for the soccer field, driving around the two dirt streets of the town looking for someone to give us directions. The streets were empty, for it turns out everyone was at the field, so we kept driving until we found it way on the other side of town. We had to wait as the men were still playing, so we ventured out into the cemetery next to the playing field.

Being *Todos Santos*-- All Saints-- which follows on the eve of *Dia de los Muertos*-- the Day of the Dead-- the cemetery was decorated with colorful plastic wreathes, streamers, and flowers. I had seen specialty shops popping up around the market square in Escuintla for the past two weeks, and now I saw where the products ended up. Families clustered around grave sites, praying, laughing, crying, and picnicking. Men gravitated to the outskirts to peer at the soccer games. I had never seen such activity and celebration alongside death and the darkness of life. Yet, the people seemed to hold the two in tension so easily; they simply poured out their hearts into their mourning and into their joy. The people were both professional wailers and lovers of laugther. They wore their suffering on their sleeves and their resistance in their soccer legs.

When the men finished their game and Hilda, Alejandra, Sofia, and I hung around the fringes of the Rosas team, awaiting our assigned positions, hoping we'd be blessed and be able to give our souls back to God on this day, in other words, "Coach, please put me in!" Surrealistic mists swirled around the game as the ball bounced along the flesh of the mountain-sloped field and off of earth undulations and grave markers. We beheld life and death together, dancing a ritual of passing and rebirth. What play combinations could we create that would cause joy and despair? The answer, we found, was not enough, for the game, like life, ended in a tie.

By the end of the rainy season and 1992, conversation surfaced among the local women's teams about holding a *campeonato*-- championship-- like the men's tournaments. Typically four to eight teams gathered and through single elimination a champion and runner-ups emerged. These were all-day affairs that brought out the crowds and local *agua*-- soda-- and *enchilada* vendors. Las Rosas and Bravo were more than ready for such an event, but Argentina didn't have enough players to field a regular team and joined with Bravo. We had to find a fourth team that would actually show up. It took four teams to build the elimination tree as the foundation for most tournaments was quadrangular. We could do it with three teams, but the math is more difficult to grasp. While shopping in Escuintla, Daniel ran into an old work buddy, Jamie, who said he had a team of women up in the foothills near Taxisco. Their town and team were called Tapeyo. He would bring the team if we could help with the transportation costs. This was not an unusual request as the home team often paid to have the visitors come, but the negotiations also specified we would have to take our turn playing them on their home field.

We agreed and began our preparations. A professional referee was hired in Escuintla, advertisements were put up, and the Q25-- 25 Quetzales-- entry fee was collected from each team before game day arrived, to ensure that they came. All teams showed up late, even the host team Tecanal. Las Rosas arrived an hour late, and while we waited, they came and went several times. Bravo didn't show up, and we had to go get them. We were figuring out how to do a triangular with only three teams when Jamie's team showed up. With this forth team present the crowd grew. They watched the negotiations of who would play who first, the rules, and how to end a tie game. The first game hadn't even started and I was exhausted.

We began around noon, and had to get in five games before the sun set. While I was playing I wished for some kind of break so I could go to Antonio's *pila*-- outdoor sink-- and stand with the rest of the women. Someone handed me the plastic bowl that floated in every filled sink, and I too drank from it as did a hundred mouths that day. Unlike the other women, I would also pour bowl full after bowl on my hair, trying to compensate for my fair skin. Rarely, given the level of dehydration at which I played soccer, did I need to urinate, though this too Antonio's house graciously offered. It was a cemented room with the usual revealing chinks in the walls and doors. Over the cement basin I squatted, voiding precious fluid while wondering how others managed these toilets that had neither paper nor a flushing mechanism. Leaving the odiferous mystery behind me I rushed back to the field, ready for another half.

It came down to the last game, once again between Las Rosas and Tecanal, the third game that each team had played that day, yet we ran as if the wind of God was our energy, and perhaps it was. At the whistle the game was tied, and the game went into penalty kicks to decide the winner. "*Un momento, por favor,*"-- "Just a moment, please,"-- said Mirsa. "We want to play overtime instead of penalty kicks." "But, Mirsa," Daniel said, "We already decided that we would do penalty kicks, and besides it is about to get dark." "It does not matter, it is not right. We think it should be overtime. Our team has decided. If you don't accept, we won't play anymore."

Daniel and I went back to the Tecanal team. "That's not fair, they just don't have as good as kickers as we do," Alejandra said. "Tell them that we'll claim first place if they don't play, because it's a forfeit." The Tecanal women gathered around Alejandra, supporting her stance. Daniel and I went back to the Las Rosas team, as the referee from Escuintla logged his time to charge us more. "Mirsa, the Tecanal team really doesn't want to play overtime. Couldn't you please relent?" No, was the answer, and they began to pack up. So back to Tecanal we went and by working on Alejandra, the impassioned one, we were able to convince not only the team, but the Tecanal supporters that had gathered around us, that we could first play two 15 minutes halves of sudden death, and if it was still a tie, then penalty kicks. They agreed and so did Las Rosas. It was a tie after a two hour game, so the game went into penalty kicks.

This was the first time that I's seen this done. Each team picked their five best kickers. Alternating by teams, each kicker got one shot at the goal from fairly close to the goal, so it was only by luck or skill that the goalie could stop a team from scoring. Of course, our skills were so underdeveloped that we often missed the goal entirely. This is an internationally accepted way of breaking a tie, but the unique Guatemalan twist is for all the spectators to form a thick rectangle closing in the kicker and the goalie. Shouting for distraction is fair game, and fans do all they can to outshout each other. It's chaos at its best.

I was chosen as one of the kickers, as were Hilda and Alejandra. As we lined up in the swirling masses, it didn't seem we'd played five hours of soccer in the 90-plus-degree heat. Each of us kicked, and Hilda scored first. Las Rosas scored as well. The next several kickers didn't score, and then I made a goal. Unfortunately, Las Rosas also scored and it came down to the last two kickers, one of whom was Alejandra. The Las Rosas kicker failed, but Alejandra didn't. I had never seen her so happy. She joined the joyful humanity and beamed pure light. The crowd went crazy and the team was mobbed by all those I thought would just as soon have seen some of us dead. Hilda, Alejandra, and I danced a merry circle in each other's arms. We had defeated the enemy and claimed our right to existence. Daniel smiled as if we'd just given birth to our child.

I couldn't glory in triumph for long because I had to drive the referee back to Escuintla and the women back to Las Rosas and Bravo. Hilda and I couldn't quit recounting plays while we drove to town. Along the way, we stopped for about 10 *bebidas*-- drinks-- apiece, me juggling the plastic bags filled with mineral water while savoring the day's memories. An hour later I was alone in my house, while others continued celebrating. My entire body ached, and nausea from the heat overcame the exhilaration. As I tried to fall asleep, I relived the dehydration, heat exhaustion, arguments, stand offs, chaos, the constant background of adultery, uncontrollable love, broken families, new families, defeat, shame, and victory. All this in a single day of soccer.

Chapter 7
THE BAND MAN
Guatemala, 1992

1992

Ram's single "Fey" is banned in Haiti because the song is widely interpreted as an anthem of support for exiled President Jean-Bertrand Aristide who was forced from the presidency in a 1991 coup.

Whitney Houston's song "I Will Always Love You" wins a Grammy for the best song of the year, and plays incessantly on Guatemala radio.

I had a bass guitar, and his name was Rhodan. Bright red, its style made up for my lack of rhythm. I rarely practiced and took only one lesson. This didn't stop me from loving music. Melodies, words, and cool rhythms were the gateless gates to enlightenment, and Rhodan was my stead upon which I connected with this alternate world. My very minor success in Alaska playing in a group (it helps to have a boyfriend organizing a band) prompted me to tote the heavy instrument and thirty-pound amplifier to Guatemala. I had hopes that I'd play with the famed guitarists of Tecanal, despite my ineptitude. Always before my enthusiasm had made up for whatever else was lacking, as in my Spanish and soccer. I suspected that in Guatemala, experts were not to be found, nor expected.

Daniel had told me of the guitarists Mateo and Diego for months before my move south. They had recently come from the Department of Retalhuleu to bring their music ministry to our *finca*, and the brothers played only *musica de iglesia*-- church music. Despite this limitation, it was the only live music for miles, and Daniel thought it was fantastic. Not having any idea what *musica de iglesia* was, but wishing so badly to be part of the community and culture, I asked Daniel to invite the brothers to my house.

Into my home walked my introduction to Latin music. Mateo, the older brother and more accomplished *guitarrista*, smiled and looked me in the eye. His non-mustachioed face and openness was a bit unusual and I liked him immediately. Diego, much younger and shyer, held out his hand, bowed his head, and greeted me as *"Seña"*-- 'Senorita,"-- which I remained to them for our time together. Also accompanying them was Daniel, our interpreter. They were unused to my accented grammar-free Spanish, and I had a difficult time with their regional use of words and accents. To make it worse, they found their guitar chords by ear and only occasionally referred to their chords as La, Fa, etc. I would later learn that their chord system of Do-Re-Mi corresponded to C-D-E, but they played mostly in minor keys intuitively; I was hopelessly lost at first.

Rescue was at hand, however, as Diego asked permission to hold Rhodan. I watched his fingers fly over the frets, amazed at his ability. He had never played an electric bass before, but since its four strings were the same notes as first four on the guitar, he was right at home. Diego demonstrated a few basic bass lines that Mateo told him to play. Rhodan was returned to me, my second bass lesson now complete. We played a few songs, the beats peppy and uplifting. They said they'd see me tomorrow at church at las *siete menos quarto* - 6:45 p.m. *"Si*, I'd love to come and watch you play, and you can use Rhodan if you'd like," because they were dazzled by his color and style. "No, *Seña*, you will play with us during the service." "I can't do that; I'll make mistakes and forget which chords to play." *"No hay problema,"* -- 'no problem,"-- come tomorrow and we'll arrange some practices for later in the week."

As they walked out the door I plotted to send word later with Daniel that I wouldn't be able to play or to write down the chord progressions. Both plans were moot because I had no idea which notes to play and Daniel was ecstatic that his *gringa* was going to his church. And I did the next evening. I went plenty early so I had time to set up and review the music. I had never been through the church's large wooden doors; it was a cultural domain outside the realm of conservation biology.

Diego and Mateo helped me carry the amplifier and bass to the front of the church as Daniel beamed. With jittery hands, I took Rhodan from Diego who had "warmed it up for me," and practiced a few progressions. "Ouch, me dio calambre"-- "I got a shock,"-- I cried as my fingers strummed the strings. Diego took Rhodan and he too yelped in pain. Several men in the choir adjusted the extension cords, dials, and switches on the amplifier, but there was no fixing the lack of grounding in the electrical outlet. The problem was solved when I minimized the shock by standing on an empty rice sack to break my connection to the floor. We were ready to rock and roll!

The kinks worked out of the system, the service began. Two lay leaders came from Escuintla in their beat up, muffler dragging car to lead the service, as they did every Tuesday night. Priests were few and far between and only came once every month or so during the daylight hours. I didn't understand much because I hadn't been raised Catholic and couldn't follow the liturgical and prophetic Spanish at all. I knew when to play when Diego and Mateo nodded their heads in my direction and the tambourines and gourd rattlers began their introductions.

We played the simple songs without too much wandering from the beat and chords, accompanied by energetic singing from the attendees. The little church probably held 75 people if it was packed. That night there were probably 30, not counting the prankster juvenile boys roaming outside and occasionally poking their heads into the open windows. When the music started, the children outside stopped playing and listened at the windows. All eyes were on the band, and booming Rhodan. This was the first time that I looked into the eyes of many of the people. I did not recognize many since normally their eyes were cast down whenever I passed them. Also, their clothes and behavior were completely different. That night their hands clapped with the music, but during the day they wrestled with diaper-less children, wiped charcoal smudges from their faces from baking *tortillas*, or swung a *machete* or a lasso in their hands. That night the men were dressed in clean jeans, cowboy shirts, and boots, and the women wore their best dresses, or at least clean house dresses. During the day the men wore ill-fitted pants full of holes and past stories, and the women's drab skirts didn't hint of their hidden joy. The realization of who we each were was probably mutual, under the loving gaze of the porcelain Mary at the front of the church.

At the end of the service many shook my hand. Perhaps our biggest fan was Alejandra, who didn't leave my side. The addition of another instrument had energized her church experience and, according to her, that of many others. A few had bristled at my toe tapping, she said, but she told me to ignore them. Mateo and Diego packed up my gear, loaded it into the *El Gavilan*, and said practice would be tomorrow night at my house. It looked like I was in the band and had finally found a way into the hearts of those who seemed distant to me, but with whom I pined to be close. Not knowing their language, their subtleties, their body language, or their culture, I could only express my love in a method that crossed cultures and time—music.

Practice happened the next night and for many nights after that. "*Hola, Seña*," handshakes, and smiles greeted me at my door. A line of men, and sometimes women, crossed my threshold, and I never knew exactly who would arrive. Supposedly it was the choir coming to practice with us, but it was anyone unable to find something better to do. After the sun went down, soccer was no longer a possibility, and visits outside the *finca* were always a risk. I was glad for the company, although rushed after soccer practice, working all day at the aviaries, and running home, jumping in the shower, and racing to the door as the first band members arrived.

Slowly, I was able to directly communicate with Diego and Mateo and laughter became our constant companion during the evening gatherings. They taught me *cumbia, bolero, corrido, vals*, and a few other beats that I can barely remember, let alone play. After several months, our playing came together enough that I decided to make a tape of the band to give for Christmas presents. Playing back the songs and conversations that we recorded I heard the variety of sounds accompanying our practices. Roaring sugar cane trucks blasted past and Exodor sang and danced to the faster beats. One song, *"Todos Santos,"* which had fast beat and low minor notes, elicited not only a rhythmic accompaniment from Exodor but also from the frog living in my indoor *pila*-- sink.

I soon found myself engaged in church and *finca* activities almost every night of the week. The band gathered not only for the nearly nightly prayer meetings, but also whenever a special prayer session was called for an ill person on the *finca* or to visit homebound people off the *finca*. Other times we were invited to play at 4 a.m. at the homes where someone had a birthday. The band arrived at my house at 3:30, and off we went in the dark. Extension cords ran into collaborating neighbors' homes, dogs were shushed, and clucking chickens threatened us from their roosts in trees as we waited for the *finca's* electricity to come on at 4 a.m. Then we blasted out *"Las Mañanitas"*-- The Little Mornings, a popular birthday song sung as an early morning serenade-- and any other requests the sleepy-eyed birthday person requested. We were invited for coffee and *pan dulce*, ourselves beginning to doze, although a full work day was ahead for all concerned.

I was now considered a member of the church and was expected to attend functions even when the band wasn't playing, such as during *el Rosario*-- the rosary. Reciting *el rosario* would only last about 20 minutes. I sat in the back of the church, mesmerized by the proceedings. Usually Daniel and Alejandra would lead the rosary, but first they had to light numerous candles and incense fires. Together they knelt in the center of the church, heads bowed towards the porcelain Mary who, with outstretched hands, stood in the center of the altar. Smoke swirled around their humble forms and sweetness permeated the air. Alternately, Daniel and Alejandra called out to us, and we echoed back the ancient words. I could only kneel, uncomprehending but enchanted by the meditative bonding of the *finca's* people.

As the only owner of a camera on the *finca*, I was asked to attend baptisms. For these occasions the priest from Escuintla came on Wednesday afternoons.

It was tough to get off work, but somehow most were excused to attend. On one particular afternoon I rushed through work to get there on time, and I sped to the church. Already the grounds were full of swirling children and gossiping adults, but no Daniel. Somewhat awkward without Rhodan or Daniel to absorb my self-consciousness I waited with the others for the priest. After a while I finally gathered that no one was entering the church was not just because it was hot, but because the keys had been locked inside.

Given a chance for action, I joined the group of young men trying to figure out a way to climb up to the roof and squeeze in under the eaves. Finally, Daniel arrived and joined the puzzle solvers. The minutes ticked by and we couldn't get into the church, and there was no *Padre*--Priest. After 45 minutes, the white jeep of the *Padre* came dusting up and stopped beside the *El Gavilan*, as a slender boy slipped into the church and opened the door. We entered the church, heads reverently bowed. Not seated a few minutes, Daniel asked permission to take the *Padre* back to Escuintla in the *El Gavilan*. The *Padre* forgot the baptismal water. "*Dios mio!*"-- "Oh my God!" That meant another hour of waiting, and then another one or two hours for the *misa*--mass. I said, "*Si, seguro,*"-- "Yes, certainly"-- handed over the keys, and returned to my infinite wait. There was no soccer practice that night because half the *finca* was at church until dark.

Our church, perhaps because of the band, volunteered at a number of revivals, both on Tecanal and off the *finca*. If played off the *finca* I stayed until the bitter end, unable to avoid boredom's black hole. One of the longest revivals was in the Finca San Fernando, a half-day drive from Tecanal. It was the home *finca* of Mateo and Diego, and I couldn't refuse, along with Daniel and others of the *finca*. Again the generator went into the back of *El Gavilan* and instruments were packed every which direction so we could make room for six adults and two children. Although the *El Gavilan* could handle more people, this was plenty for a long drive.

To reach San Fernando we drove through Escuintla and headed west towards the Mexican frontier. This road, like all too many roads in Guatemala, went through mile after mile of sugar cane. Lone towering Ceibas would mark where cattle fence rows or forests had once breathed. We passed through Mazatenango and stopped for a brief leg stretch and a stroll in the market area. Quickly our group scattered and it took over an hour to find everyone and get on the road again. After Mazatentango, we headed up toward the volcanoes. The terrain began to shift, and for the first time I saw rubber plantations. From the road all we saw were tall, slender trees with spiral designs cut into their bark. Occasionally, we were hit with a whiff of a *finca's* rubber processing plant. The odor was worse than sugar cane and coffee, but it heralded the same thing—a monoculture replacing beauty and biodiversity. There were plenty of jokes about the smell of rubber-- *ule*-- masking the bean farts that seemed part of any ride in a cramped car. Soon we arrived at the *iglesia* situated on a relatively level street in a town perched on a rocky hillside. All around town were the ghost-like *ule* trees, barely visible in the fog, mist, and occasional soft rain, but obvious because they stank.

The wet, cool conditions made the generator hard to start. As we fiddled and tinkered with the equipment, the towns and *finca* people slowly gathered. Much to my surprise, another band showed up, and they looked professional. Their generator was permanently anchored onto a truck, and the bass amp was triple the size of mine. Also, all their guitars were electric. We envied their loud music while we tried to avoid getting grease and gasoline on our church clothes. Once the equipment was set up, we were invited into the home of Mateo's family for tamales. For once, we arrived early and didn't need to rush.

Typical of other revivals I had been to, the cycle of testimonies, singing, and preaching was endless. Toward the end, our band was invited to hook into the other band's electrical equipment. Oh, boy, happy days for us all! Mateo and Diego at last played music that carried beyond the bass's echoes, and I only barely touched Rhodan's strings for the notes to bounce off not only church walls, but the surrounding volcanoes.

At the end of the set, I was glad the group was breaking up. Alas, people were only leaving the church to form a procession. Out of the dark night came the town's people, carrying torches, candles, and the bulky platform of the *aldea*'s—town's— celebrated saint. I whipped out my camera. Before I knew it, requests for having pictures taken with the *gringa* delayed the procession. Being the only blonde bass player they'd ever seen I suppose, I was a celebrity. Soon they began their chants and mournful singing. Our group brought up the rear, trying as we might not to stumble on the wet, rocky road. Along the way we toured the *finca's* work houses where the *ule* was processed. Mateo and Diego were proud of their knowledge of this product. They might not own property or make more than $2 a day, but it was the land of their hearts.

Up the climbing roads we at last came to the center of the *finca aldea*-- village. The saint was deposited in a building with more than a hundred candles. People knelt and prayed, while others asked to be photographed. After midnight I asked Daniel for a chance to get warm and sleep before we headed back. Picking our way carefully down the hill, some of the town's people helped settle us for the night. I slept in *El Gavilan* after saying my goodnights to all. Daniel joined me after a discussion about who got to sleep in *El Gavilan*.

The few hours of rest passed slowly in the cramped, cool confines of the car. Finally, a knock on the windows told us to rise. Thank God. I don't think I could have stayed another 5 minutes slumped over the 4-wheel drive throttle in the front. I gave Daniel the luxurious back seat. Silently, under the stars and fading moon, we were guided into a home for *cafe* and *pan dulce*. By 5 a.m., we were on the road again; the growing daylight seemed like gratitude for our worship the night before.

Now that we had a tried-and-true road show, the invitations came in for us to perform. Not many weeks later we were asked to play at a wedding. I was unsure of the distance, but tired of always being the driver, I announced that the *El Gavilan* wouldn't go this time. I had hoped that would put an end to this trip, but funds were found to rent a truck. All those going to the wedding met at the front of the *finca* one later afternoon Swinging my amp into the back of the pickup truck, owned by a man I'd never met and headed to a place I'd never heard of, I recalled the sage words of my recently deceased father, "Don't do anything stupid." Heading off into the ever later afternoon in a small, open, overloaded pickup truck on the back roads of guerilla and robber country was not the smartest thing to do, nor the most comfortable. Usually in the driver's seat, I was unused to the kidney jarring road up to Cartago and beyond.

I wondered where we were going and asked Daniel, who didn't know either. By evening we reached the end of the dirt and rock road, but there was nothing but one small house, appearing deserted. Mateo and the hired driver walked up to the quiet, dark house, and repeatedly knocked. The occupants finally decided that we weren't a threat and gave us our bearings. Apparently we had taken all the right turns because we were where we were supposed to be, except there was one slight problem. We had to walk two miles up into the hills.

Typical of Guatemalan ingenuity, a plan was soon devised. Daniel and Diego walked into the brush with a *machete*. They came back with two young trees. These were slid through the handles of the generator and rested on the backs of rotating porters, us. Cables, gasoline, extension cords, and instruments were divided up amongst the rest and into the hills we climbed.

The path that we followed was like a small-game path, but it was the only one. Even though we were on the right track, I wasn't sure that the night was going to end well. We wouldn't find the right *aldea* and worse, when we returned the truck and driver would be gone, or at the very least, the truck wouldn't start. Everything was out of my control and I could imagine my father rolling over in his grave.

Yet we arrived at the houses without incident. I wouldn't call it a town by any means. Not only was there no electricity, running water, or phones, but it was scattered homes in a family compound. Trees surrounded one home from another, so perhaps the population was greater than I imagined. We walked up to the first, dark homes that were more like shelters made of tree walls and thatched roofs. We asked where we were to go, and out spilled a multitude of weary children and one smiling grandmother. Chirping excitedly in a mix of Spanish and some Indian dialect, she guided us to an open courtyard that was being prepared for the *fiesta*. She invited us back to her home for food and cafe after we set up our gear.

Stumbling around in the dark, we looked for a place to set the generator as far away as possible from the activities. Stretching out the extension cords, we found that the only location was among the town's tethered *cuches*-- pigs. Estimating the length of the pigs' restraints, we cranked up the generator to ensure its function and, evading younger, free roaming piglets, we returned to the grandmother's home for refreshments, where we heard the clamor of the wedding party walking from some distant church toward the *fiesta*. Gulping down our *café* and *dulce*--coffee and sweets--, we rushed to our instruments to greet the bride and groom with music and hand clapping.

The newly joined couple didn't seem happy to see us, or happy at all. I didn't know if it was the strangeness of having a band at their wedding or Guatemalan shyness at work. Regardless, they sat stone-faced at the only table during the entire night of singing and eating, while the rest of the *aldea*'s people celebrated. During the band's breaks the guests clamored for the evenings culminating event, tamales. Great, deep pots of steaming *tamales* were delivered, and each guest fished out their leaf-wrapped tamale. In Guatemala, eating *tamales* is like eating Cracker Jacks. You never know what the surprise is until you eat most of it. Sometimes it's a piece of unnamed avian or mammal bone, a hunk of meat or just red sauce. The mushiness of the corn meal around the sauce and the unknown I was putting in my mouth always turned my stomach. Yet, I couldn't refuse a meal of celebration, which would be like declaring myself a heretic and declining communion.

Not soon enough, Mateo finally called it quits. We had played every song we knew and then played them again. Packing up the equipment, many scrambled for one more *tamale* to eat or a few to take home for others in Tecanal. Guests volunteered to guide us out of the *aldea* and back down to where our ride was waiting, we hoped. Walking along the dark, sloping, narrow trail, I imagined robbers and guerrillas behind every rock. It wasn't a paranoid fantasy because this road was infamous for violence.

That night there were no attacks as we hiked under the fullest moon I'd ever seen. She guided us down the hills and onto the flat plains. Lifting our voices and laughter to the clear late night's miracle of survival and hope, the final mile was one of remembered peace and our hopes held true. The truck and driver were there, and the ride home was uneventful, but cold. Here along the tracks where desperation spawned tragedy, we traveled as if protected from evil. We were after all a church band, man!

The next morning back at my house, the heat woke me early, so that night I crashed with the sun, longing for rest. Knocking on my door at 1 a.m., and "*Seña, estamos Mateo y Diego,*" "It is Mateo and Diego"-- yanked me out of bed. Pulling on shorts under my long night shirt I stumbled to the door, planning which way was the safest direction to a hospital at this time of night. Mateo, Diego, and Nicolas entered, Mateo's face contorted and tight, his usual smile replaced by concentrated pain. Diego softly shook my hand, greeting me with, *"Disculpe Seña, pero mi hermano esta enfermo"*-- "Excuse me, Miss, but my brother is sick." I fired questions at Mateo, "Where do you hurt?" "Deep in my ear, *Seña.*" "For how long?" "Only for two hours. The pain woke me in the night." Before I could speak, Mateo loudly moaned, and his hands cupped his ears in acute pain. Using a strong flashlight to look in his ear I was told the pain was dull but constant until every few minutes it significantly worsened. I could see nothing, but like them, I suspected the worse. Some insect had climbed into his ear and was trying to chew through his ear drum so it could burrow into his brain and turn Mateo into an alien like some horror sci fi flick

I quickly thought of what supplies I had to remove or kill the insect without going to a hospital. A drive to the aviaries would not be pleasant or safe at this time of night, but we could go on the back road and avoid the danger of *la carretera* if we had to. Not relishing that, I heated a pan of water and with a large syringe tried to flush out whatever was in his ear. No luck, and in fact, Mateo screamed and squirmed so much that I stopped the flushing. Surely in a few more seconds the bug would take over Mateo's life, and we'd lose the best guitar player with whom I had ever had the honor to play. Pushed to the limit I knew I had to bring out my worst for that creepy crawly. A can of Raid.

Spraying a toxin onto a possibly open wound near the brain isn't anyone's first choice, but I had no alternative. Star Trek's "Dammit Jim, I'm just a country doctor" played in my head as we wrapped Mateo's face in a towel. Raising my attack weapon I aimed carefully, while Diego and Nicolas held Mateo still. "Pssst, pssst" the sound of modern if desperate medicine. Mateo fell silent, as did we all, waiting for the cyclical cry, but there was none. To make certain, I sprayed again and we waited to make certain Mateo was cured. A smile came to his face, success. The syringe flushed out only a few flecks of blood. Handing Mateo two aspirins and a glass of water, I told him to meet me at *los aviarios* at 6:30 in the morning.

Off the men went for a few hours' sleep until the light of day. Escorting shy Mateo into the aviary hospital the next morning, I sat him in a low chair and took out the otoscope and peered into his ear. The canal was red, inflamed, swollen, and had linear oozing scrapes. Difficult as it was to get my bearings, for birds' ears are not at all like mammal ears, I saw his ear drum. Nearly dropping the otoscope I quickly turned my face away from Mateo so he wouldn't see my expression. As it was I had to hop up and down a few times in revulsion. Aware that my bedside manner was nil, I told him, *"Es una cucaracha, una joven--* "It's a cockroach, a young one." We shared our surprise that one small cockroach could cause so much pain. Using my alligator forceps, their long, slender reach perfect for the insect extraction, I tried to remove the cockroach. The instrument, however, was still too bulky and Mateo writhed in pain. Not having any mammal local anesthetic I suggested that if he couldn't hold still, he'd have to go to a doctor. But he'd have to decide because it was unadvisable to have a decaying insect in a body cavity and it was too gross to think about.

The band lost Mateo for a few days while he went to Guate to see an ear doctor, who told him that his case was not at all unusual. He had pulled out cockroaches, crickets, spiders, you name it. Figuring it was all due to folks sleeping on the floor, as many did on our *finca*, he advised them to put cotton in their ears. Armed with this new insight, Mateo returned to us, the church, and the band. He was grateful for my help and offered me a chance to ride the polo ponies that he cared for on the *finca*. I didn't know much about the horses, and hadn't been around the polo barns since the one time I examined a sick gelding. The regular vet had not been available and I was the second string. I knew enough to say, "*Si, es neumonia,--* "Yes, it's pneumonia,-- "and you better get some really good antibiotics, but the $30,000 horse eventually died. I was irritated because the horse needed better care, as did Mateo and his family on his annual salary that was less than 1/30 the monetary value of the horse.

I wasn't having any luck with the equids in the area. One time I'd been called to treat a zebra foal at the zoo. They told me to come quickly because the zebra was dying. I arrived within 30 minutes, and the foal was cold and stiff. I looked around at the Safari workers trying to work out how a living animal could go from being alive to cold stiff in a half-hour, but my Spanish wasn't up to the task. As I walked away, I wondered if I was being framed for the death, and then wondered how I'd gotten so mistrustful of those with whom I shared *finca* life. A saying that I learned in that first year was, "In some countries if you have a sick goat, you hope your neighbor's goats get sick too. Here, if your goat gets sick, you kill your neighbor's goats."

As I mounted the mare, I hoped I'd have better luck riding than caring for a horse. My mare, Mateo reported, was a gentle player and would help me play polo. Grabbing two mallets and a ball from the barns he mounted and joined me on the field. No sooner had he handed me my mallet and struck the ball out in front of both horses, I was nearly left behind as my mare leapt in the direction of the ball. I had only slightly leaned forward and yet she had responded. As we approached the ball and I took aim with the long-handled, awkward mallet, I let up a bit on the reins to lean over for the hit. Automatically, she veered to the correct side of the ball so I could get a clean swing. Amazingly, I actually made contact, but nearly lost my seat as she galloped off after the ball. I was ecstatic with the horse and myself, sensing each other and reacting as one, much the same as we did in the band.

Though I loved the band, I was itchy for non-church music. I could occasionally pick up scratchy music on my international radio, but the beat and vocals moved so fast that I couldn't make much sense of it. When Daniel asked me if I'd like to go to a dance up at Tienda de la Ceiba, I jumped at the chance. Something to do other than church or soccer, at last! The music boomed from the amps heard a kilometer away, and by the time we got there communication was impossible. Daniel led me through the crowd of cowboys and some armed soldiers, all with beers in their hands. We headed straight for the dance floor, a cement pad where a truck usually parked. There wasn't room so we danced in the dirt. Every eye turned to watch the *gringa* dance. I had no idea how to dance to this music. It was a *merengue*, or as they say in the Dominican Republic where it originated, *perico ripiao*-- ripped parrot. It's fast-paced, full of guitars, rhythm, and accordions.

I watched those around me and started bouncing, nowhere close to how the others danced. The next song was *salsa*, even harder to dance to. At the end of this song the soldiers walked toward Daniel and me. Daniel said, "Don't worry; they are just here to protect you." For the rest of the night I danced with Daniel and other partners, with the soldiers jammed up against us the entire time. I thought it was more like square dancing or doing the bump than anything Latin. Whatever it was, I loved it, and when it was time to go, when the cowboys got too drunk and loud, I asked when the next one was. "It's the season of dancing as the rains end before the field season begins," Daniel said. Hah, I thought, I could live a normal life here—sports, church, and evening entertainment. How hard could it be?

LORAKIM JOYNER

CHAPTER 8
ON THE FRONT LINE
Guatemala, 1993

1993

On May 25, 1993, President Jorge Serrano Elias suspended the Constitution, dissolved the Congress, disbanded the Supreme Court, and declared himself dictator for the next two-and-a-half years.

Serrano's actions met with massive protests by most Guatemalans. The self-coup failed and Serrano fled the country. Vice President Gustavo Espina took over but was also forced to resign because his actions were deemed illegal.

---

*Continued from prologue...*The two armed men walked toward each other, a drama that was ruining our winter parrot count. I feared that my peers suspected my counts were inaccurate, and they would never believe me when I said the guns went off just as the birds flew over and I couldn't get an accurate count. Our *finca* guard, Ramon, walked farther from us and closer to the man who had a rifle pointing at the ground. When they were within single meters and easy shots of each other, Eric and I crouched, ready to run. The two men talked, their guns still lowered. Ramon turned and walked towards us, and the other man ran to his truck. He was yelling what I imagined was, "Let's charge them." Ramon quickened his step and shouted, "*Vamos!*"-- "Let's go!" We ran to a grass pasture, climbed through the barbed-wire fence, and stayed low as we wove through tall reeds. Looking back I saw men pour out of the forest, pile into the truck and speed off. We had moved from a standoff to an escape by both parties. Ramon said he asked for the man's identification and told him he was on *finca* property. The man said his *cedula*-- ID card-- was in the truck and he'd return with it. Ramon didn't know what the man would do and was afraid he'd come back with reinforcements. I said, "Fine time to wonder what an armed man will do. We could have all been shot." "No, they were just poachers." But he and I knew no one could predict what poachers would do.

We shouldn't have been surprised that the fields around La Montana were always full of poachers, especially the field Corozo. There were plenty of places to hide, it was far from the center of the ranch, and it bordered other, less protected *fincas*. Yet it was a shock when Daniel climbed the Corozo 1 nest and couldn't find the three chicks. They were a special challenge to find because they could scamper down the long horizontal nest and hide. I assumed the chicks were deep within the cavity and I pushed Daniel to search farther. I couldn't believe that someone would take the chicks. Not many people came here, but cowboys and the polo horse workers were always in the area. Surely our own wouldn't steal them. Besides, just because the chicks were gone didn't mean a nest had been poached, as we knew from the Rosita incident when hawks ate the chicks. But as we searched the area for evidence, we found broken sticks at the base of the tree that had been used to hook the chicks out of the nest.

Seething with anger, we loaded up the gear and drove to the *finca's* office. I asked for the *finca's* administrator, Samuel, just as he drove up. I confronted him with the news. There was no way those chicks could be poached without him knowing about it, and I demanded his help in finding the poachers. I was blowing off steam and really had no idea if he knew anything. But I needed his cooperation if birds would ever be safe on the *finca*. Samuel sped away, leaving us stunned in a cloud of dust. He and Daniel had never seen me so angry. I was driving the car and looking for my next victim as I mentally wrote a letter to Sebastián. He had to know that his rule against poaching was ineffective.

The next day Sebastián told me that two workers were accused of poaching the chicks and had been fired and left the *finca*. The evening before I was met at my front door by drunken *finca* workers. I didn't know who they were then, but later learned they were the poachers. One was the brother of my neighbors, and another was a polo worker. They had a reputation for trouble, and this was the *finca's* excuse to get rid of them. An example had been made, but Samuel knew all along who was stealing chicks and that my neighbors, to whom I gave vaccines and took to the hospital, were the robbers. I wanted to know why I hadn't been told sooner because finding drunken men at my doorstep would have alarmed me more than it did. As it was, I greeted them, and briefly considered inviting them into my home when it became clear that I couldn't communicate with them due to my Spanish ability and their inebriation. Something in their eyes warned me away from that tactic, and instead I shooed them away as politely as I could, and as a second thought locked the door behind me.

One of them later gained a reputation for provoking others and robbery, and eventually he landed in jail for murder. This man's angry glare had lasered at me because I dared to deny him his job, home, and ancillary income. Dian Fossey, the gorilla conservationist, had been killed with an ax for similar reasons. To this day no one knows who the culprits were, but many suspect it was poachers angered by her strong-arm techniques to reduce gorilla poaching. She was my hero because she stood up for the rights of wildlife, like I was trying to do in Guatemala. But she didn't love the people and they knew it. I kept her in mind every time poachers attacked our nests.

Not long after, Joaquin ran from the fields near the forest shouting, "Poachers!" I jumped into our jeep, *El Gavilan* and Ramon swung onto his horse, drew his gun, and we kicked up a dust line to find the poachers. We didn't find them that time, but the next week another biologist ran to the volunteer center with the same news. This time the poachers were down the muro road hiding in a tree line, where biologists were lying behind the rise. Fighting words were exchanged, a real standoff. *El Gavilan* and Ramon on his horse scared them off. We later learned the poachers were Elena's husband and sons, with whom we played soccer. Poachers were everywhere and everyone.

I couldn't go anyplace without seeing wildlife poachers and killers. Even though signs prohibiting hunting were posted along the roads edging the *finca* and the forest, the allure of much-needed money was too great. When I spotted someone hunting from the road I chased them away in my best Dian Fossey imitation. One day I stopped with a car of biologists and visitors who dropped their jaws when I approached a gang of men with rifles. Truth be told, I hadn't seen the rifles until I was near them. Luckily, their incomprehension overruled their anger and they left. This time I accepted that someone could get hurt and our anti-poaching efforts weren't helping. "Don't be Dian," I repeated to myself, and "Find a way to love the people."

With this intention, I volunteered to drive the women to their daily morning maize grind. The motorized mill at our *finca* was broken, so the women had to grind the dried corn into *maza* -- cornmeal dough-- slowly and painfully by hand, or I could drive them in our project truck to the next town where there was electricity at 5:00 a.m. I didn't look forward to getting up so early to drive on potentially dangerous roads in the dark, but I thought we could handle most anything because the women were fierce and Daniel brought a couple of *machetes* for weapons. I hoped helping the women would keep peace in the area and bribe the families to leave the parrots alone.

I turned in early the night before the maize-grind run and was fast asleep when an explosion echoed off the walls. The doors slammed shut and the windows shook just short of shattering. I rolled off my bed and onto the floor in a cold sweat, wondering if volcano Pacaya had finally blown its crown or if we were under attack. I crawled to the bathroom, the safest place in the house from gunfire, and huddled under the sink. After a half an hour of silence I crept to a window. There was no haze or falling ash, so it had not been Pacaya. The next obvious source was the *finca* bridge over the *Micaela Linda*, if it had been dynamited. I didn't see any unusual lights and heard an occasional truck grinding gears in that direction and passing over the bridge. Other than that there wasn't a sound, not even the constantly bickering roosters.

I assumed that if the *finca* was under attack someone would rescue me, but it would be foolish to go in search of answers. Like my neighbors I left my lights off and slept on the bathroom floor for an hour. At 4:30 a.m., Daniel stopped *La Paloma* in front of my house, and I stepped out into the dark. With Daniel were women from most of the houses on the *finca*. They didn't know what the noise was either. I jumped into the back with the women and we pulled onto the *carretera* and lumbered up the hill to the *Micaela Linda* bridge.

Daniel was driving over the bridge but abruptly stopped. The other women and I jumped from the truck and walked to a blasted hole in the bridge. Chunks of the bridge were strewn at the bottom of the Micaela Linda, and a stack of live dynamite was taped under the boards where we stood. With a flutter of muted voices and pointing, the women climbed back into *La Paloma* to get on with the day. The bombing really didn't come as a surprise. Almost all the other bridges south of us had been blown. Just a few weeks earlier, at the Las Esperanzas bridge, burned trucks were left with a huge sign wishing everyone a *Feliz Navidad*-- Merry Christmas-- from the guerrillas. Perry told me later that he had heard the guerrillas placing the dynamite from his *casa* near the Micaela Linda Bridge. Having no radio or phone he could only sit on the floor of his bathroom and wait for the explosion. When it came, concrete rained down, breaking windows at his home and throughout the *finca*.

During this time I was frequently woken up at night with booming and the bed shaking. Every other time it was due to an earthquake or a volcanic eruption. After each episode I'd ask others if they'd felt the earthquake at such and such a time, and often the answer was no. Then I'd hear on the radio that there had been a small earthquake in Central America during the night. I began to wonder if I was just imagining the tremors when it happened repeatedly. I'd visited northern California friends a few months earlier during the Christmas holidays when I was woken by tremors and a sense of the bed spinning. I wrote down the time and the next morning asked my friend if she'd felt the earthquake. She said no, and then I handed her the paper where I'd written the time. We turned on the radio and went in search of newspapers and, sure enough, there had been an earthquake at that exact moment in southern California. Though I was sometimes frightened during these explosive awakenings, never knowing if it was an attack or a dangerous earthquake or eruption, my nights were full of wonder at sensing so much of the earth, whether I was in Alaska, the Philippines, California, or Central America.

The military usually responded to what appeared to be symbolic gestures on the guerillas' part, for bridges could soon be repaired. A sudden loud noise could mean a helicopter landing on our *finca*'s grassy airstrip. Sometimes the helicopters were from the USA. Kids would run to gawk at the huge war machines, and I would join them to see what was up. The Americans informed us they were fighting the *narco*-- drug traffickers. I wondered, "What *narcos*?" I was told I could take pictures of the kids with the helicopters, but not the pilots or serial numbers. One day, a helicopter was flying low when gunfire erupted from the ground. The helicopter made an emergency landing on our air strip, where either the pilot or a passenger died. The army swarmed over our *finca* for several weeks, making it tricky at night to go to church or soccer games.

Sometimes the helicopters or planes performed military maneuvers. During one parrot count I noticed specks in the sky flying erratically. They were paratroopers dropping near the air strip, which seemed unusual, but Daniel told me they always practiced parachute drops over our *finca*. He showed me the indentation in the ground where one soldier had fallen when his chute didn't open, and near it a stone monument and plaque for another soldier who died. For some maneuvers foreigners were training the troops. I snuck up once and took photos of blond-haired, dark-sunglass wearing, tall, white men in nondescript army green directing the drills. I naively believed that the U.S. was doing nothing more than helping to fight the drug problem in Guatemala, but later I saw how my governemnt was sneaking military aid to the Guatemalan government forces.

Despite all the violence, my days were usually spent figuring out how to find, study, and protect our nests. That year we found a nest in the middle of Finca Arveja's community houses. We named it *Arbol de Futbol*-- Soccer Tree-- because the nest tree was near the cow pasture that doubled as a soccer field. It wasn't much of a soccer field, dotted with cow patties, but then it wasn't much of a cow pasture either. This nest was in the perfect location for our education and conservation awareness program. The *finca* school was also near the tree, so children and soccer players alike could watch us climb the tree, pet the parrot chicks, help coil our ropes, and change attitudes ingrained over centuries of poaching. We felt it could be the greatest show on earth, thrilling children into adapting conservation behavior.

First, we had to learn how to climb the tree. We were challenged by two bee nests, which meant we had to pick our approach just right so we wouldn't startle the bees. No matter which approach we picked, the nest towered some

24 meters, and the upper branches were even higher. *Ceibas'* massive trunks rise out of the land with no branches until their heights bloom in the heavens. There in the clouds the massive limbs reach out for meters and provide towering highways for many species, in this case, bees as well as large iguanas. Without any lower limbs, getting a line up over the towering nest branch seemed impossible. We had gradually improved our techniques over the years using a variety of fishing, hunting, and rock climbing equipment, and so were optimistic that this tree could be conquered.

Language difficulties melted away as testosterone-laden volunteers lined up to shoot a slingshot or bow and arrow. I always went first, choosing a bow and arrow to place our first line. After two misses, a visiting seasoned parrot biologist gently pried the bow from my hands and whispered the ancient prayer to testosterone, "Let a man do this." It was windy and I was having difficulty arching the arrow over the highest branches, so I let him take it. I was already pushing the three strikes and you're out rule. He held up a saliva-moist finger, measured the wind speed and direction, calculated his shooting angle, took steps away from me, and fired. Up, up, went the arrow until it was lost to us mortals below. "Where did it go?" he cried. A moment of suspense hung in the still air, then out scurried a fluff of green, the quickly retreating mother parrot fleeing her nest. Yup, he'd done the impossible. He shot the arrow into the nest, which a climber later removed along with two other arrows caught in the branches before we shot a successful line.

The school made a project out of the tree and named the chick "Paco." The school house was one room, made of old planks, with open windows, but still it was stifling with 30-plus children. It erupted when the wild-eyed, jumping children spied *El Gavilan* crossing the soccer/cow/soon-to-be-sugar cane field. *El Gavilan* was something to be excited about, for not only was it reminiscent of royalty coming in a royal carriage, but it was coming for them, to honor them, to pay attention to them.

Unfortunately, tiny Paco suffered from a severe case of skin mites and underdevelopment. He nearly crossed over into parrot heaven during one exam. With gangs of children oohing and aahing over Paco and grabbing for my stethoscope, I considered crossing over with Paco to escape the chaos. Each time we climbed the tree I wondered who was more immature, the excitedly scampering fiends or me thinking I could save anything in this chaotic situation in which I had found myself, let alone do no harm. Birds can be delicate to do physical exams on, especially if they're sick. I didn't want to be in the position of having the children's adopted parrot die in front of them and then have to go into some dead parrot sketch by saying he's just sleeping. But Paco had a courageous heart, like most of Arveja's younger children and mule riding cowboys. And brave he was with bees constantly swarming around his nest, iguanas hunting parrot pie, and his beleaguered health.

CONSERVATION IN TIME OF WAR

In April it was time for Paco to fledge, as he was about nine weeks old. The school children were anxious for the *fiesta* they'd earn if Paco fledged and wasn't poached. We too were anxious to have the chick out of a nest and on his way. But Paco didn't budge. The days went by and he stayed in his refuge. I went to the nest one evening to do my watch and was joined by the locals. I had to question the validity of evening watches with scampering children, courting cowboys, and sweaty soccer players asking to look through my binoculars. We could build our observation blinds only so big. While trying to do my job like a good biologist, the children whispered they had found green feathers at the base of their tree. I lowered my binoculars. This wasn't good news. They led me to the tree and there were the remains of Paco, scattered brittle feathers that could only have belonged to our chick who spent his life fighting mites and death. He had won over the mites but not over whatever secret darkness had kept him from a successful first flight. We gathered his feathers that had a sweet decaying odor. I spoke to the children about life and death and that Paco had followed his life cycle that was naturally interrupted by a hawk or iguana, or maybe a mammal after he had fallen to his death. I reminded them the life cycle lesson had been in our environmental education class earlier that year.

The following day we gave them a *piñata* party because Paco had not been poached, and they made a poster of our project's work with drawings of all of the biologists. A drawing of Paco was adorned with his own feathers and a partial wing bone. The kids looked seriously at us biologists like parents would crying children, the children being us. We thanked them for giving Paco a chance to live in the wild and not as a pet. In the blink of an eye they celebrated amongst balloons, candy, cake, soda, and a swinging *piñata*. But we could barely smile. The graven image of Paco with his feathers had seared our hopes and souls, and we longed to make sense of this confusing world. The children understood their world, knew about tears, and needed no buffering. Theirs was a world of constant death and sickness – all had lost a brother, sister, or cousin in early childhood. All knew that robbers, assassins, soldiers, policemen, rapists, and drunken fathers were the predators of their lives, waiting to violate them as they had so many others. The children taught us the life cycle of humans is easily interrupted but spins on in others, always. So why not dance, letting out our anger while battering *piñatas*, slamming players into cow patties while racing for the goal, and drinking our wretched souls into oblivion.

Paco was not our only loss. Our first year of extensively studying the yellow-naped amazon yielded dispiriting data. Poaching and other nest problems, such as predators and inadequate nest cavities, resulted in over 90% of the nests failing. Some nests were at risk from both poaching and natural causes, such as the Puerto Coaches nest in Arveja. We posted anti-poaching signs on the tree, where they were ripped apart by machetes. Poachers had climbed the tree to inspect the nest. Like us, they were waiting for the two eggs to hatch. On the third straight day of nest observation, I was anxious because I hadn't seen the parents for two days. I feared they had abandoned the nest, or the chicks had hatched and been poached already. If nest trees were climbed in the first few weeks after eggs were laid, the probability of parrots abandoning the nests was higher. In this case, not only had we and the poachers been climbing the tree, but a pygmy owl was nesting in the same tree. It swooped at us when we climbed the tree and had also chased the parrot parents.

After my morning watch, Daniel and Lucas joined me at the base of the tree. We decided to climb to see what had happened to the nest. Up went Daniel and down came the bad news. There were two eggs, one nearly buried in the nest litter and one half-buried. Burying eggs was a sign of abandonment. He carefully held up each egg to the light. They were dark but he couldn't tell much else, so he brought them down for me to examine. I hate to move eggs, but if they were abandoned there was no choice but to take them to the laboratory and do a necropsy. At the base of the tree I did a superficial candling of the eggs by holding them up to the sun and examining them through a short, dark pipe. The embryos were older than the second trimester of incubation and there was no movement.

Thinking the eggs were dead, for nothing could survive three days without parental incubation, I placed them in our field padded cooler, which I placed in *El Gavilan* whose windows we raised and doors we locked as we walked to a neighboring *finca* to climb two more nest trees. By the time we returned to the car it was 95 degrees and the relative humidity was near 100%, as our soaked clothes testified. Anxious to get home because this was Saturday and a half-day of work, I quickly drove through the back fields of Arveja and onto the bumpy Puerto Coaches road. About half-way home I asked Lucas to hold the soft cooler on his lap so the eggs wouldn't become addled before necropsy. Nothing could have survived the heat and bouncy car.

After dropping off Lucas at his home in Bravo, Daniel and I returned to the aviary. Before opening the eggs I candled them with a professional candler in a dark room. Daniel followed me into the incubator room at the aviary and there, in the focal light of the candler, beat a heart that had defied all odds, alive after three days without incubation or parent protection! We might have been overjoyed, but we knew that the chances of this chick hatching were minuscule. Variant temperatures over the last three days and rough handling on the way to the lab would surely weaken the embryo, and it would die before hatching. It's usually in the final few stressful days before emergence that chicks are likely to succumb. They have to not only switch from egg membrane respiration (air exchanged through the shell and across a placental-like membrane) to full lung use, but they also have to peck out of the egg. We didn't give either egg much of a chance.

A week later our fears were realized. One egg wasn't developing and its bright-red blood vessels were dissolving. The second egg had grown quiet. No movement was detectable through its dark shadows, not even a kicking leg or raised beak. I was about to necropsy it when I felt a movement in the egg. Returning to the candler I saw a small beak rise up out of the ball-like creature, and through the egg came a faint chirp. I placed the egg into the incubator, and over the next few days it cracked one dent into the egg shell, but no more. A delayed hatching was worrisome and usually meant that we had to help the chick out of his egg.

We scheduled this one Sunday morning, and I was able to get the chick out. He was alive, but barely. Smaller than he should have been for hatching and affected with scoliosis and opisthotonos (curved back and head extended back over the spine), he would probably not survive his first week. To give him the best chance I took him home. Fighting his sluggish digestive system, I got enough food into him that he began to gain weight after a week, despite my horrendous field work schedule. By the end of the second week his back and head were normalized and he had become a strong and demanding chick.

His survival perked us up, after the poor reproductive success of the birds in the wild. Of the 23 active nests, only four had successfully fledged young. The native biologists called our chick *Moises*-- Moses--, the prophet telling them of a promised land. These amazons have a tremendous ability to survive despite poachers and diminishing habitat, and if Moses could survive then so could the rest of the species and the people themselves. Perhaps a brighter future awaited us all.

Moses was old enough that I could leave him when Avery, my Alaska travel companion, and Julie, another veterinarian, visited me after the field season, in mid-May. Despite the dangers, both women came anyway, and I tried my best to show them a good time. I was nervous about picking them up at the airport. They were arriving early and I had elected not to spend the night in Guate, but to drive up in the morning. This meant being on the roads by 4 a.m., but as the buses began to run about that time and pedestrians would fill the roads, I judged I'd be safe alone on the roads. Later I would hear of a robbery at 4:30 a.m. not far from Tecanal.

As I pulled out of the *finca* my intestines rumbled, which I attributed to hunger and the early hour. My intestines had mostly adapted to the amoebas, but every once in a while they erupted without the usual fever and vomiting. The little bugs had grown subtler in their tactics, and I could never predict when I would be affected. By the time I reached Escuintla the gentle tumbling was a full-scale attack. Driving up the grade out of Escuintla I couldn't hold back the onslaught. There was nothing to do but stop the car in the dark and hope no one passing would seize on my helplessness. Barely free of the car I jumped into the tall grass beside *El Gavilan* and blew the most violent diarrhea ever. The foul smelling debris of unicellular organisms covered my clothes and shoes, and about two square feet of the roadside. Scared to stay outside the protective confines of my car, I jumped in and planned to clean myself in the city.

With the windows rolled up, the smell was overwhelming and I wondered how I would explain this to my friends. Welcome to Guatemala, but I'm too sick to take you around the country. Outside the airport, on a deserted side street, I did my best with the car's plastic rice-bag rugs and the gallon of drinking water that *El Gavilan* always carried. It was improvement enough that I could enter the airport without too much embarrassment. There I greeted my friends happily and apologized for the car's odor and explained what had happened. Perhaps it was the power of suggestion of me constantly popping pills that they suffered nausea their entire trip. I was taking a combination of metronidazole (Flagyl) plus an iodine compound to ease the infection because Flagyl was no longer strong enough alone. Unfortunately these medications left me almost sicker than did the amoebas, so I joined my friends in avoiding food while we traveled.

Our big trip was up to Rio Dulce, where we rented a little cabin near the water for two days. It was cool and rainy, but that didn't stop us from renting a boat and a pilot to navigate us down the river to Livingston, the only truly Caribbean town in Guatemala. On our way we stopped at the Manatee Reserve, where we were greeted by a spider monkey. Being animal lovers, both Avery and Julie were delighted by the friendliness of the creature, but soon his embraces became aggressive and frightened them. As veterinarians we all knew what a monkey bite could do to a human. We pried the monkey off Julie and walked along the slick hiking trail weaving in and out of the forest. On our way back Avery spied the outhouse, always a welcome site for someone in our condition, and excused herself, as Julie and I walked to the visitor huts and warily watched for the approach of the spider monkey. After a long time Avery finally joined us, looking distraught. Not far behind her loped the monkey. Without an explanation she said we were leaving, and we hurried down the boat ramp.

In the boat Avery told us that in the outhouse she dropped her pants and heard a loud thump on the metal roof. She started to pull up her pants but not before the monkey slipped under the eaves and wrapped itself around her. She struggled to pull her pants on and the monkey off without getting bit. It was a test of manual skill and controlled panic, but she was successful. As we floated away with our blue-eyed, brown-skinned guide, we laughed through the mist that the reserve should be named the Crazy Monkey Reserve because no one I knew had ever seen a manatee there.

After a long day in a boat we returned at sunset to the hotel, where we learned there had been a coup. We tried to gather as much information as we could from the hotel restaurant because no TV, radio, or phones were in our rooms. We called home to report we were okay, but those at home responded with, "What coup? Where?" We didn't know if we could get back into Guate and if the airlines would be operating for their flight. By morning we had a fuller story. President Serrano, angry about wide-spread government corruption, had locked the senate and judicial offices and was ruling the country as the sole leader. The army had split ranks on their support. As of yet, no one had been killed.

Closer to the city, along the same road that years before took me to Sierra de la Minas, we saw evidence of the coup. Tanks and more mounted machine guns were patrolling the streets than usual. Roads into the city were nearly deserted and tanks blocked some roads. At our hotel we learned that Serrano had been run out of the country, only to have the vice-president demand control of the country. Following this second coup, the army intervened and took control of the country. Three coups in as many days. Let no one say that I didn't show my friends a good time.

Avery and Julie left Guatemala the next day and I drove to Anita's to hear the details. She had a lot to say, though she was in shock. Serrano had come to their house late the night before his coup, but he mentioned nothing about his plans. She said both she and her husband felt betrayed, as did his many other supporters. His brash move put them in danger, in particular his closest friends and advisors. Anita emerged unscathed, or at least not arrested. Her harm ran deeper because she was part of the "old government." Not only was she no longer a key advisor to the president, but she was a *persona non grata*. Over the succeeding years many of her conservation efforts would be blocked, including our project. Her dream of preserving Guatemala was crushed in the coup. I returned to Tecanal and retired my medical record titled "President's Birds" to the back of the medical records cabinet where no one would see it. Camelot had fallen.

Chapter 9
ON THE SECOND LINE
Guatemala, 1993

1993

USA President Clinton sends six America warships to Haiti, enforcing UN trade sanctions against the military-led regime in that country.

Playoffs continue to determine the participants for the 1994 world cup to be hosted in the USA.

Now that the field season was over, I could do errands that I had ignored. I needed to visit *Guate* to get a visa for Daniel. On one of our city trips we were searching for the consulate and were lost as usual and had to ask directions. Daniel began to roll down his window to ask a woman pedestrian when I said, "No, Daniel, *yo puedo,"*-- "I can-- and leaned out the window and asked, *"Disculpe, pero donde esta el consolador?"* The woman averted her eyes and sped away. *"Disculpe, Senora, donde esta el consulado?"*-- "Excuse me, M'am, where is the consulate?"-- asked Daniel. This time she pointed up the street. Crabby at the usual prompt replies Daniel got and the blank looks I got, I said, *"Porque, Daniel?*-- "Why Daniel?"--, I asked her the same question you did?" "No. Kim, I asked her where the consulate was, you asked her where her dildo is. *"Hay una gran diferencia!"*-- "There's a big difference!"

Coming back from Guate later that day, we stopped in one of the big *mercados*-- markets-- that sold diverse and international foods. We were wandering the aisles searching for baking powder. With more time I could now do some cooking. Baking wasn't done much on the coast because most cooking was on open wood fires. Surely in Guate I'd find baking powder, but it was as hard to find as it was in Escuintla. I asked one of the store employees, *"Disculpe, pero donde esta su polvo de orinar."* The man blanched and turned to Daniel, who said, *"Donde esta su polvo de hornea?"*-- *"Where* is your baking powder" I couldn't hear the difference in the questions but, as usual, the man pointed to an aisle where we found baking powder. Daniel began to smile and I asked, "Okay, Daniel, *que paso"*-- "What happened?" "Oh, Kim, *mi amor*, did you see the face of the worker?" "Yes, but what was the problem?" "Un momento," he begged as he choked back the impending belly guffaw. Once collected he said, "Kim, it's better if I ask the questions from now on." "But I need to be able to communicate when you aren't by my side." Daniel's dark eyes burrowed into mine. "Maybe *esta correcto* but, in the meantime, you should learn to ask for baking powder instead of urination powder."

After that trip, we used our extra time to gear up for the *futbol*—soccer—season, rationalizing it as our conservation education program. I wasn't sure how much energy I had for this effort because of the way *futbol* season ended the year before. Daniel had been coaching while playing with us when the women were scrimmaging against the men of Tecanal, when I heard a snap across the field and Daniel went down. One of the polo cowboys, who was also on the Tecanal men's *finca* team, had challenged Daniel and left him rolling on the ground, holding his knee, as the cowboy ran with the ball. Daniel was out of commission for a long time and never again played futbol with the same abandon. He didn't consider medical care because that might do more harm than the violent attack had done. Instead, he'd ask someone to lean onto his leg so the knee joint popped back in place and he limped for the next month. I was angry that this cowboy had damaged Daniel's physical perfection on purpose, and that he was the cyclical lover of Daniel's brother Chema, had tried to rape Daniel's daughter Hilda, and would later try to seduce (or did) one of our team players, while he kept one or two wives.

I knew the challenge of organizing games and practices. One of our last games had been against Tapeyo in the campionato. They had lost badly, and wanted another shot at us. We had promised that we'd go to their home territory and arranged a game in a few weeks' time. Joining our team would be Nora, Susan's oldest daughter. She and her family were on the finca for December, and Nora had practiced with us and her father, Steven, had coached us. I was ecstatic to turn the practices over to someone else because I was exhausted from all the arguing and confrontations. Steven just looked at me like I was crazy, how could it be so hard?

He soon found out as we journeyed up into the hills to play Tapeyo. First of all, their was field. It ran a steep downward course and was peppered with grazing cows and their defecacious gifts. How could anyone play a game on this? Poorly is the answer. We couldn't do anything but fight and argue. The opposing team didn't want Nora to play because they thought she was a boy with her short haircut and coordinated play. They wanted to bug us with their whining, which could lead to winning. It worked.

During the first half we were getting slaughtered. The game was rough as girls and women slammed together in tight balls, more like rugby than soccer. During one of these brawls my shirt was grabbed and I was nearly thrown to the ground. I came out of the melee with a girl's neck in my hands, as angry as I had ever have been. The mini war was brought into line when Steven took the referee's whistle for the second half. The physical abuse diminished, but we were still slipping and sliding in cow goo, our tennies and bare feet spattered as brown as the ball. We left that evening beaten, but promised a rematch in a few weeks' time. Surely we'd beat them then. Steven, Susan, Nora, and the younger daughter, Violet, would not be with us during that last game because they'd be in Tikal for Christmas.

Despite Steven's attempt at civilizing our game, negotiations for the next game with Tapeyo turned manipulative. For the third game between the two teams, the opposing coach refused to play on our home field. He wanted a neutral field, and we were not about to return to their soccer field from hell. I was still burning from having been bullied on the field and for having lost my cool. It also didn't help that he called me "*nalgas de aqua*"--water butt-- and Alejandra "*cuchiflus de elefante*"-- elephant ass. Sure, we jiggled a bit when we ran, but did he have to taunt us?

We decided to play on a field between the two teams. It was tall in grass but more than doable. We carpooled the players, now with three new team players. We had picked up *Doña* Isabel and her two daughters, Amanda and Camila. These daughters were long of limb and coordinated, and would one day rival Hilda with their ability to score goals on the run. I thought nothing of the additions, but Jamie's competitive eye picked up on the changes right away as we lined up to play. "*No, hombre, estas muchachas no puedan jugar*"-- "No man, these girls can't play."-- Walking close to Jamie to avoid the ire of my team I said, "What do you mean they can't play?" "*Pues*-- Well--, they are not on the Tecanal team." "Yes, they are. They practiced with us for the last two weeks," I said, "and they're no longer on the Las Rosas team." "It's not fair. When we played before they weren't on your team, and we'll only play you as the team that challenged us, no changes!"

Once again, I played the role of arbitrator, although I was far from neutral. Ole Water Butt was angry at this foolishness and the response from Tecanal. "If they don't play, we don't play. They'll forfeit and we'll win. Go tell them that. Kim!" So I did. Jamie's response was the expected, "No, you're playing illegally, so you forfeit, and we win." I could have slapped everyone present. All I wanted was for the women to transcend their country lives and bond through the game. Who won or who played seemed hardly the point. This went on for quite a while and it looked like we wouldn't play the final game of the season. Soon it would be breeding season and we'd be too busy in the field for soccer.

Then I came up with an idea. "Jamie, what if we play the game, let the new girls play, and we will give you all the game. You automatically win, no matter the score." "*Hombre*, that works for me." Convincing Tecanal was more difficult, but I finally convinced them that if we won, it would be to the embarrassment of the other team, for they could only claim victory through a loophole. At last, both teams lined up for the whistle, but the pregame madness was a prelude to what was to come. It was the most run-away game ever. Fights broke out on the field and the sidelines, I couldn't pull girls off the field for substitutions, and Jamie yelled insults at every Tecanal player. I swore that I would never organize another soccer game, provide transportation, or speak to these wild creatures who were my neighbors and teammates. By the end of the game, which we "won," I was disgusted and exhausted, and yet players on both teams were animated. Great fun had been had by all, except for the outsider who didn't understand that complex, messy human interactions were a part of life, and were enjoyed.

The tensions within soccer continued to mount as we finished that first soccer season. As agreed by teammates, a different family would clean the uniforms after each game. After that last game, the duty fell to my closest neighbors. Four of their girls played on our team, despite the constant restrictions to their freedom from their mother, Paula. As the weeks went by I became concerned about what had happened to the shirts when the family didn't return them. I was going to store them in between games because Daniel's sister, Hardee, who had purchased the shirts, wanted me to keep them safe. In a sense, whoever had the uniforms had control of the team, and right now that was Paula.

After brief discussions with the eldest daughter, Martina, Daniel told me that Paula wouldn't give us the shirts unless he spoke to Paula. Now, this was no easy matter. Paula was known as a sharp tongue, a brutal gossiper, and an angry beast kept caged too long within the social-political system of *finca* life. I thought it best that I accompany Daniel so that the fallout wouldn't be so great. The opposite was true. Paula seemed to glory in the humbling presence of the *gringa* knocking at her door and tore into Daniel's hide with the venom of a maddened she -bear. I turned redder than the flowering bushes leading over the bridge that connected our homes as she degraded Daniel and his ancestors. I kept trying to butt in so we could get the uniforms and leave, but Paula wasn't to be denied her moment of power. Daniel took the abuse and apologized if Paula thought he had slandered her daughters, which was the complaint. I could take no more and directly asked Paula if we could have the uniforms and to please excuse any misunderstanding—we loved her daughters and their ferocious playing (and now I knew where their Tasmanian devil-like soccer play came from).

"*No puede tenerlos, yo los quemo*--"You can't have them, I burned them." Not believing I had understood I turned to Daniel, who was as red as I was, which was difficult considering his dark complexion. "What did she say?" "She said that she burned the shirts." "What do you mean, she burned the shirts? Did they try to dry them over their trash burning pile? Ask her again!" "No, Kim, she means she burned them and there are no more uniforms." Like silent soldiers, we both turned, let the door slam, and marched off the combat field, beaten to the core. She had destroyed her own life, her daughters' precious footing in another world, and the *finca's* cohesiveness that was so necessary for organized soccer to happen, and all out of spite.

This was the final straw that broke my soccer spirit. How could Daniel and I save the world if it was our enemy and didn't appreciate our efforts? I vowed to never return to soccer, as did Daniel. Let those women continue to reside in their kitchen prisons, literally barefoot and pregnant for all of eternity. That was how my thinking was of soccer during the 1993 breeding season when we worked 80+ hours a week. But I longed to be with the women of Tecanal when they continued to play Bravo and Las Rosas.

But my female companions and I were crazy for soccer, so as our schedules relaxed and the last chicks fledged, I schemed once again. Oh, how quickly irritation wanes in the tropics! The Tecanal team couldn't go much further without Paula's daughters, who had been forbidden to play with us. We needed more players, players we could control. "What if we made a regional project team, combined all the talent from Bravo, Las Rosas, Argentina, and Tecanal, and used the team to promote avian conservation, self-esteem, and discipline?" I asked Daniel. Money could be budgeted from our conservation education funds to pay for gas, uniforms, and advertising. The project participants huddled around this idea and came up with Juan-Pablo and his soccer playing brother from the city as our coaches. Daniel and I would take a back seat, me only a player instead of the mind blowing task of leader, and Daniel the transportation specialist with a bum knee. He finally got his driver's license through bribery and paperwork. He would be the first on the ranch to have one. Others didn't have the opportunity to drive a car or, if they did, they drove short runs to the tiendas to buy drinks for official *finca* guests. So the project had two drivers and two cars, both of which in the non-breeding season were recruited like soccer mom vans to haul soccer players. All we needed was Susan's approval, as our out-of-country co-director, and she loved the idea.

With a husband soccer coach and two daughters that would one day play competitive soccer, how could she think otherwise?

We began by visiting all the women's homes and telling them of the new super team that would play together, not against each other. In some homes, we had to again ask permission from the husbands and fathers before the women folk were allowed to practice or to play. Up went notices, uniforms were ordered, and the biweekly practices began. Compared to previous practices, these seemed like military training camps. Attendance was taken, drills were dictated, and no arguments or fights were allowed. Anyone not following the rules could be banned from the team or have to sit out the next game. Only the most disciplined players that attended practices would be picked to play first string.

One of the first things Adrian did was to see how we ran. He did drill after drill in an attempt to gauge our speed and endurance. Then he told us to line up, sweating and gasping, according to height. I went to the front of the line, always the shortest on any team. But this time I wasn't the shortest and stepped back a few spaces. Adrian, monitoring our positions, kept moving me toward the taller girls. By the time he had rearranged us, at not even 5'1", I was one of the tallest women on the team. I'd found my home at last!

Daniel and I were thrilled at how the team was shaping up. Over 20 women came to each practice, sometimes as many as 25. Into our cars we stuffed them, dragging them to the various fields for practice. We had to keep changing the locations of practice so we didn't show favor to any one *aldea*. While practices were ongoing, Daniel and I went in search for teams to play. We drove to the larger towns where we'd heard about women playing soccer. Tracking down leads, buying drinks at *tiendas*, leaving messages that would be answered by hand-written notes delivered by bus drivers, we were finally able to come up with the season's games.

These games were the stuff of champions. One of our first games was against Escuintla, the killer team we'd heard so much about. We ended up playing them several times. For each of these games where we were the visitors, we had to rent transportation. *El Gavilan* and *La Paloma* simply weren't big or reliable enough to haul the 25-plus women, the coaches (Adrian and Joaquin), the fans and children, and all the gear. Usually we rented a truck owned by Andres, the brother of Mirsa.

For our first game, we scheduled the pick up so we could swing by each *finca* and town. First Andres's truck would go to Tecanal, where we had to honk the horn, go to homes, and even leave women behind as we pushed ahead to the next stop. I followed in *El Gavilan*, and into this safer, enclosed vehicle went all the children and babies. In front of me I'd spy the women, many of them in skirts and make-up, laughing and pushing their way into the pick-up truck. Once all the women were gathered, Adrian distributed the uniforms to be worn over their shirts. This was to ward off the policemen, who ticketed trucks overloaded with passengers, which was every truck on the road, except those transporting soccer players. This worked for us, except once. The whistle blew at the traffic circle in Escuintla, and all the men piled out from our cars and trucks to go argue with the police. After a Q25 bribe, we were once again on our way.

At the field, we drove around looking for the captain of the team. Of course she wasn't at the field, nor were any of the players, although we were late. And so it went for all our games. Scheduled times were a reminder that this was the day of the game, and whenever God and country decided to go, that was when the game began. But first, the women had to scatter, find bathrooms, trade skirts for shorts, put on their second-hand cleats that had been donated from the U.S., and, of course, add red lipstick to their brown faces

I wore colorful shorts, the same white long socks as everyone else (donated by my Californian friend Avery, of tennis renown), and the uniform shirt, which was our project T-shirt with green numbers on the back. We were proud of the team T-shirts that were printed for our project and read, "*Vivan Los Loros*!-- "Long Live the Parrots!-- The team players weren't thrilled with the white uniform with little color. It didn't have the sexy appeal of the more modern uniforms. Plus, they were cotton, and they were hot!

As we lined up after our warm-up, Adrian read out the starting positions. The back field--la *defensa*--was Alejandra, Elena, Mirsa, and Salome. Three of these were mothers of three or more children each, and they had seen the reality of the world—no one could get past them unless they were willing to spill some blood. The midfield—las *volantes*-- was made up of me at center, Amanda on the left, and Sofia on the right. I was the passer, Amanda the runner, and Sofia the hard pusher. Our three forwards-- las *delanteras*-- were Hilda, Camila, and Sherri. Hilda was the kicker, Camila was the dribbler, and Sherri was the crazed youth from Bravo. Adrian then read out our plans for offense, pointed out the location of holes, mud spots, and broken glass areas on the field, and gave us a pep talk, not that we needed one. We were like colts at the starting gates.

The game wasn't spectacular. We lost, but only by one goal. The Escuintla team was flabbergasted because no one had ever made them work so hard. We were also riding high as a team to be reckoned with; we had three coaches, our own uniforms, a growing fan club, and were the talk of the town. We returned to our homes that night, our skin sticky with sweat and spilled soda flung at each other, now more than mere spectators in a man's world.

The biweekly practices grew our power and gave the women options on how to make decisions in their lives, other than fighting. Harrumph! Fights broke out between rival families and within families. One of the worst was ongoing with Alejandra and Hilda. It was as if they weren't mother and daughter, but two competitive sisters. Whatever complex family relations existed off the field were only magnified on the field. They yelled at each other, whined to the coaches, pouted, and stalked off the field. Their family dynamics were so inclusive that it was hard for the greater world to not get sucked into their black hole. In one practice, Alejandra body-blocked me play after play and then threw a tantrum when the ref called foul. Thank goodness I was only a player now and not a responsible coach, although I did have a hand in getting both Hilda and Alejandra suspended after one of their more violent disagreements during practice.

Not dropping a beat, Alejandra shone in our next game in Masagua where she drew the gathering crowd into a maelstrom. The game was a brutal one in the heat and on a hard field. There were a few hundred fans, a couple of whom couldn't stop taunting. I was playing midfield when Alejandra ran off the field and away from the ball, and spectators scattered. She grabbed rocks, of which there were plenty, and threw them at a fleeing man. I was too dumbstruck to move and stayed to protect our goal while our center fullback was starting a riot. Daniel joined the melee and tried to hold back his wife, but to no avail. Adrian and Joaquin ran to Alejandra who was throwing punches at the man. The crowd ate it up as chaos reigned down on the game. Alejandra had been teased too much about her maneuvering bulk and finally snapped. It took a long time for the two to be separated, then the crowd quieted, and the opposing team argued that the rock throwing fullback had to be ejected, and we returned to the playing.

With Alejandra gone, we were bummed and at a disadvantage. Daniel and Hilda wore the Guatemalan blank face as if nothing had happened. We had a game to win, which was 1-1 at the end of the second half. Used to the typical arguing at this time I watched as the coaches and captains negotiated on how to break the tie, or even whether to. It was decided to play sudden death with 15-minute periods. Despite having played for the entire game in one of the more grueling positions, I was honored that Adrian let me play the overtimes. I wasn't the oldest (Alejandra was then 37, Elena was 36, my age), nor the least fit, but I was the most vulnerable to the heat, even if I didn't have the lightest skin on the field. Sofia was also called *canche*, which means blondie, at least she was before I came. Afterwards I was the more *rubia*, but we both had a hard time in the heat.

A big part of me, other than my ego and intense desire to be a part of life, wanted out of the game. The constant running, body slams, sprints toward both goals, and strategizing left me exhausted, and dunking my head in water was doing little to keep the heat exhaustion or even stroke at bay. I didn't know how I could continue as we went into overtime after overtime. I entered a zone of exhaustion that left me no choice but to become the ball. A pass came back to me and I let go with an awesome kick. Some say that I was running nearly at midfield when I contacted with the ball, others say that I was much closer in. I can't say because I was flying in slow motion and melding into the world around me. The entire assemblage looked up at the ball as it arched towards the heavens. It seemed that the ball would never come down. During these split seconds, from my hovering soulful mindset, I looked around and was given one of the rarest gifts one can receive, a view of the complete authenticity of one's fellows. Adrian's mouth opened in a loud groan, Joaquin was yelping and jumping, Daniel stoically frowned his extreme pleasure, and Alejandra led the Proyecto cheering section. The fans rose to their feet, hugged each other, and screamed "GOOOOOOAAAAALLLLLL" at the top of their lungs as the ball slipped under the cross bars. Before I knew it, I was mobbed by the team and our fans and Alejandra and Hilda in a sweaty embrace. As I had remarked to the captain of Masagua before the game began, "Scoring a goal is better than sex." It most certainly was. For who would be content with a solitary man when she could embrace the entire community?

In other games, my universal appeal and connection to the greater world didn't shine through. Take for instance the game against El Arveja. We tried to get a game against our sister *finca* in the project for about a year until they finally agreed. This time it was only the Tecanal team and we were supposed to go to El Arveja. Then they would come play with us in the next quadrangular we had planned. The invitation was set for *Dia de la Independencia, 15 de septiembre--* September 15 Independence Day. This was a day of grand celebration for all, and the attraction at El Arveja was a women's game. The *Don* of El Arveja had agreed to transport us and sent a tractor pulling a large hay cart. In we jumped for the long slow haul to Arveja.

Our patience had worn thin from the long ride in a tractor, and how good could some back water *finca* be? We knew them because we'd taught their children and admonished their men folk to stop poaching parrot chicks. It would be good entertainment for the locals and we'd be good sports about it. We waited for people to show, and then had to exert patience for the speeches, the parades, and then finally the hand-over of a new ball. We were invited to join the children's parade around the soccer field, a cow pasture, complete with unmowed grass, cow patties, and mud swamps in the far corners.

Our smugness evaporated when the kickoff whistle sounded. These unprofessionals ran our butts off, threw us into shit and mud, and bruised us with body blocks and fouls. I knew they were our project's *finca*, where we'd spent days. I knew it was just a game. I knew it didn't matter that a hundred men were shouting "*la gordita*"-- chubby-- whenever I had possession of the ball. But despite my awareness, self-control fell in a puddle, and I tripped, pulled, blocked, fouled, and whispered "*Su madre!*"-- "Your mother!" This wasn't a term to be casually thrown out. In fact, it was the worst anyone could use. Our team had picked it up when I used it during our scrimmages. Sides would be chosen, I would spy Hilda or Alejandra on the opposing winning team, and I'd shout, *"Su abuela!"*-- "Your grandmother!"-- or *"Sus primas!"*-- "Your cousins!" On the tractor ride back to Tecanal I wondered how telling someone you are family had turned into a curse.

Chapter 10
TRAGEDY STRIKES
Guatemala, 1993

1993

In the USA, 40,150 died from auto accidents and 1.2 million globally. Over 90% of the world's fatalities on the roads occur in low-income and middle-income countries, which have only 48% of the world's vehicles.

2.5 million people a year die from alcohol-related deaths.

Somebody died. That's all I can write. If I told you more, I would put others in danger. I might never be able to return to Guatemala. And they might come gunning for me and mine.

LORAKIM JOYNER

As an undergrad at the University of California at Davis, I did everything birdy that I could, and graduated with a degree in Avian Sciences. I am attending to a red-tailed hawk there in 1978 (top). In 1987 I went to Panama to surgically sex parrots in between trips to Guatemala. It wasn't all work! (below).

I began our field work in in 1990 (right). Investigating a termite mound in a tree, I discovered it was an orange-fronted parakeet nest. A few days later the top of the nest had been removed so poachers could extract the orange-fronted parakeets for the illegal wildlife trade. They left behind cracked eggs, which we tried to save, but couldn't.

Every day, such as here in 1993, I organized about 12-15 volunteers and staff, making sure each team had a machete and other gear.

Above is typical parrot habitat from the late 20th century in the South coast of Guatemala. Here I am in the early 1990's out in the field, having to cross one of many fences typically found in the habitat of wild parrots. The forests are long gone and replaced with agricultural and ranch operations.

In the 1990's (and earlier) the illegal wildlife trade removed thousands of parrots every year from Guatemala. Literally boxes full of birds made their way to domestic and international markets, such as these orange-chinned parakeets (right) in Guatemala.

The combination of landscape, population and economic opportunity makes for rampant poaching of wildlife in Latin America. Poachers climb the trees, such as this one in Guatemala in 1993 (left), risking their lives for monetary reward.

Moses' (right) parents abandoned him when he was an egg, we presume because too many poachers had been climbing the nest tree. The competition between poachers is stiff. We rescued, incubated and raised him. He nearly died, but he is still alive today in Guatemala.

Here (right) I am shooting an arrow attached to a nylon line, which will then be used to place the rope that climbers will use to check on parrot nests in Guatemala in the early 1990s.

Once the rope is set up, climbers scale up the line using ascenders, such as this conservationist climbing a Chinga Ceiba tree, which is cradling a nest that is over 30 meters high and also has three Africanized bee colonies in its branches (left). This is why the climber is in protective clothing and wearing a face net. Whether poacher or conservationist, there is plenty of risk and excitement in this work.

Our first years of placing artificial nest boxes were not successful, at least for the parrots. The boxes filled up with bees, which we had to take down because of the risk of Africanized bee attacks (right).

Even with bees and poachers abundant, there were a handful of successful nests, such as this nest where three seven-week- old chicks (below) flew free, and might still be flying to this day. However, their chances to successfully reproduce are slim due to poaching, population decline and habitat loss.

Once the chicks were on the ground, I could conduct physical exams and also take samples, such as where I am taking a culture to assess the oral and upper respiratory micro flora of this three-week-old amazon chick in 1993.

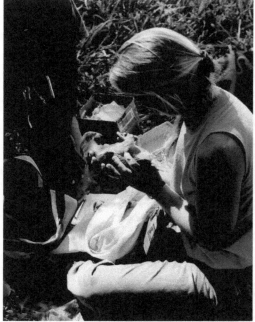

Here I am examining an older chick ready to fledge. Because we were often short-handed, Daniel had to climb down the tree to assist me on the ground.

This is my big night attending an evening at the palace with the President of Guatemala in 1990.

It was fun to play "dress-up" but I couldn't wait to get back to the field. Here I take a penalty kick after a tie soccer game, and yes, I scored!

Doing my best as mid-fielder to get in scoring position (above). During my last game in Guatemala in 1995 I was the goalie, and gladly accepted the trophy on behalf of my joyous teammates (below).

Here I am with the band warming up before the church service begins (above).

Climbing (right) on Tikal's Maya ruins when friends came to visit was a wonderful experience. It allowed me to get above the birds and tree tops and to imagine what the ancients had seen before me.

Here is half of the yellow-naped amazon roost site in Guatemala, which no longer exists due to the encroachment of the sugar cane agribusiness (above). Once there were 250 parrots here, now there are none. People in tractors in 1995 not only attacked the roost site, but also trees with yellow-naped parrot nests (below). These too are no more.

The sugar cane agribusiness decimates native habitat, requires a lot of water (which there is less of because of the tree loss) and puts chemicals and smoke into the environment. They are burning the sugar cane field here to prepare it for harvest (above). Harvesting is tough work (below). In the 1990's workers were often Maya families including children.

From 1995 onward, I often moved my belongings and parrot companion Exodor in my Chevy van (above). I added a travel companion in 2000, marrying Meredith with Exodor's and Moses' feathers woven in my hair.

Exodor (right) continued to
keep me company until 2003
when he died. I promised him
that I would never have another
homed bird. During the 2000's I
served as minister to several Unitarian Universalist congregations (left above).
Later I wore veterinary scrubs with a clerical collar, such as during the People's
Climate March in NYC in 2014 (below), to serve as a witness to the beauty and
worth of all individuals and to call on people to care for all species

Beginning in 2005 I slowly started extending my ministry back to Central America, such as in Guatemala starting in 2009 (above) and 2010 in the Petén region of Guatemala (climbing Yaxha Maya ruins below).

Fernando Aldana, who was critically important to our ability to restart yellow-naped amazon parrot conservation in Guatemala, braves all kinds of weather to count loros at the historical roost site (left).

Colum Muccio, out counting loros at one of our hot spots in Guatemala, continues to be a steady and passionate influence for wildlife conservation (right).

Hector assisting with an examination of a five-week-old scarlet macaw chick in La Moskitia, Honduras in 2011 (left).

Maria Eugenia (Maru) demonstrates her glee after helping to push our stuck truck out of the mud. She is displaying her solidarity "Hasta la muerte" ("Until death") with the parrots and people by raising her hand and showing off her "Parrots Fly Free" wrist bands.

Pascacio shows his solidarity with the parrots by raising his hand with the "Parrot Fly Free" wristband. (above). Alicia takes her turn riding in the back as we pack out of the field site in 2011.

Santiago, brother to Pascacio and Alicia, demonstrates the technique for climbing parrot nest trees (above). Anayda, Santiago's spouse and Co-Director of the Rescue and Liberation Center cares for Rosa.

Tomás in 2010 shows me his scars from the four bullets that nearly killed him only five months earlier (left). He tells me that he is not afraid, for the people and parrots are worth everything we can do for them.

In 2014 we drove by this grave marker at the base of a macaw nest tree (right). A man poaching some birds made a mistake, and fell. The parrots have not returned to nest, though in 2017 one pair showed interest in the tree. If it were an active nest, we would probably confirm it by observation, as our climbers are reluctant to go up the tree.

In the beginning, released birds in Honduras were fed, and sometimes treated on the porches of homes (above with Tezla of ICF, below with villagers).Here I show the villagers how to care for parrots as I examine and treat Rosa in 2013.

Honduran soldiers accompany us due to the danger in 2017 (above). No matter, we seek the liberation of all. The Mabita Research Center (below) says in Miskito "Macaw Fly Free" which can only happen if we all are free.

Chapter 11
BUZZZZ, BANG, THEY'RE DEAD
Guatemala, late 1993-1994

1994

This is the 40-year anniversary of the 1954 Guatemalan coup carried out by the USA CIA that deposed the democratically-elected Guatemalan President Jacobo Árbenz. It ended the Guatemalan Revolution, and installed the first in a long series of USA backed dictators and political instability.

The Wild Bird Conservation Act was enacted to protect exotic bird species from international trade. After this act, the number of parrots imported in the USA declined from over 100,000 annually to only hundreds annually.

Instead of going home for the 1993 Christmas holidays, I spent them in Tecanal. I had invited the two girls, Daniel, and his mother over for *Noche Buena*-- Christmas Eve. While other households were busily stuffing and boiling *tamale*s, I was cooking a ham and stocking the fridge with Gallo beers for his mom and me. This was an important event because it symbolized I had become a member of the family if I was with them that night. Dinner was at 7:00 p.m. and when no one showed up by 7:30 p.m., I wasn't surprised. This was a land where punctuality didn't exist. By 8:00 p.m., I was anxious and wondered what happened. Just as I was about to try to find them, there was a knock at the screen door. In walked a long line of nieces, nephews, in-laws, Chema, Fabiana, and Daniel and the two girls. But no mother. Apparently she'd already had one or two beers too many, as had these party goers. There they were in my home, however, and I offered them platters of food and cool beverages. It was a fine evening, and I went to bed wondering how many people hosted dinner parties where the first guests were an hour late and weren't who you invited.

I began gearing for my annual New Year's party. I invited all the neighbors and Daniel's family, about 50 people. I found a large Santa *piñata* and filled it with candy and coins. On my dirt patio I placed chairs and tables, which soon filled up with people, cake, and a traditional hot punch. We took turns hitting the *piñata*, a tough one to crack. By the time Santa's fat stomach finally burst, night had fallen. Usually by this time I was bored with entertaining because I couldn't bridge the language and culture gap. But this year was different. I found a social tool that spoke to every one of all ages, colors, and economic backgrounds. With this secret I threw the best party ever in Guatemala.

I asked Daniel to help me pass out my secret. Into each child's palm we placed safe, colorful fireworks. And into each adult's hands we placed firecrackers the size of their heads or rockets that had the power to take off an arm or put out an eye. My guests went crazy. Stern Paula giggled as *mariposa*-- butterfly-- rockets shot across her face, and Lucas and Chema cleared the back yard when they lit two of the largest firecrackers. The blast was nearly as great as the dynamited bridge the year before. In the front yard we had a clearer launch area for the rockets, while teenagers scurried about relighting smaller fire crackers with short fuses that quit burning. I don't know how we did it, but no one was injured and we didn't set any roofs or fields on fire. Instead we spent an hour in mass pandemonium and chaos, daring deeds, and constant laughter.

The year started off with a bang that just kept going with popping sounds outside my house one evening. I rolled off the couch and reached to turn off the lights before tucking into a ball on the floor. Someone had machine-gun strafed my house! I belly crawled into the bathroom, the safest room in the house, and waited for what surely would be a bloody end. The night went silent, and not a peep was heard from my neighbors. That meant something was surely wrong because they were two adults and six children in a two bedroom house with constant conversation or fussing. Squeezed under the sink I eventually fell asleep until light crept under the metal door. Inching my way, I opened the front door and walked out. Along my wall was a stripe of bullet pockmarks that led to the house next door. My neighbors and I stared at the evidence of a gun battle that hadn't targeted us, but was between cars passing by. We never heard of any deaths or bodies, and the event remained a mystery.

CONSERVATION IN TIME OF WAR

I didn't use my couch at night for some time, but was soon back on it for my daily *siesta*. Almost in dreamland one afternoon, I heard squealing brakes on *la carretera*. I held my breath, but that did no good, and the crunching sound of impact seemed right outside my door. I ran outdoors barefoot, hoping it wasn't a child, and instead a farm animal. The incident happened next to the bus stop, and a crowd gathered around a prone body. I pushed through the crowd to a man with joints out of alignment and a barely recognizable face due to cuts and blood. But he was alive. I asked if anyone knew him and if anyone had a car. The muted silences and imploring eyes were all too familiar. I ran to find our work car in the field with parrots (never, never eat a huge bowl of hot soup and then go running in 100-degree heat). Daniel and I loaded up the man with his two cousins and were racing to the hospital twenty miles away. Luckily, this accident had happened during the day and the only danger to us was my nervousness. I had no idea if the man was bleeding internally or had a cerebral hemorrhage. Sure as heck I didn't want him to die in my car. While we were speeding along, he regained consciousness and asked us to empty his pockets of the money because it would be stolen in the hospital.

There was little reaction at the national hospital when we stopped at the front door. The only movement came from the two policemen who inspected my car, hoping to find evidence that I hit the man and they could collect a bribe. No help came, so I managed to lift the man and hand him to Daniel, and we carried him to a room. A trail of blood covered our tracks from the car sprinkled with bone fragments from his leg fracture. The man's blood dried on us because the washroom was locked. And there was no doctor. We insisted and argued until someone finally came, and then the door was shut, barring us. I wasn't family, just a *gringa* driving a nice car. There were no thank-yous, no questions, no acknowledgement of our existence, typical in these situations. On the drive back to the *finca*, my bloody hands stuck to the steering wheel. I wondered how a car that hit a man could leave the scene. What did the children in the car think as their father sped away? How could the policemen be more interested in extorting money from me than in helping a hurt man? What kind of world is it where doctors and nurses steal from their patients?

Later I drove the permanently stained *El Gavilan* from a meeting at the project houses (were the visitors slept and where we led the field work) towards home. As I drove up the dusty, palm-lined road to *El Portom*-- main gate-- more people than usual were gathered around the gate. It wasn't a bus stop, the other one being up the road where the man was hit, but often a few folks congregated there before either leaving or entering the *finca*. Seeing a crowd, I wished like hell that I didn't have to pass through them. At the open gate, Sargento asked if I could help *un hombre*. A man was guided to me, supported by three *compañeros*-- co-workers. His wrist was tied with a dirty, bloody, handkerchief. His friends said he hurt himself with a machete during work. The buses had quit running that late, and they asked if I'd take him to the hospital in Escuintla. I asked to see the wound, hoping it was something that I could patch up and avoid the night hospital run. Nope, it was gashed to the bone with tendons and muscle showing, but it wasn't bleeding profusely so there was no need for a tighter bandage or tourniquet.

I didn't recognize the man and asked where he lived. Not on the *finca* came the reply. Oh, a stranger. This was what my father would call doing something stupid, taking four strangers in the dark along a dangerous road by myself. I suspected the wound happened during a *machete* fight, for the wound was on the right, his *machete* wielding hand. The men were angry, violent, and had probably been drinking. I kept on saying I couldn't do this, and more spectators surrounded the car to catch some Saturday night entertainment. All eyes turned to me to see what the *gringa* would do.

A saving face way out of this was to demand that Sargento ride shotgun. Surprisingly, he said yes. Now I had to do it. *"Muy bien--* very well,-- Sargento. Please search them." If I was going to do something stupid, at least I'd have the pleasure of saying the tough phrases that one hears only in movies, "Search 'em" and "You're riding shotgun." No weapons were found, and I told *Sargento* to hold their *cedulas*—ID cards-- until we reached Escuintla. As they were loading into the back seat, I whispered to Sargento to keep his machine gun ready and sit in the front with me. The drive to Escuintla was uneventful, a welcome letdown after the excitement at El Porton. When I told Daniel and Perry about the incident, they were torn between amazement at my stupidity and my bravado.

I thought I was careful in that situation and in others like that. The rule usually was to never give a ride to a stranger, and never by myself. If someone wanted a ride, I asked Daniel if he knew them. For instance, once we were coming back from Escuintla when we passed the usual crowd on the outskirts, waiting for buses or hitching a ride. *"Espera, espera"*-- "Wait, wait--" said Daniel, "I know someone." The man was a stranger to me, but Daniel knew him, so we gave him a ride. I didn't think any more about that until a few weeks later when the *finca* to the north was attacked, and the owner's wife and daughter were killed. "Who killed them?" Daniel said, "The man you gave a ride to last week." I shouldn't have been surprised because guerrillas were everywhere, causing me to quip at a bird conference in the States, "Yes, the guerrillas know all of our movements in Guatemala. They know I'm here giving a talk, and I wouldn't be surprised if they could even give my talk by now." For this reason, we didn't keep a schedule and told few people of our plans. Everything was a secret because ambushes were harder if no one could predict our movements.

Still, we were occasionally surprised by the guerrillas. Lucas had been tracking a fledgling when he saw uniformed men walking through the *caña-- sugar cane--* on the other side of our *finca*. He hid until they passed, but immediately reported to the casa de proyecto-- -project house-. His concern was that if we wore green camouflage clothes, which we did, carried radio equipment, which we did, and had binoculars, which we did, we could be mistaken as the enemy and shot by either side. We agreed but saw no way around the dilemma.

Daniel had to hide from the guerrillas one afternoon, when he was far from the *finca*, in northern Esperanza. As anything north of the *carretera* was considered unsafe because of the hilly terrain that hid insurgents, we stayed away from there when possible. But the fledgling parrots he was tracking were there, and so he followed. He heard voices before he saw the troop approach. The only place he could hide was in a large *laguna*. He waded in up to his neck in the dark, tannin-laden water, holding the radio telemetry equipment over his head, like Vietnam soldiers walking through water with their rifles over their heads. Although as a *campesino* he had nothing to fear from the guerrillas, their possession of military equipment and him being alone in an isolated area were not the way to make the acquaintance of armed men on a mission.

Our military looking equipment continued to put us at risk. At Finca Arveja with Daniel one evening, we were on what should have been a deserted road, with our gear in the back. Ahead were a couple of trucks and uniformed men with guns. As we drove closer, we saw the uniforms were anything but uniform. They could have been guerrillas, but cars that could be traced were unusual. Robbers were not likely to stop people so boldly, but that couldn't be ruled out. The group was either G-2 (private assassin squads) or robbers, neither of which was cool. I had decided to go down with a fight when a farm truck headed toward us coming from the other direction. If the men had meant to stop us specifically, at least there would be witnesses. We pulled over and were immediately surrounded by dangerously tense men brandishing a variety of weapons but wearing no insignia.

We were told to exit *El Gavilan*, and the interrogation began. It was awkward unloading our gear with their guns in our faces. They took Daniel to one side of the car and me to the other. I could see Daniel grow angry at our treatment. The farm truck stopped, and out jumped the Don of El Arveja, Miguel. With a smile as big as his heart, he walked straight to the leader of this para-military gang and shook his hand. They knew each other or at least pretended that they did. A smile from behind the pistol wielding leader broke the tension. Miguel explained who I was and what all the radio telemetry gear was. We showed them our propaganda sheets and I even delivered a conservation lecture. Daniel was still angry as he returned the equipment to *El Gavila*n. Miguel escorted me to *El Gavilan* and waited until we left before he returned to his truck where, he told us later, a pistol lay loaded. In the rearview mirror, I watched until he left as well.

That stop wasn't bad compared to what happened to others. Perry walked into the aviary out of breath one morning and told me guerrillas had entered his home. The night before he was watering his garden, which was the joy and diversion of his life. Just as he stepped toward his door, a man pounced from the shadows and pushed Perry inside. With a gun at Perry's head, he asked for money. Perry said that it was in his wallet in the other room, but asked to close the door so his dachshund Fausto wouldn't escape. The robber/guerilla let Perry shut the door and then took his money. It was part of the money that Perry kept in his house, but the rest was hidden. The man said, "Remember that you are always being watched," and warned him not to alert the *finca* security guards. He then slipped out the back door, leaving behind shaking Perry who never again left the security of his house when it was dark, or at least not on a regular, observable schedule.

Miguel of El Arveja also had trouble dodging the guerillas. "*Hola, Don,*" I greeted him a few weeks later as our afternoon group passed him on the Puerto road. He was headed out and we were headed in. We stopped and talked through the rolled-down windows. "*Coma esta?*"--'How are you?" I asked. "Not so good," he replied with a grin, but sad eyes. "I just spent an evening kidnapped by the guerrillas." He now had our complete attention, even the usually rowdy group in the back seat. "They surprised me in the rear of the *finca* where they were hiding in the small *bosque* (forest). Actually they were quite nice, even the woman leader that kept pointing her uzi at me. They threatened to burn down my *finca* or kill me if I don't pay a large amount of money. You know, the Guerilla Tax." We had heard of this scheme of the guerrillas demanding "protection money" in exchange for not harming *finca* operations or personnel. As far as I knew, Tecanal didn't pay this, but many other *fincas* did. "I'm going home to get the money and will be back in the morning." He had to pay Q500,000 which was about $90,000. Having no idea of cattle *finca* economics, I didn't know if this was an outrageous amount, but suspected it was.

One night later that year, the guerillas burst through the door of Miguel's cabin on the *finca* and demanded another large payment. This time when he paid he stopped at our place and left his radio phone and pistol for safekeeping. When he came back he seemed harried and said that he no longer could spend nights at his *finca*, let alone bring his young son with him. We rarely saw him after that, where before he'd been the host offering coconuts, lemonade, and even horse rides to our guests and volunteers. When we did occasionally run into him, he hinted there was no way he could manage a cattle ranch under such conditions. Sugar cane would be so much more profitable and safer. I shrugged off the possibility, knowing how much he loved his cattle fields. Besides, he knew what sugar cane would mean for the parrots.

CONSERVATION IN TIME OF WAR

We never did meet the *Don* of Esperanza, one of those absentee owners who managed from afar. Instead we arranged to work on his *finca* through letters, and worked instead with the administrator, Alfredo. We saw him regularly, and sometimes his wife. We had just finished a count at the roost site when we stopped on the side of the road to speak to Alfredo's wife. As always, I was nervous to be out at night, so I kept the engine running and the lights out while Daniel quickly told her we'd be by in the morning to pick up two blocks of white cheese. She and her husband lived in one of the run-down shacks provided to permanent *finca* workers. Every day she made a white cheese from the *finca* cow's milk, with salt, water, and a curdling enzyme. It was a staple of ours, despite the risk of it being unpasteurized.

A few days after we had stopped by their house to buy cheese, Alfredo was murdered in the night. Stories differed on what happened, but we eventually put together that he'd been warned by the guerrillas to improve the poor conditions of the workers at the *finca*. And maybe he'd been involved in other enterprises that pissed off the guerrillas. Whatever it was he did, he didn't live past forty. Waking him and his cheese making wife in the night, they came to his house and held a tribunal right there. They found him guilty of various crimes, and before he was assassinated they asked him if he had anything to say. He asked not to be killed in his home near his family. They took him into the sugar cane fields and shot him in the head.

A few days later we visited to give our condolences to his wife, but all we found was a cross marking the spot where he died. It was easy to see, standing alone in the charred remains of the sugar cane harvest. Slowly we approached the cross as if we were inviting fate to turn its head toward us. The dark scattering of burnt cane reeds clawed at our pants like begging skeleton hands. At the cross, we looked down at the small wooden monument that bore the name of the dead, which was almost as depressing as our uninterrupted view of an empty and scared land. Sugar cane had replaced cattle fields, which had replaced forest. Gone were the trees, parrots, lagoons, and Alfredo.

Despite the violence at Arveja and Esperanza, we increased our presence there because more and more parrot nests had been found. The daily risk to us wasn't coming from the people, but from the stinging insects. We had stationed artificial nest boxes the year before to see if the wild parrots would use them. Through Joaquin's study of tree cavities we knew there weren't enough suitable nesting cavities available and poaching was high. If we could place nest boxes near the protected inner sanctum of the *finca* where people lived, maybe the parrots could be protected also. Unfortunately, 14 out of 15 of the boxes became colonized by honey bees. Maybe we couldn't save the parrots, but we helped the local production of honey.

The lure of gaining bee hives attracted two local apiarists to our project, who agreed to help us remove the bee-laden nest boxes near the ranch homes.

We couldn't risk leaving them up in case they were significantly Africanized. These apiarists weren't experts, but they'd worked with bees. Both had bee colonies in patios behind their homes in Las Rosas and made spare change from selling the honey. They were anxious to get free bee colonies and we wanted to salvage our nest boxes (bee colonies normally cost about 80 *quetzales*, which is about $16 or a week's salary). They assured us they could climb trees. Considering ourselves by this time to be expert parrot biologists, we took all the necessary precautions. Each person had bee nets over their heads, the *La Paloma* and the apiarist's truck were parked a distance away, and the ever-present mob of curious children were backed off to a safe spot. The first boxes they attempted to remove were located around the *Rancheria*-- the ranch community.

For the first tree, Pedro, who was about 70, simply took a ladder, climbed up to the nest box, covered the entrance hole with cardboard, and lowered the box-- *la caja*. Piece of cake we thought! The next tree had a slightly higher nest box, so Andres, being considerably younger, went up the tree. At this point, very few of us had our face bee nets on (but at least they were still in our pockets), the car was closer, and the kids were only several meters away. Nearly to the box, he called for a bee face net, and was able to carry the box down without being stung. By the third tree, no bee face nets were in sight, the *La Paloma* was parked under the tree, and the kids were helping us handle the climbing ropes. I think that you can see what's coming here. As Andres climbed the tree, the bees exploded. Not only did the bees go for him, but they swarmed toward all the spectators. First the kids took off screaming as bees chased them. Daniel and I, sensing responsibility and a chance to get macho points, stayed close to the tree and sent up protective clothes and a smoking pot (By the way, sending a hot smoking pot swinging precariously on a rope up a tree to smoke down a nest of wild bees is, in retrospect, a very silly thing to do). Like in other traditions with swinging, smoking pots, its usage is more symbolic and used for calming human fears.

By now, the biologist rank had diminished as clouds of bees singled out those most likely to yell and some demonstrated unusual running styles. Andres was one of them. As he was coming down, the swarm followed him, and when his bee mask slipped, he nearly fell out of the tree. The bees streamed inside his bee face net, and he was lucky to get down alive. But his trials were far from over because the bees chased him, though he never ran. Daniel and I slowly backed away, but we had to take off running. From a distance we watched the bees engulf Andres, his truck, and *La Paloma*, which presented a problem. We had work to do elsewhere and had to use the car. Not wanting to be deficient in macho points for the day, I made a mad rush to the car, wearing my bee mask. Once inside, I used alternating hands to smash bees, operate the stick shift, and steer the car like a maniac away from the wall of bees. Andres was still pacing alongside his truck, and the bees were right beside him. He signaled that he was okay, so we loaded up and headed to the aviary.

Our work at the aviary kept us beyond sunset, a situation best avoided, which I explained to Susan as we drove up the gravel road to the locked gate. "Not too many years back a man was murdered and strung up to the Safari gate, slashed and dismembered. Do you remember Perry telling us that story?" "Ugh," she said. "Also, the head of a young girl was found in the ditch just a few hundred meters up the road last summer," as I continued to set the mood as we neared the dark gate. "Is this a good idea that we're leaving out the main gate?" Susan muttered. There was another possibility, the back way along the *finca* dirt roads, but that wasn't an option that night because of flooded fields, consuming ruts, and the low slung *La Paloma*. "No problem, Susan, we have a routine to get out the gate as quickly as possible. Take the gate key and jump out when we get close. Run to the gate, unlock it as quickly as possible, and Daniel will help you swing it open. I'll gun through and wait in the shadows with the headlights off, while you all shut the gates, lock them, and come running to the car as I swing onto the road. I'll turn the headlights on once I'm sure no other cars are near and we've reached escape speed." Susan studied my face hard, realized that I wasn't kidding, and began to fumble with the keys. At the appointed moment, she and Daniel jumped into the dark and the routine went as smoothly as possible. Almost.

As they jumped into the rolling car, we suddenly leaned into the roadside shadows with *un pinchazo*-- a flat tire--, the third for the day. Susan turned to me, terror stricken that we'd be unmercifully slaughtered . We backed up inside the gate, locked it, and the tire was changed with only moonlight so we didn't lure murderers to us like moths that smother a small light.

After the tire was changed, once again we ran through the routine and headed towards the main finca gate and an armed guard a mile down the road. Slightly embarrassed by our lack of survival skills, we laughed at the day's follies. Dead bees adorned the dashboard and an occasional buzzing accompanied our joking and reflections. The red tongue of Pacaya's fiery lava flow licked away the evils of humankind and left us feeling relative serenity. We had a few minutes of travel before reaching the safety of El Porton, with Daniel sitting between the seats, straddling the stick shift, and leaning into Susan and me. Once safe, I swelled with pride. The previous record for car problems for *gringo*s at the *finca* was three flat tires in one day. We not only tied the record, but we took a step higher with a car full of Africanized bees.

Though we made light of the bees, they were a serious threat in Guatemala. A group of school children were attacked in Guatemala City the year before. They were walking down a narrow canyon trail when a few climbed up a steep bank. Apparently, they disrupted a bee colony that was super Africanized, and they may have been attacked by more than one colony. We'd heard that one attacking bee colony can excite neighboring bees to attack as well. Whatever happened that day, children fell down the slopes or died. Those on level ground couldn't run fast enough down the narrow trail. Many were hurt and seven died.

The bees caused death in the country as well. Every few months we heard about farm animals being killed because they couldn't run from the attacking bees. I was glad our bee boxes had caused no harm, at least until the end of 1994. One of the larger nest boxes had been placed high in a *Cenízaro*-- Saman-- tree in the field Chaiute. Due to its height, we didn't attempt to remove the box or the bees. One day the head cowboy, Emilio, was repairing a fence near the tree. It was a lazy day for him with no pressing concerns of cattle movements or shipments. He was out to enjoy the day on his horse of 15 years, his favorite and most beloved. While he worked, he wrapped the reins around a log to keep her from wandering into the field to graze with the ever curious, gathering cattle.

All it took was a few taps of his hammer and he heard a roar and rush like biblical scenes of judgment day. The bees descended on him and the horse and he took off running to escape death. By the time he'd gotten a hundred meters he saw his horse hadn't bolted with him. All she had to do was step away and the reins would have slipped loose. Instead, she screamed, buckled to the ground, and died, her brown flesh swirling under a black carpet. He was powerless because moving closer would have meant his death as well.

We didn't hear the news until a few days later. Emilio was the closest neighbor to our *casa de proyecto*, and his wife sold cold soft drinks to our workers. Yet, they said nothing to us. Instead, we found out indirectly. Several of our *cajas* had been torn down from their high perches. After asking around and being met with cold looks from cowboys and polo horse workers, we figured it out. Groveling and apologizing to Emilio, his smile surely hid contempt for us and our project. To make amends we set out to take down this *caja*. We worked in conjunction with the new *jefe de seguridad*--security chief-- who'd been commissioned by Sebastián to help us rid the *finca* of the killer bees.

We rode out with the jefe in the *El Gavilan*, and Samuel rode out in his truck. We explained there was no way to climb the tree, day or at night without great risk. Our next plan was to hoist up a rope with a whole pesticide strip attached. The strip, hanging by the box, might cause the bees to leave, if not to die. The macho men looked at us, the guilty ones, as they grabbed their rifles from the back of the truck. We barely had time to run for the *El Gavilan* before their shots splintered the box and bees cascaded down on us. Somehow windows got rolled up before the bees torpedoed the windows. We roared away anyway before the raging insects could find their way into the car, as they did in horror flicks. Samuel and the *jefe* were not as lucky, but were stung only a few times. Only a few bee-ridden boxes remained intact, and this was the most famous. It became a favorite for target practice over the next few years whenever a new *jefe de seguridad* came onto the ranch.

Though the bees were aggressive, so were we. We needed to know if chicks were in nests, even if bee colonies were in the trees. Bee colonies rarely kept us at bay, and were one of the best ways of protecting a nest because poachers feared them. Alonso, our hired scout at Arveja, had once been an active poacher. We met him one afternoon so he could show us possible nests. Out walking we told him about the horse's death in Tecanal, when he pointed to a large *Ceiba*. "Look up there. Do you see that *hueco bonito?*-- pretty cavity?" Our hopes rose that *loros* would come to the cavity. "There are *muy malas abejas*-- very bad bees-- in the tree. I was climbing up that tree with Olga, my wife, hauling me up on my rope perch, when all of a sudden I heard death coming for me. I was so close to the cavity that I fell and nearly died from the fall and the bees. Olga too got many stings. The bees went *loco* and stung all three chicks to death. Such a waste. No matter if there are chicks again in this tree, I will never climb that *diablo* -- devil-- again."

We assumed he wasn't poaching anymore because we hired him to show us the nests on his *finca* because he was the savviest of all the wildlife husbandmen. As much as we relied on him, his shifty eyes and the stories from his neighbors hinted that his conversion wasn't complete. Alonso kept some of his smaller, less financially rewarding conquests at home. There was always a contingent of roaming *pericos*-- parakeets-- in his trees. He never caged them and only sometimes clipped their wings. Wishing to complete his conversion, we gave him nest boxes for his conures. We had barely walked up with the first nest box and placed it on his patio ground to explain how it worked when he placed two conures on its roof. They went berserk, crawled to the entrance, and made a variety of excited calls. We beamed at our success, for if these birds bred, perhaps Alonso and others would quit poaching.

We went back the next week to ask Alonso the status of the nests he was protecting from poachers. He was a tractor driver and after asking several mounted *vaqueros*-- cowboys--, we finally saw him on his tractor in a far field. We were halfway across the finca by the time he saw us and stopped the tractor. He left the clamoring engine running, and perched atop his mechanical beast, he whistled. Out of nowhere dove a green phantom that lit on his shoulder. It was true. Alonso hadn't lied, at least not about this. He had a winged friend that followed him everywhere, and of his own free will. I thought Alonso was the most blessed man alive, and Alonso's smile indicated he thought so too.

Though the field season was advancing, we suspected that one new tree might have an undiscovered, active nest. Over the past few years we observed pairs of *loros* in the trees and *termiterias* in the Tecanal fields of Jano. These fields were near the center of the ranch and the eyes of the cowboys and polo workers who could be poachers. Despite this risk, we so wanted another nest in

Tecanal where we had the best chance to protect them. The year before, a pair chewed on a *termiteria* in the tree, but never settled into nesting. This year, a pair came and went from a cavity near one of our nest boxes in the same tree. Their behavior was erratic and we couldn't confirm whether the birds were actually with eggs. The only problem, of course, was bees. The bees were in the high nest box, but they caused no particular fear for us as we set up to climb the lower, possible nest cavity.

The bees chased us, and Daniel was stung while the rest of us ran breathlessly. The direct attack wasn't going to work. How about toxins, we wondered? The next day the team tried to hoist a line with a No-Pest Strip on it. Again, the bees chased us. During all our attempts, the *loros* kept coming and going and enticing us by spending the night. In the words of John, if a bird spends the night in a cavity, it's a nest. This may not have been a true maxim for this species, but was true enough to keep us inventing ways to get a look in that nest cavity.

Finally, we were left with our last choice, a night climb. We planned this carefully so no word or unwanted movement would disturb the tree. During the day, we quickly rigged a fishing line so we wouldn't have to muck around the base of the tree in the dark. A moonless night was chosen. We parked *El Gavilan* a soccer field away, and as we stepped out adorned in our bee suits and climbing gear, I had a sudden image. Music set to macho drumming hummed in my ears and I pictured us with our suits, gear, and bravado walking up to the nest in slow motion, much like American heroes walk to and from space rockets in outlandish films. Clutching at dangling carabineers to silence our approach, we crept up to the nest. Because of the awkward branches, only one ground repeller was hooked in. The job of this person, other than getting a crimp in his neck, was to never let his eyes drift from the climber so he knew when to lower the climber, which was often Daniel. As they were the anchoring weight for Daniel, they couldn't run until Daniel was unhooked from the line and running too. Attracted to the drama of the moment, I elected myself as the anchor.

For this climb we agreed that Daniel would jerk on the line if he needed to come down in a hurry. No flashlights were used because the bees were too aggressive. Up he went, clanking a bit, but to me he was like a quiet, dark, mournful ghost haunting the warped ways of the world. Inch by inch, foot by foot, he neared the possible nest and success seemed ours. We would settle the status of this nest one way or another and be done with the uncertainty. Just as my mind was beginning to drift away, my harness jerked. As I unleashed the rope and let our hope slip through my figure-8, I signaled to the others to run, which they did without looking back. Daniel's twirling body met mine with an onslaught of bees. We faced each other with a ton of gear and bee masks between us as he frantically waved at the bees and tried to unhook his ascender.

We fumbled, and we panicked. The gear had entrapped us, forcing us together to dance with erratic moves. At last, we managed to get unhooked, and as agreed upon in our exit plan, Daniel ran one direction and I another. The bees swarmed after the man who'd threatened them.

There was another tree with a lot of Africanized bees, three colonies total. We hadn't figured out how to climb it years before, hence earning it the name *Chinga*-- screwed-- *ceiba*. The challenge of climbing was not so much the bees, but the height of the nest, over 30 meters from the ground. I had no idea how much taller it was than other trees until one afternoon Lucas came bounding into the *casa de proyecto* and told me to go with him. Rushing to the landing strip he pointed to the sky to a multitude of swirling cones, called kettles, of hundreds of hawks, slowly rising on thermals and spiraling from the ground into the clouds. And this was just one spiral out many lining up in a march from north to south, following the chain of volcanoes and the ancient Indian's movement from the Arctic to the tip of South America. Daniel, Lucas, and I jumped into *El Gavilan* and drove up the Reforma road for a broader view of the mass migration. Lazily the variety of species floated up and around, making us dizzy with their movements and numbers. In the distance towered the *Chinga Ceiba* miles away.

Our first attempts at climbing the *Chinga* were long and arduous. The nest was in the upper central trunk, which was rotting, probably from a lightning strike. The height of the nest was thirty-four meters, and it took all of our knowhow and persistence just to get a line up. During one attempt, we had visitors, Stan and Wiley, who were filming us for a documentary on the project. That morning Stan was out of it, having contracted the usual intestinal bugs. It was about all he could do to man the camera during the climb, when he wasn't rushing off to the bushes. Wiley, on the other hand, enthusiastically wanted a chance to shoot the bow that let loose an arrow attached to fishing line over a branch above the nest, which then was attached to a rope to pull up our climbers. Shooting the bow was my area of expertise since I couldn't climb, but he was a big guy and I relinquished the bow to perhaps more capable hands.

His first shot sent an arrow high but off the mark and it fell towards us. This was particularly dangerous because a lead weight was soldered to the end of the arrow, and if it struck someone it would be serious. Seeing the arrow plummeting at us, Wiley dropped the bow and ran, as did we all, except for Stan who in his diseased, obtunded state couldn't grasp the reasoning for our shouts of "Run for your life!" We watched in horror as the arrow struck the earth only a few feet from Stan. He stared at the arrow as we rewound the line for another shot. There he stood trying in his nauseated fog to put together the events. Given the relative success of the first attempt, surely the next shot or two by Wiley would arc the arrow over the branch. Lucas told Wiley we'd name the tree after him if he helped us conquer the tree. Wiley drew back with all his might and sent the arrow up and over the highest branch, a perfect shot, except it was the wrong branch. Lucas said, "I guess we'll call it Wiley's Branch."

It was not only the height of the tree that made this a hard climb, but also the flooded fields that prevented cars from getting close to the base. Vehicles were left behind, and the crew had to negotiate the mud and the sink holes while carrying heavy equipment. Even worse was we had to start before daybreak to avoid the heat of the day because it was a long climb and we all had to wear bee gear. Eventually climbing this tree became routine, even with the nest located along a branch that required the climbers to scoot on their hands and knees at a height of thirty meters. The tree was loved because it represented what we had accomplished and because there was no way we'd lose this chick. It was just too hard a climb.

We'll never know how the poachers got up that tree. Perhaps they had the long climbing rope we lost that season under the *Castaña* bats tree. It was left behind and when we returned for it, it was gone. With the tall ground cover, it was amazing anyone found the rope, unless the poachers had been watching us, which we suspected. They too used sling shots to cast lines, and with our long professional rope they could do the deed. So it was a blow when the *Chinga Ceiba* chick disappeared, having nearly fledged, despite lots of lesions due to the burrowing fly larvae. We knew it was poachers because of human tracks near the nest. *Que Chinga!*

We had another beloved tree, an *amate*-- fig-- in *Campo Santo* 4. I loved it because I had discovered it as a nest in 1991– my first nest ever. It shaded a good portion of one pasture, a refuge for animals of all kinds. Its ancient trunk anchored us into our work, telling us that the cycle of time brought amazing and complex life. Within its many branches insects flew, mated, and ate, over its branches hawks danced out their urges and exchanged food between grasping talons, and on the branches *loros* stood side-by-side, clucking like chickens as they ensured the survival of their species by coupling, and whimpering when it was time to feed each other.

Due to age, major branches within the tree's depth slowly died, leaving the inner recesses open to decay. It was within one of these upward thrusting main limbs that the nests were located each year. The progressing death, however, each year sunk the bottom of the cavity deeper into the trunk, which resulted in varying nest entrance sizes. This year the nest entrance was just a sliver, and Daniel always grunted and whined when he had to pull a reluctant chick from the nest. That year's chick was a wild one. He began hissing before he came out into the light and was a lunger at fingers from the minute his eyes opened at about three weeks of age. Most of our chicks weren't like this. The majority sat complacently while the team moved around them, and only in the last weeks before fledging did the birds scramble away from our prodding. But not this young creature. He bucked and flapped the entire time Daniel struggled to bring him into our world.

Near the end of the bird's nestling period, Daniel sported a few bite scars from lowering the wing beating child to the ground so I could exam it. By now the bird was nearly fully grown and for some reason was calm on the ground. I was anxious why it submitted so easily. My heart skipped a beat and then flew wildly when I saw a reddish swelling near the elbow of one of the wings. "Oh dear God, don't let this be a broken wing!" I manipulated the wing and sure enough the bones were broken, though not severely displaced. My only hope was that it was an old break, one we hadn't caused and for which we we'd be damned. But no matter how much I wished and prayed for a miracle, the bruise grew beneath the skin, indicating the fracture occurred when Daniel moved the chick from the narrow cavity. Probably the bird had an outstretched, flapping wing that got caught on the entrance.

Melissa and Simon, a couple volunteering their biology skills for the summer, listened aghast to my mutterings. We had long awaited this chick's flying freedom. Cane workers and poachers were at high tide, and this was a particularly vulnerable nest due to its easiness to climb, its lowness, and its proximity to other fincas. We had posted guards during daylight hours for weeks, and this was one of the last chicks to fledge for the year. We held our happiness at bay until the bird flew from danger. More than once one of our guards or biologists had sprung from the blind to scare lurking poachers from the tree. We were going to save this bird! Instead, with our invasive techniques, normally harmless, we had doomed this bird. Though I didn't say it aloud at that time, I never wanted to climb another nest tree or examine any more chicks. I just wanted to climb into a hole and not have to be so connected to bird harm, either as a witness or as an agent of pain.

But I put on my professional face and explained to those present how we had a difficult decision. Should we bring the chick into captivity, and damn his future as well as ours, or should we place it back in the nest in hopes its wing would heal and that it would fledge on its own? It wasn't a bad break, and I didn't want the bird in captivity. I wanted it to wander like its ancestors, undefiled by human hands. We struggled and discussed its future in the shade of that great tree, and the plan was set. Back into the nest the bird went, and we wouldn't remove him from the nest again so to the wing could mend. What we would do, however, was continue to guard him during daylight hours. We did this anyway when birds approached fledgling age, which was from about 52 days onward. We watched the chick to see how it would fly and if they had problems we could "rescue" them and bring them into the relatively safe but restrictive life of an aviary bird.

We committed ourselves to this plan and the waiting days turned into weeks and still the chick didn't fledge. No doubt it was delayed in its fledgling time, but this was good. Perhaps the wing was mending, as there was no room within the narrow cavity for the anxious chick to flap its wings. Redemption seemed right around the corner as we went into our third week, not an unheard time for a bone to set. We thought we were about to win this waiting game, however, when one morning the parents didn't enter the nest and were behaving erratically. Daniel climbed the tree while we silently prayed. Shaking his head from above, we grunted, kicked the dust, and seethed. Poachers had climbed the tree during the full moon night. It did no good to think of such a wild, unruly, broken-winged youngster fighting for his life in smoke-filled *casitas* -- little houses. Truly, he couldn't avoid suffering if he survived.

By the time we lost the *Campo Santo* 4 chick, the field season was almost over. Of the 28 active nests, 8 had fledged. This was much better than the previous year. With the year closing I could concentrate on RESCAVES, our education and rescue center. Anita and I dreamt of stopping the poaching, so we built RESCAVES as a home for confiscated parrots. If authorities were going to enforce the no-poaching laws, they needed a safe, registered place to bring the parrots. Policing the illegal bird traffic fell under the jurisdiction of the Guardia de Hacienda. Anita arranged for me to meet with them in Guate, where I shared with them about our center that took in parrots that were confiscated from poachers. The meeting went well and we procured a letter with the necessary impressions, stamps, and glorious letterhead. Daniel and I went to Escuintla, the closest *Guardia de Hacienda*, and presented this letter, our plans, our hopes, and our desires to the Captain to join us.

Before leaving, we made arrangements with the Captain for his troop to come to *los aviarios* to be instructed in avian care, identification, and conservation. The troop arrived in a big blue hacienda bus that matched their blue uniforms. I knew that the *Hacienda de Guardia* was like a militarized Fish and Wildlife Agency, but when they actually marched into squads in front of *los aviarios* I was surprised. Such orderliness wasn't common in any previous meetings and lectures. But it didn't last long. I began by attempting to relax them and welcome them with a joke with the phrase *"que jodido."* The ranks broke file and laughed, resulting in a sharp whistle blast from the Captain's second-in-command. I thought I'd said something was irritating, but I said we were screwed or worse.

We had built three rows of large cages at RESCAVES, and they were all full. Most of the parrots had arrived in one batch of 35 chicks earlier in the year, all of them young enough that their eyes hadn't opened. Juggling them, the 16-hour-a-day field season, and little Moses had been exhausting, but had paid off. All but one survived and now they were the center of our off-season education efforts. We bused in groups of children from all over so that they could receive conservation coloring books, hear songs about conservation, and take a tree home to plant. We had grown seedlings of the two most common nest trees, *conacaste* and *cenízaro*, and distributed and planted them wherever we could. One of our big projects would be to plant the seedlings around the *futbol* field in Tecanal, hoping that one day they'd provide shade for people, as well as food, shelter, and nests for parrots.

During this time, another large group of parrots arrived, brown-hooded parrots. They were young birds, illegally removed at some point from northern Guatemala. Notorious for being difficult to keep in captivity, they remained true to their reputation. These small, timid parrots may not have been the brightest colored, but they were mesmerizing with their stoic presence and chattering calls. The first day most of the birds appeared to have good health, but then they began to deteriorate. Their illness was confusing, and they responded sporadically to our arsenal of medicines. As the disease spread to all the birds and they began to die, my treatment regimen became more and more aggressive. The birds lived their last hours in "avian intensive care," full of tubes, injections, and invasive techniques that caused visitors to gasp at the brutality of health care driven by modern technology. The day came when there was only one left, and when he died, I kept him in my hands for an hour weeping. I began to seriously doubt if veterinarians had any right to be working with wild parrots, ever, in field, in rescue centers, and certainly not in homes.

Deep into in, there was no way not to respond to injured wildlife. In the hospital after the brown-hoodeds died off, we had a convalescing grey hawk. She had come to us when Daniel and I were out walking on the far side of the *finca*, a long, hot walk home. There she was in a *zanja*" ditch-- her big eyes following us. Daniel threw his shirt over the bird's head and upon quick examination I found a broken wing, likely from a sling shot. We decided to take her to the aviaries for either treatment or euthanasia. I thought she would mend, but not enough for flight. I called over to the zoo, and they said if the bird survived she could live on one of the islands in the drive-through park. There she'd be unable to escape and protected. It was a good idea, but would be hard on our avian friend. Grey hawks are high strung and her time in the aviary and later in the small flight cages were terror filled. She continually reinjured her wing and other parts of her body. Eventually I had to amputate the wing at the wrist, after which she quickly healed. With the field season over we could set her free on the island.

We waded across the lagoon, and as soon as we placed the grey hawk on the island, she flapped and flopped into the water and would have drowned if we hadn't been there. After several more attempts she finally stayed perched on a tree, too exhausted to escape on her phantom wing. Daniel and I took turns standing guard for two days in case she nearly drowned again. We lifted our guard on the third morning, and when we returned in the afternoon to check on her, she was gone. Nowhere to be seen, nobody in the water, nothing. We searched in the grass, in the *zanjas*, and on the other islands. No sign of her anywhere. Giving up, we headed out of the enclosure through the gate system that automatically opened and closed gates between the different animal collections. Actually, the gates weren't all that automatic because people had to honk to gain the attention of workers on tree-top level platforms. Each platform worked ropes hooked to a pulley and weight system that opened and closed the gates. Some of the human gate tenders had rifles in case a rhino or lion went rogue. To leave the lagoon enclosure we had to pass through the lions. There we found our grey hawk, or what remained of her. She had survived the painful rescue attempts, treatments, surgeries, and placement, only to flop over the fence into the mouth of a lioness or two.

We weren't set up for wildlife rescue and release. We didn't have the cages or resources to do it correctly. Before releasing the grey hawk, we rescued a pygmy kingfisher. Her sparkling colors demanded our worship. She was just too beautiful to believe. She was taken into the bathroom, our critical care quarantine unit. Apparently hit by a car, we were waiting for her to recover her strength to release her. Unfortunately, she came out of her semi-conscious state sooner than expected and willed herself to be free. She escaped her little intensive care box and flew right into the cage of the grey hawk. She didn't survive.

RESCAVES teamed up with *Proyecto de Loro* not only to care for parrots and wildlife, but also to bring aid to the people and the land, and deliver a conservation message. One of these projects was our poultry and pet vaccination program. We figured that it wasn't enough to preach the gospel of the earth without helping people. After all, the root of the birds' problems lay at the feet of the country's socio-economic status. In a sense, we were bribing the people with our goodwill. If we saved their domestic poultry, perhaps they'd think twice before poaching. In the meantime, we could increase their meat and egg production, and hopefully their health.

We targeted our three main *fincas*, Esperanza, Arveja, and Tecanal, as well as our two closest *aldeas*, Micaela Linda and Las Rosas. Vaccinations were purchased from Guate and included pox and Newcastle's for birds, and rabies for dogs and cats. All homes were notified of the day we'd appear so their poultry and pets could be gathered. This would speed up and organize the program. Right! It never worked out that way. We'd show up in our veterinary uniforms and a volunteer or two helped speed up the process and pass out conservation propaganda sheets. "You need to protect your wild birds, as well as your poultry. The poultry, parrots, and the environment need the same preventative care!"

Chaos reigned. Children scampered off in search of baby ducks, mothers rounded up hens, older children chased roosters, and dogs flushed out the shyer flock members. Grandmothers even got into the act as they half-carried, half-dragged their beloved turkeys for us to admire their size, beauty, and potential for filling up a hundred or more *tamales*. Feathers and shit flew everywhere! Children screamed and beamed, the women waved their fingers trying to remember each and every bird, and smiles popped out on every face. These women and children loved their birds, a love that was based on the food chain, but it was deep and true. This love didn't spill over into caring for the birds as pets. Indeed, birds were tied up, held upside down, and transported great distances to markets without food, water, or relief from the heat. But they were portable food and greatly prized. Although the price of poultry meat and eggs was comparable to that in the USA, these people weren't making $100 a month, and that would feed countless children, extended family, and less privileged neighbors.

This vaccination program was a great success. Over 1200 birds were vaccinated in the surrounding area. Consequently, there were many fewer deaths (until dinner time) than there would have been otherwise, as evidenced by frequent invitations for us to share meals with those in the area. We'd be passing by a quiet house on one of the *fincas*, where the people usually ignored us and stared at our parrot conservation antics. After the vaccination program, children came running to us, held our hands, and led us to the dinner table, where platters of poultry bits were served in soups and tamales.

With the vaccination program winding up, the field season over, RESCAVES stabilized, and most of the sick birds dead, we had plenty of time again for soccer. We started practicing, slowly rebuilding the team, but Elena never showed. We went to her home to ask about her, but her family said she was *desaparecida*-- disappeared or missing. She'd left six months earlier for the USA to work, leaving her six children behind. No one had heard from her and the worst was feared. Even without her and other players who just seemed to not be around, we put a team together and began playing. For one of our last big games we once again played in Escuintla. This time, however, we had the privilege of playing on the big city field and many spectators. Somehow, we all knew that this might be one of our last games, and I was desperate to have it be a winning end to my late blooming career. Plus, I wanted to beat Escuintla on their home field, which we'd never done.

We struggled and fought but we couldn't break their 1- 0 lead. As center mid-fielder I was frantic to get a goal before the whistle blew. The harder I played, the lazier my teammates played. It was as if all the injustices of the world were being played out on this field, and it was always someone else's fault that the game didn't go as I wanted it to. I was fighting to win just as I was fighting to stay in the game of life. Then, out of nowhere, Adrian signaled during a throw in, and I looked around for the player he was pulling off the field. He kept pointing, Joaquin joined in, and Daniel too, until I realized they were calling to me. I stomped off the field, enraged at being taken out in my prime. After whining to Daniel, I marched up to Adrian and demanded to know why I was removed when all the other players weren't giving it their best shot. "You looked like you were getting tired," he murmured, his eyes never meeting mine. I returned to Daniel's side, his eyes too fixated on the field and not on mine. I couldn't believe it, they were treating me like I was some crazed, loco-blooded *Guatemalteca*-- Guatemalan woman-- whose eyes couldn't be met without risking a violent confrontation.

I sulked the entire ride home, after which I immediately went for a four-mile run to prove I wasn't tired. But I was, and I had heat exhaustion to boot. I spent that night in aches and chills, which wasn't unusual after a day of soccer in the sun. In the morning I was finally sober, and wondered what I'd done in my soccer stupor the day before. I found Daniel, Joaquin, and Adrian and apologized for my poor sportsmanship. Later in Daniel's arms, I heard him snicker. "What, what, I know I was quite a sight." "*Si, mi amor*, you were. But it was worth it. You gained the *apodo*-- nickname-- of '*La Rino Blanca*'-- the white rhinoceros-- and we laughed all last night remembering your anger. *Es verdad* -- it's true--, Kim, you are truly a *Guatemalteca*!

To get ready for the 1995 field season, I headed to the USA for a long month. I felt shame that I could so easily and safely travel across borders, and as we flew over Mexico I wondered if Elena was somewhere down there, and alive. I was to meet my mother in Seattle and we'd camp our way across the USA. She'd never seen the country and I wanted to make that happen for her. My Chevy van was waiting for me in California, and I drove up to Seattle. By the time we reached Utah, the October air had turned chilly, and on the road to the Grand Canyon snow began to fall. The low clouds, mist, and thick snow kept my mother from a view that normally stretches for miles, both horizontal and vertical. Disappointed and cold, I sought to brighten us with another tactic. From my days in Florida, I'd brought a large phallus-shaped art piece made of cement. It was gifted to me because of my bawdy humor and lack of boyfriends, and had been good for laughs. I'd left it buried on the Alaska-Canada border for a couple of years, but recovered it when I left Alaska. Now it was time to be rid of it, with no chance to take it back. On the edge of the Grand Canyon, only able to see a few meters, I said some words that resembled a prayer, and flung the penis over the edge.

Chapter 12
LOSING THE WAR
Guatemala, 1995

1995

Efrain Rio Montt, ex-dictator of Guatemala, named president of Guatemala's Senate. Though responsible for the massacres of the early 1980s, he continued in power. The Supreme Court strips Rios Montt of immunity from prosecution.

Before the beginning of the 1995 breeding season, Daniel knocked on my door and pried me off of the couch. He wanted me to work with a visiting parrot biologist from Brazil, who came to gather ideas for his country's avian conservation program, including radio telemetry. That afternoon he and Daniel were scheduled to track one of the Pilas nest fledglings, and he wanted me to go. Reluctantly I agreed, trying to muster the energy to explain the process to a biologist. In the middle of a field, a storm suddenly came on us. Daniel quickly disconnected the metal antennae from the hand-held receiver and laid it against a tree along a fence line. Once the lightening attracting device was dumped, we ran to a wooden cattle trough to wait out the storm. Closely wedged onto the salt lick and crouched under the small roof, we continued to talk over the booming and flashing, flinching each time lightening hit trees and shook the earth, or at least I was. I suspected that the two men were playing a macho game, trying to look calmer than they were.

They didn't have long to play at that game because even more suddenly the storm retreated a surreal distance. A bright golden glow descended on us. The falling rain fell all around us, but not on us. It was like we were under paradise's umbrella, shielded and bathed in the light's glory, seeing the world through lenses made of gold. Finally, the men grew excited about a double rainbow that arched over from afar to end with us at the rainbow's golden finale. I reached out to hug the kaleidoscope of colors that shone through the darkness and the tempest.

Soon it was early breeding season, but I still had plenty of work to do at the clinic and RESCAVES. One morning Alexa was helping out at RESCAVES before the field season geared up. Working with her was quiet because she rarely spoke, and only then could one get a glimpse of the adornments on her teeth. She had metal stars and moons affixed to the front of her teeth, I guessed to correct cavities. We were busy preparing for an educational experience for school children when Daniel drove up in a cloud of dust. He was scheduled to work elsewhere on the *finca*, so he cringed when he said *"Kim, disculpe, pero tengo una ave enferma,"*-- "Excuse me, but I have a sick bird,"-- he said. "I can't stay." Alexa and I peered into his cupped hands and there was the most beautiful hummingbird I'd ever seen. Though still alive, its unmoving body contrasted sharply with the spark of life that it gave each of us to behold such a wonder; so small, so close, so iridescent, and so perfect. Daniel quickly transferred the patient into my hands, jumped back into *El Gavilan*, and sped away. "Alexa, it looks like you're my veterinary assistant today for this bird." *"Esta bien,"* "That is fine,"-- she said, never a woman to say more than necessary.

We drove in the *La Paloma* to *los aviarios*, the stick-shift driving made difficult because I was holding the blessing in my hand. Driving through the cattle gate that Alexa opened, I felt the hummingbird stir. Maybe it had been hit by a car and was only stunned. Wondering why I had to be in control of both driving and holding the bird, I asked Alexa to take the bird. She quickly held out her hands, cupped as if in prayer, her eyes saying that she couldn't believe she'd been given the responsibility. She was the newest hire and hadn't been given more responsibility than simple observations. Her timidity kept her from the more aggressive field assignments.

At the aviary doors I asked Alexa if the bird was moving. *"Si, Kim, esta vivo."*-- "Yes, it's alive." *"Pues*, Alexa, I have an idea. Maybe it was only stunned and now it'll be fine." Brilliantly sensitive, I refrained from explaining the characteristics of neurogenic traumatic shock. "We can let the bird go, but we have to be careful that it doesn't fly *borracho*--drunkenly-- or we'll have to chase it and bring it into the aviary for more recovery and treatment." Alexa then started to hand the bird to me, knowing that it wasn't her place to release our charge. "No, Alexa you do it. Just slowly open your hands away from your body, up high so it will have a chance to get clear of the ground, and keep your eyes on where the bird goes." As if she was carrying the weight of the world in her hands, she walked a few paces into the pasture. Concentrating, she didn't seem to realize I was only a few feet from her. She lifted her hands and eyes to the heavens and opened them slowly, carefully, and hopefully. Up and away sped the smallest bird in creation. We followed its progress, quickly losing site of it as it headed toward the smoking volcanoes. I glanced at Alexa, who was in an ecstatic trance. It was if her soul had flown away as well and was only now returning. "Kim, *es la cosa mas bonita en toda me vida*"-- "It's the most beautiful thing in all of my life. Stars flew from her smile as she spoke. My thoughts echoed her words, although the most beautiful thing in the world was not just the recovered hummingbird, but also Alexa's rapture at having held beauty and given it healing and freedom.

Inspired by her reaction, I thought of how to keep RESCAVES alive. We had received only two deliveries of confiscated birds. The rest were wildlife rescues. The education efforts were beautiful, but it would take decades and a changing economic status, if not world view, to stop the poaching. Yet, if people could handle birds, like Alexa did, and have a conversion experience to birds, perhaps there was hope. We could set up a banding station at RESCAVES, where not only visitors from all over the world could come and know beauty, but locals, students, government officials, etc., would help staff the nets. They would be with birds, and with minimal harm and manipulation of birds and humans alike. Almost.

To test this project, Randy, a doctoral student came from "*Los Estados*"-- the United States-- for a mist netting experience. He and Joaquin went out in the mornings and evenings to set up the nets. Mist nests are fine nets that are stretched out between long poles driven into the ground. The height of these nets depends on what kinds of birds you are trying to catch. For song birds the nets went from ground level to six feet. To catch parrots, elaborate pulley systems and telescoping poles are required to raise the nets high enough. Randy in his pilot project, however, was seeking migrant song birds, as well as the natives. In the winter months, our *invierno* and breeding season for the native birds, scores of migrant birds came from the north, much like our volunteer biologists. During these months, our fields and forests looked like they blossomed in a mix of tropical and northern gardens. Species normally only seen at home, wherever that was, would suddenly appear in our midst, reminding us that the world really wasn't so small. Cross-continental travel had existed for millennia for many species, long before airplanes.

Each session Randy and Joaquin invited one of the biologists so that they could have an Alexa experience. Each person would crouch hidden by a net and as soon as a bird hit the net they would run to untangle it. Much like our conure experience using butterfly mist nets, this was taxing for human and birds alike, as the fine hair-like strands were untangled from feathers, nails, and beaks. Sometimes the manipulation of birds was too much and they didn't survive. Others were so exhausted that their weak flights away made us doubt they would be able to escape predators, of which there were plenty in the dusky evenings. Later I read of the disadvantages of using mist nets to capture birds. Even this apparent benign education tool had a dark side, and I became wary of it, even while enthralled. To hold a painted bunting is to hold the glory of God. Colors crisscross this tiny body, a master's hand beyond our imagination. For just those few moments, by holding all that is perfect and right, one suspects one's own perfection, though at a cost.

One late afternoon I was monitoring a tree to see if it was an active nest, and Randy and Joaquin were staffing the nets. The sun had just set, so they began to lower the nets, but not quickly enough. Flying beings hit both nets. Randy went running to one net, Joaquin to another. As Joaquin worked his net, he heard Randy exclaim, "Shit, these little birds can bite!" Randy clutched a bleeding finger, and Joaquin said, "Randy, these aren't birds, but bats."

At dinner that night there was much laughter and some discussion about whether Randy was at risk for rabies, and his final decision was that there was no risk. Several days passed and Randy was bombarded with faxes from concerned relatives and his girlfriend. Professional opinions from experts in the USA alarmed them and, as a result, Randy too. There was a definite risk of rabies, and Randy had better get to a doctor quickly. He grew frantic to begin searching for the rabies antiserum. The morning Joaquin arrived to give him a ride to the city, Randy woke up sick as a dog. Randy was sure that the rabies virus had begun its work. It turned out that he had caught some other innocuous bug, but it was a tension-filled trip to Guate and to various hospitals until the injections were found. They returned later the next day, vials and syringes in hand, armed to resume their work, which was occasionally interrupted when I gave Randy one of his injections.

Given our experience of previous years, we knew we had to step up our protection of nests if we wanted the chicks to fledge, especially those nests closer to human activity. This meant protecting the nests over the weekend as well, and asking our biologists to work. Because they were there protecting the birds, they were also collecting data for our nest-time budget analysis. Hidden from view, our field workers recorded all parental activity. One weekend Daniel and I were giving the biologists rides to and fro, to and fro, and then all over again. Mirsa had done a back-to-back watch (7 hours!) and Alexa was about to do a double as well. The least we could do was to escort them to their stations at midday. When we approached the back of the blind at one nest, we noticed Mirsa was outside the blind, visible to the parrots. When questioned, Mirsa pointed to the blind. I couldn't imagine what would cause one of our most vigilant biologists to ruin a watch by being visible. There, piled heroically in the entrance on the blind, was a major dump. This was one of those dumps you only hear about in other's dreams. It was big, it was granular, it was fibrous, and it was orange. Within this excrement one could see Third World symbols; a diet of mangos, dysentery from Rio Micaela Linda's water, lack of digestion due to alcohol dinners, and an underlying native artistic ability.

It was as if time had stopped as we gathered around to pay homage to the incredible creation. I slipped into another time continuum considering the implications of someone purposely defiling our blind, one of our many perceived and imagined enemies. How could they have possibly timed this massive expression some two miles from the nearest home? I knew not the world in which I lived, nor was I sure I wanted to be a part of this human experience. I must have mumbled my thoughts aloud because Alexa opened her mouth, the universe broke open, the glorious heavens sparkled as she spoke a great truth in response to my mutterings and meanderings. She said, "*Dios es grande*-- God is great." I was lost, not she. Within the putrid pile perching so tentatively on the ditch wall, she saw a miracle. I saw betrayal, lack of hope, no respect, self or otherwise, and, most of all, amoebic dysentery. How could she be so hopeful? I looked into her eyes, but the moment of truth had passed, the view into her universe had closed. Once again, the wall came up, and the shutters closed.

Others waited for action. There was only one I could see. Tear out the bastard's heart or make him come clean up the mess. I say "he" because one person came to all our minds. We named him, *El Cargon*-- The Shitter. He was a disgruntled ex-employee, who was seen eating mangos and drinking copious beers the night before. This was all the evidence we needed. But instead of violent passion, we shoveled the masterpiece into the far bushes, but the art wasn't lost. I never miss a photo opportunity.

Despite the cleaning detail, Alexa refused to sit in the blind the rest of the day. I wondered what she thought that day as the sun baked her and the shoveled dump. What had given her the ability to see God in a pile of dung, where all I saw was shit? That a mango digested could be a vengeful object was not new to her, but still she saw mangos as great. As for me, I'll never look at a mango the same way. Her faith brought her interpretation of the event beyond the ordinary

Although I was mostly on the "climb tree" crew, I did occasionally pull a time budget watch, like Mirsa and Alexa. These watches always challenged me because I had a hard time tracking birds in and out of their nests. All it takes is scratching your nose one time and, poof, the female is out of the nest and out of sight. Sometimes I believed the birds waited for me to be distracted and that's when they flew to and from the nest. Their special ploy was to move just when I was writing in my notes, "no activity last 15 minutes." On the time

143

budget sheet was a column for "birds lost," which means we don't know where they were. In the biologist world we avoided having too many minutes in that column, and I always seemed to have a lot. Now I could claim that I had a hard time tracking large, green, screaming birds because of my poor vision and partially paralyzed eye, but I was not convinced that the cause was not something more deeply flawed within me.

My turn had come to do a fourth-quarter watch on *El Cargon*, a tree named after the man we suspected had defecated in the blind. He had discovered it, glad to earn a "finder's fee" that we paid anyone who showed us an active nest. The pair had fooled many observers because the blind was awkward to watch from and the birds were quiet. I snuck up to the tree, eyed potential observation points, checked the wind, looked for signs of aggressive insects, and settled into my nest for the evening, confident I would master this watch.

The hours ticked by with no bird movement. Then up from behind came Daniel, who had a reputation for being unable to stay still on his watches, but being 1.5 miles from his watch nest was even extreme for him. He too like me was a climb team member and didn't pull that many watches. I'm sure that the biologists were amused by my time budget forms. In the early years, Daniel and I did watches together so I could help him through the time budget form and the math of minutes. Fitting two folks into some of the blinds could be a challenge, but being more than just friends we managed to fit and find something to do in between the brief moments of true wonder when the parents returned to feed their chicks.

So what does Daniel do but show up in my blind, ruining not only his watch but mine. Once again, I was losing biologist points, and Daniel sensed my disappointment. "But, Kim," he said, "I ran most of the way here chasing poachers who had climbed part way up my tree. I need to know if we should go after them." He was at Arbol de Samuel and it was no surprise that he saw poachers. It was close to sunset, so I told him to forget it and please, please, sneak quietly away so I could salvage my watch.

Once again alone, I honed in on the nest. After Daniel left I scurried to avoid some *wintas* -- large, fierce, black ants that sting worse than a bee-- but surely I hadn't bothered the birds. I was getting worried that perhaps the birds had seen me or Daniel when I heard footsteps behind me again. Daniel brought me a cold soda from the local *tienda*. Something I learned over the years was to never, ever yell at a Guatemalan when they had screwed up while trying to be courteous. I thanked my man and shooed him off. He promised to return at the end of the watch to take me to one of our biologist parties, which we held when volunteers returned to their country.

Although I was pissed at Daniel for again disturbing my watch, again, I still hoped the birds hadn't noticed and again turned my attention to the nest. It became late and still no birds. The worst time of a watch when it's nearly dark and the parents don't show up. Had the nest been poached or predated, did the parents decide not to feed that night, or even worse, had I missed seeing the birds? Just when I was about to give up, I saw a flash of green (as I was writing "No activity for the last 15 minutes"), and there were the two parents near the nest. And that's when it happened. There are rules to observation watches, and common sense could have avoided an embarrassing scene. However, if you have a case of amoebas and your colon has a strong reaction to caffeine, do not drink a cola while confined to a small blind near people's homes, where at any movement you could lose control.

After many years in Guatemala where bathrooms are scarce, I had developed a muscular sphincter. So I clamped down and kept my eyes on the nest. During one of those waves of anal terror I was so intent on keeping my pants clean that I missed both parents leaving. "Shit," I cried, and shit I did. Right there, in the blind, in my pants. It was an explosive event. I was covered. I tried to clean up as best I could, while stumbling around the blind and avoiding *wintas* in the dark. I was brought so low that I cried and wished for my mother. What worse could happen did.

Daniel drove up with boys in tow to take me to the party. With underpants sloshing around my ankles I waddled behind a tree, sobbing and shouting, "Don't come closer." Thank goodness no Americans were in the car, because the Guatemalans have a habit of not questioning actions, just following orders. The headlights had caught a flash of my white butt bowing out from a tree and Daniel immediately recognized the familiar silhouette. He quickly doused the lights, jumped the fence, and beheld the sight, once again demonstrating legendary Guatemalan facial control. Without much discussion, he said he'd be back to get me, and drove off with the boys. We never knew what the boys thought about the incident and how I appeared showered and in fresh clothes for the party. They never did question why I had ordered the blind site moved, although it didn't really matter because the next day we found that the nest had been preyed on by iguanas. That's why the parents had been hard to see; they realized their year's efforts had been eaten, and they were no longer interested in the nest. That's what I told myself, looking back on yet another watch with "lost birds."

The long shifts and days were wearing on our conservation team. It was time for a break. One of the best women's soccer teams in the country had heard about us and wanted a game. Even better, they played regular soccer on a full field in Guatemala City. Often, cities only supported six woman "*Papi-futbol*" teams that played on a reduced field, which was an outdoor asphalt basketball court. We were in the middle of the breeding season, but with a little fine tuning of the schedule we might be able to make it. But the trip required funds for transportation, and the project couldn't swing it. It was already looking like we wouldn't have the funds to continue next year, but since this might be the last chance for me to play, and perhaps the last chance for the *Proyecto Loro* team to ever play, I went for it. I was considering accepting a position at the North Carolina State University School of Veterinary Medicine, which would mean this was my last field and soccer season.

We rented the bus and driver that regularly drove by our homes. The bus was bright and sparkly, with paintings of nude women on the interior walls, and colorful streamers flowing in the air. We tied our *loro* mascot banner on the front, which was a parrot kicking a ball. The great thing about having a whole bus was that there was room for everyone and I didn't have to drive. Joaquin, Ricardo, Adrian, Adrian's brother, Diego, Daniel, and boyfriends accompanied us, Otilia's toddlers and infants spilled over easily into welcoming hands, and not only could Gloria's sister come but also her younger siblings. First, the bus swung by Tecanal, horn honking and men whistling as women piled in. A crowd gathered at our *porton*, wishing us well as we went off to play in the big leagues. Then we went by Isabel's home by the Micaela Linda, Andres's *tienda*, to pick up the Las Rosas group, then various stops in Bravo, and finally the girls whose parents worked on the Finca Argentina. Each stop raised the decibel level a fraction higher so when we reached Escuintla it was a mad house. This time we breezed through the traffic circle as the driver honked at the policemen. Today there would be no fines, no breakdowns, no sunburns from riding in the back of a truck, and no cold, drenched people from the afternoon storms.

We arrived in the city and drove through one of the *colonias*- - neighborhoods. Approaching the field, we suddenly grew quiet. The field was a littered, hard-packed, grassless area surrounded by corrugated tin homes and *tiendas*. Great cracks ran through its surface from runoff that gathered momentum and flowed over a sudden drop-off by one of the side lines. The slope wasn't unusual, for we were up in the volcanoes, but the debris, rocks, and broken glass strewn about the field were a surprise, as was the extreme poverty of the area. Playing on this surface would be like playing on inner-city asphalt, complete with the garbage of urban existence.

While we imagined the various injuries we could incur, our coaches went off to find the other teams and arrange the game. This took a good hour, during which I wondered from group to group, wishing I could just hang with Daniel, but we were in public and he wore his indifferent mask. So I wore mine and joined Alejandra and her girls to eat lunch. We munched on Alejandra's chicken and my banana bread, sharing a communal meal in silence, as we had for years shared a man. By this time, Daniel had moved out of Alejandra's home, had temporarily lived at Lucas's in Bravo, and now stayed at his mother's, and he had annulment papers. But who can ever divorce, especially in a culture that never really marries.

CONSERVATION IN TIME OF WAR

The coaches returned with the verdict. We were to play a quadrangular. Our project team would supply two teams and they had two teams, one of which had beaten every other woman's team in Guate. There were grumblings as we split our players into two teams, one obviously the first string. Some threatened to not play at all, especially if they had to wear the alternate uniforms, a grey mesh. These conflicts were almost ho-hum conflict level status, soon conquered, and the games began.

I was chosen for the first-string team, but not a running player. My time for that honor had passed. Long stretches of relative inactivity during our busy work season and my gut adapting to the parasites had added a few pounds and taken the edge off my ability to keep up. But I was the *goleadora*-- goalie-- and would earn the scars to prove it. The first game was won, and I had bleeding knees from trapping the ball on the rough surface. Luckily, not too many shots came my way and I had time to pick up most of the glass around the goal. I must have made an impression because after the game, during our break, several men offered to buy me a beer. I went to a bar with Daniel as a chaperone, and sipped mineral water as the men smoked, drank, and relived the plays of the game.

It was a long wait before we played again, and there wasn't much to do that my foreign eyes could detect. I couldn't find most of our team from the coast. Where do they all go? I watched other games and looked at the volcano Pacaya, now seen from the other side, completely different from a mile's elevation. Still the clouds clung to her and smoke flowed down her slopes so all of her was never seen. Her hidden reaches beckoned me upwards, knowing that to go there was to invite robbery, murder, and eruption surprises.

A whistle blew and I was jolted from imagination to reality. This game was for the championship, the winner would be the best team in Guatemala. Once again, I was the goalie, this time with dozens of men gathered around the back side of goal cheering me on with raised Gallo beers. There was no move that I made that didn't inspire comments from the crowd, cheers, gasps, and groans. I was getting pummeled as the ball came at me from close kicks because of the reduced size of the field and goal area. Fingers were resprained, or even rebroke. I was never sure about my right ring finger. Years later it still curves where it shouldn't, a lasting trophy to all those deflected balls and body slams against goal posts.

Despite the support of our team, I was soon tiring from the constant stress. The game was tied and I didn't want it to go into penalty kicks. My fingers and heart couldn't take it. But when in Guatemala did wishing get anyone anywhere? The whistle blew and chaos ensued as the crowd flowed onto the field. There was no way that each and every fan wasn't going to have their face right in the action as the five kickers took their shots at the other team's *goleadora*. Our team was at a disadvantage because the goals were smaller and the distance shorter. The kickers seemed to be an arm's length away, and the balls flew in at speeds too great to react to. Like so many times in my life, I didn't want to be involved in such intensity, yet couldn't refuse.

The kicks came in fast, and although I'm a mediocre goalie, I made a few good stops. Finally, we were down to the last kick. We were up by one goal and if this kicker missed, or if I could stop it, then we'd be the champions. The ball came in high, direct, and fast. I barely had time to get my hands up, when my ring finger bent back as I tipped the ball. Throbbing in pain I looked around, unsure if the ball had cleared the goal. Without a goal net, balls rolled down the hillside and into the gutters without leaving any clues if they'd sailed through or around the goals. The crowd's silence baffled me. Did we win, did we tie, was Pacaya sending us an earthquake? In that split second I was in another world. I didn't understand the secret dead-pan face of *Guatemaltecos*.

Then they swept me from my feet, freeing me from my self-imposed prison. They hadn't scored, and I had. The event was a success, I had connected, we had a good time, and we won! I was elected to receive the championship trophy, although I wasn't the best or most beloved player. I was the sponsor. We won because of the beauty and power of those women, to whom I felt a deep bond. Despite my sun- and wind-burned face I smiled and laughed with all the women. Nothing like a national championship to break down our silly little human walls. We had so much to be proud of. In just a few years, our team had come together from divergent backgrounds. There had been losses, struggles, and explosive events that threatened and ended lives regularly, but still we won.

There was one lesser soccer game a few weeks later, in which I barely played. My friend Linda had gone to this last soccer game, having finally managed to get to Guatemala. Leaving her children in capable hands at home, she came to see my life before it once again dramatically changed. Wanting to help me transition, she also hoped for some vacation time, so we toured Panachel, Antigua, and Tikal. I had done this same loop and similar ones with other visitors over the years, but this would be the best trip yet. Perhaps it was because I had gained some confidence and autonomy in this foreign land. For example, I knew not to use the cheap, small airlines for a flight to Tikal. I had more than learned my lesson a few years ago when Barbara and I went to the Petén.

Both Barbara and I being tight for funds, I hadn't booked our flight on Aviateca, the major airline in the country. Instead I chose a small company that Perry had recently used. Knowing of Barbara's fear of flying, I asked what size planes they used, and they responded that we'd be flying on an eighty-seater prop plane. Proud of my thoroughness to such details, I nonetheless was anxious as we drove up to the main terminal past wrecks of airplanes raised up on cinder blocks. Entering the small two room office that also served as a ticket counter, we were ushered out the back door to board a small ten-seater prop plane. They didn't ask to see our tickets, but only asked for our names. We were the last to board, or so we thought, as they placed us in the rear by the entry door. Sitting in the revving plane, the single pilot didn't greet any of us. The co-pilot's seat was given to a passenger, who wasn't there long because an office guy told this standby passenger to deplane and let three more on. I knew where one would go, where there should have been a goddamned co-pilot, but the other two? There were no more seats. *No problema!* The office guy handed wooden planks to the two remaining passengers and demonstrated how to lay them on the inner frame of the tail behind Barbara and me. Trying to not inhale exhaust fumes through our open, incredulous mouths, the two men from Scotland climbed over us, placed their wooden boards across the width of the tail section, and settled in.

At about this time Barbara reached for her Valium, perhaps explaining how she weathered the trip so much better than I had. After completing her rite of passage, she noticed that although the door had been shut, it hadn't been latched. I leaned over and did the honors and saw the date of the last inspection of the airplane. Barbara, feeling her drugs, asked me nonchalantly what was the date of the last inspection? "Oh, 1964," I giggled. But hey, maybe they didn't mark inspection dates anymore, which was my mantra as we took off and cleared the volcanoes. The worst was over because the terrain was basically flat from here on out.

Except that a low altitude thick fog and storm rolled into Northern Guatemala, making for marginal visibility. Surely the pilot had instruments that would guide him, but even this I began to doubt as he circled and circled in the wet blanket. Trying to control my nausea and fear, I was relieved when we broke through the clouds, except that we were only a hundred feet over Las Rosas Lake. This was too close for comfort, and during our three days at the park I grew more and more anxious about our return flight.

Asking Barbara to keep the Valium ready as we were taxied to the airport, I couldn't have been happier to see the promised eighty-seater, even if it looked like it was the first plane ever flown in Guatemala. Our flight back was uneventful and I saw Barbara off to *Los Estados* the next day. I didn't think much more about it until five days later when an airplane crashed and an American Peace Corps volunteer died. She'd taken the same airline, the same flight, and the same airplane, but it crashed into a volcano, killing all onboard. After that I flew only the huge Aviateca jet to Tikal, and I recommend the same to all travelers that venture to this tropical land.

Once in Tikal, Linda and I couldn't hold still. Even in the middle of the day she was game to go exploring, and, like me, learned to appreciate the rush of a caffeinated soda in the afternoon heat. Her enthusiasm for climbing reminded me of my mother, who visited Tikal at sixty years of age and with a broken arm. Furthermore, it was the rainy season and all surfaces were slick and treacherous. But that didn't hold back Mom, who hiked up Temple IV before I could unsling my backpack. She had heard my stories about how wonderful the view was above the canopy, and a little measly broken arm wouldn't stop her. Up the angled ladders and over muddy roots she ascended, not needing encouragement from me. We spent a while at the top, and while she was busy clicking pictures I plotted how to get her down without her other arm breaking. This was the same stretch where Daniel had torn up his ankle a few years back. My brother had warned me to not let anything happen to the mother unit, his words echoing as I worked out a plan.

Just as I was about to tell her of my carefully thought out route of descent, she started down. I had planned to descend in front of her so I could break her fall if she slipped, but now I'd have to double her speed to get in front of her. No mountain goat myself, this was tricky and I never managed to do it. Instead she descended the last wooden ladder by herself, and when she touched ground the crowd at the base applauded her achievement.

Linda too seemed to be of the same mold, and she climbed everything possible, leaving me halfway up the only temple I had ever failed to summit. I couldn't step across the inclined rubble as she and Daniel had done before me, so it would remain that I couldn't conquer all that the ancient Mayans had challenged me with. But what I couldn't conquer, I could defile. Not that it was intentional, but Freud might argue that. I blamed it on the caffeinated cola.

The ultimate edifice we climbed was the *Mundo Perdido*-- the Lost World. One of the last jungle-covered mounds to be discovered, once rebuilt it provided a difficult climb only in its large steps and sharp angle of ascent. My limbs shook only occasionally on the way up, and I was relieved that the top was a large, flat expanse. Here we could view the peaks of all the other temples emerging out of the green, pulsating canopy, and with such a view, we sat down to dine. Something magical clicked with the combination of good food and spectacular ambience, but my intestines decided to contribute to the experience. Mumbling to Linda about my condition, both of us paced back and forth across the top and decided that there was nothing for it except to do the deed right there in plain view. Dropping my shorts and leaning as much over the back slope as possible so my exposed white derriere wouldn't hang in stark contrast to the terrain, I voided sloppily.

My aim of going to Tikal was to honor my experience in Guatemala, for this park had delightful birds, intriguing history, and was relatively safe to walk around. I had hoped that this experience would allow me to leave Guatemala with positive images to counterbalance all the negative ones. But instead of embracing the country, I shit on top of it.

I traded Linda off at the airport to pick up John, where once again we were honored to have him. He had continued to consult with us over the years and in 1995 had a few days available to work with us. He volunteered to take a fifteen-hour nest watch at the Serengeti nest, a brutal shift that our biologists were reluctant to pull but invigorated this seasoned pro. The day of his watch I was startled from my bed by gunfire, a sound I would never grow accustomed to. Daniel came to my house for work, but also to offer to show me a murdered body. He had seen it. I declined his invitation to the site, less than fifty meters from the nest John was observing. Violence was so prevalent, and I thought how experiencing any more than absolutely necessary would mean I had crossed some kind of line.

That evening, I waited for John to return and share news of the vicious attack near the nest tree. His notes were famous for detail and I wanted to read them. Sure enough, John had recorded the mad race of cars to the nest, the slamming brakes and crunching metal, the repeating gunfire, the frantic yelling of a man trying to get out of his car overturned in a ditch, the riddling of the car with bullets, and the speeding escape of the attack car. John had drawn a picture of the murder in relation to the nest tree and compass directions. A great biologist, he was perhaps an even better crime witness.

Because of our watches at Serengeti and the nest's proximity to the armed gate at Tecanal's entrance, those three chicks successfully fledged. We also had two chicks fledge from a rotting palm tree in the forest. Somehow it had escaped the notice of the poachers, and as it was too far and remote for us to guard, we were glad that the chicks survived. We still had a few nests left to fledge in April, including *Campo Santo* 4. At first, all went well. The same parents returned to the same field, the same tree, and the same branch. As in previous years one youngster came into the world. This time the chick was a calm one and the nest opening was wide enough to easily remove the living, breathing contents of its inner recesses. I still sucked wind though whenever we climbed, repeatedly shouting up the tree, "Fold the wings in, fold them tight!" I didn't think I, let alone the chick, could live through another wing broken for the sake of science and conservation. Especially after last year, this nest simply had to survive. More than anything, we needed this chick to fledge so we could place a radio transmitter on it. All was calm until one day, Africanized bees settled right above the *loro* nest in the same branch.

On came the bee suits as we carefully studied how to now climb the tree. No ropes could brush the branch, Daniel's body couldn't send vibrations along the branch, and all must be quiet below. If the bees erupted, we'd survive, but the chick wouldn't. Our hope hinged on this one event. Despite the bees, we climbed the nest and studied the chick for the first few climbs. Then one morning we got an early call from the guard/biologist on duty—she hadn't seen the parent birds come in to feed the chick. Up drove Daniel, myself, and Mauricio in a huff to analyze what happened. As we approached the protective overhang of the tree, we found evidence of the desperation of poverty. Dead bees littered the ground, a man's red kerchief was in the dirt, and grass was burned away. Poachers had apparently come in the night to take the chick and burn the bees out. By the looks of things, chaos had reigned, for the bees were still angrily buzzing above and a few chased us away. It was no wonder that the parents didn't come to the nest—the bees were ferocious. We'd have to wait to climb the tree in the night to see if the chick was still alive or present.

That evening we all met at the biologist's house to plan our approach. The climb was to begin at about 8 p.m., a good 15 hours after the work day had begun, but a life was at stake. Whenever more than four of us gathered it was usually mayhem, with jokes, pranks, and spontaneous singing. Instead, we drove in silence. Our headlights shone on the ground near the tree, and silence was the order of the night. The afternoon observer reported that no parents had been seen. The appointed ground rappelers donned bee suits, and the rest of us put on long sleeve shirts and had our bee masks ready to slap on if needed. Sending the line up in the dark, silently and without undue vibrations, was a long and difficult task. Finally, however, the ropes went up, as did Daniel. Flashlights followed his ascent. Those holding the lights were careful not to shine them on the bee colony and had been instructed to turn off the lights if the bees descended. Bee experts had told us that in the night they followed lights, and we had learned the hard way that they could attack 24 hours a day, even on the darkest nights.

Daniel struggled at the nest entrance, doing his best not to put his face and hands into the swarming bees. Breathlessly we waited below, watching Daniel manipulate a flashlight into the cavity. Even in daylight hours, deep cavities can be difficult to inspect. After what seemed a millennium, Daniel signaled a thumbs-up (thumbs-down meant to get him the hell down quickly), and up we sent the chick bag. And glory to the anti-poaching god, Daniel placed a green, shiny chick into the sack, and lowered her to the ground below. There we inspected her as best as possible. A few bee stings, a little weight loss, but she was otherwise simply stunned by the evening's maneuvers. Quickly and with silent prayers the chick went back up the nest, and Daniel came back down amid much quiet back slapping and thumbs-up signals. Despite a few more poaching scares and difficulty placing the radio collar, all came to fruition and the little girl took off on her maiden flight, much to the joy of our thankful group. She stayed near the tree for most of that rainy season, her parents never leading her far away. The tree was an anchor for her and had been perhaps for generations of her family.

Though we were successful in placing the radio collar and tracking her for several months later, I was unconvinced about the need for anchoring this permanent device around the neck of a parrot. Some chicks did well with them in the nests, and others did not. Some would hook their beak on them, some would flip out unable to adjust, and some seemed to be having trouble getting clear of the ground on their fledgling flight. I assisted in putting on the radio collars because I was the project veterinarian, but the potential harm didn't seem to outweigh the knowledge we gained. In some projects, radio collars can give valuable information as to the movements of parrots, their foraging behavior, family structures, and survivability. What did all this information matter in terms of welfare for the bird, if poaching was nearly 100% in nests that we did not guard? Radio collars, though sexy in scientific studies, would not stop the poaching or the population decline, which we were direct witnesses to.

So far all three of our fledged nests had been on the Tecanal *finca*, but we were having worse luck in Arveja. Miguel of Arveja had made good on his past hints that he might have to convert his cattle *finca* to sugar cane one day. The repeated expense of the Guerilla Tax and his inability to manage the *finca* when he could no longer risk spending the night had pushed him to a decision. I couldn't believe he would ever do it because he loved the *finca* too much and he knew what *caña* would do to his beautiful fields, to our precious nests, and to his beloved people. *Caña* made a desert of the land in typical monoculture fashion, as it had to other *fincas*. First the *caña* cooperation would bargain with the *finca* owner to lease certain fields. Once the arrangements were agreed on, the land owner stopped managing the fields and left them in the hands of an economic beast that spoke only the language of profit. Then came the surveyors, the engineers in their city trucks, and finally the mechanized earth destroyers that ripped trees and life from the land. Once a field was flattened and removed of all visible life, except around the fence lines or *toma*-- irrigation channel-- wanderings, the *caña* was planted. Up it quickly grew, amazing in its ability to produce a commodity that would be shipped abroad, while the natives of the land were displaced, struggling to find other work or trees that could support their way of life.

The ultimate insult of the *caña* is the harvesting techniques. To cure the *caña*, the fields were set ablaze, and whatever animal had relented and sought protection within this artificial habitat, was burned to death if unable to escape. Once darkened and lifeless, in came the temporary *caña* workers, almost as darkened and lifeless as what they cut, bundled, and loaded into the waiting *caña* trucks. For several months of each year we saw these trucks head towards Escuintla carrying death, now the dominant product of the land.

Miguel had told us his decision to allow the ravaging of Arveja in the middle of my last year's breeding season. I stood there disbelieving as he introduced our work group to his two brothers, who now owned part of Arveja. Instead of it being a large family *finca* whose profits were shared amongst the sisters and brothers, it became a divided parcel, where every person decided for themselves. We had seen new fences going up around the *finca*, but had only vaguely registered concern because we were too busy protecting the nests. Miguel knew how this impacted me and could only smile and say, "We have to eat, you know." I looked from my native biologists that were as slender as they come to Miguel and his family with their bellies slung over the belts. My thoughts were harsh and included not only Miguel but also myself. I was rounder myself those days, and had applied for work in the USA that offered an annual income that could support over thirty families in Guatemala.

Miguel approved the leveling of several fields, including Traconnes and Silencio, each of which had five nest trees. Where would the parrots go from what had been their territories for more years than I'd lived? The final blow was that the *caña* company would begin the destruction mid-1995 during the breeding season. Miguel said we could tag trees that would be spared this breeding season, but there were no guarantees for the next year. We would spray paint in big orange or red letters "NO" on the trees that the tractors wouldn't devour. It was a mournful run to Escuintla to pick up the paints and return down the Puertos road that afternoon. We painted as many trees as possible, those currently with nests and those that had nests earlier in the season or in the study. The last tree we marked was *La Arca en Silencio*-- The Ark in Silence-- not yet poached at the time, and alive with *loros*, bees, iguanas, and bromeliads, its diversity a bastion of hope. The sun pulled away and left us standing under *La Arca*, wondering how in the world any of us would survive the darkness that had descended on our world.

Over the weekend we bitched and moaned, and sure enough on Monday afternoon when we returned, the initial attack force was already in place. We followed their gutted tracks to the back of the *finca* and there the heavy machinery belched as it dug into the roots of living communities. There was no way that we could have marked every tree because Miguel knew roughly how many nests were on his land. So we watched the slaughter, hating the process and, after the course of the day, ourselves as well. Each day we watched the tractors come closer and closer to the front of the *finca*, until they finally reached Traconnes. Here there was still an active nest, *El Principe*-- The Prince, but that was about all there was in the entire field because it was all naked earth, its dead inhabitants stacked like so much worthless kindling into great piles for burning. Climbing the tree was unsettling with the roar of the killing equipment and the heat that reflected off the stripped earth. The chicks were still there, as were the bats that shared the nest cavity, but no parents could be seen. I elected to stay and observe the nest, while the others took off to observe their nests. What once had been a car full of biologists to handle all the nests in Arveja had been whittled down to just a few of us. To hide, I picked a fence line that also served as a dump for the ancients that had been felled. I picked a spot to wedge myself into, willing to meld with the dying branches and their diminishing vigor. Like a child, I curled into a ball and wept.

CONSERVATION IN TIME OF WAR

The parents did return that evening to feed their chick, but ultimately they couldn't overcome their aversion to all the people and machinery around their tree. They circled the tree, called frantically, and even landed a few times in the *Castaña's* upper reaches, but they couldn't stay long. Everything was gone, there was nothing. Finally, they left in silence, echoing my despair. Perhaps the parents would come back in the night when work stopped so that they could feed their hungry chick. I wondered if the youth would weaken from lack of feedings or if the parents would abandon it. The next week when we climbed the tree, the chick was gone. If poachers got it, which was likely, it might have been the best thing for the chick. At least the chick wouldn't starve, or at least we hoped not. By this time, I thought that, relatively, poachers weren't as evil as other manifestations of humankind's disenfranchisement from Earth.

The carnage we witnessed that breeding season was extensive. Of the twelve nest trees in Arveja, seven were in the path of the *caña* conglomerates. All were marked except for the low Oscar nest, which was rotting to the ground and didn't offer much of a refuge for any creature, let alone for the hunted parrot. The rest we assumed would make it to the end of the season. But not all would escape that first year, even when our word "No" cried out from the trees. *El Gitaron*-- the large wasp-- was burned badly at the base during the fires that were set to clear the fields of any evidence of life, and we knew that was just the beginning. Those trees that were left standing were right in the middle of the proposed *caña*, and when these killing fields were sent aflame, there was no guarantee how long they could survive.

That is of course, if the trees even survived until the *caña* was harvested, for *La Arca* fell that very month. The chicks had long been poached, but it was still a great loss, for it meant that our pitiful demands to spare the trees were easily ignored. We don't know why this tree was targeted while others were allowed to stay, but the story we heard from the inhabitants on Arveja was that the bees had been giving the workers hell while they cleared the field. After the constant bombardments from the six bee colonies in the tree, toppling it would easily stop the nuisance. *La Arca* didn't die without having the last word because when it toppled the angry bees chased the tractor drivers who fled on foot to escape the wrath of thousands of bees and over a hundred years of tree life.

This ongoing drama occurred throughout the second half of the breeding season, and it was almost a relief to have no more active nests at Arveja because the desolation was just too much to bear. The few remaining nests at Esperanza and Tecanal offered us hope and dispelled our despair to tolerable limits. *Caña* had already come to Esperanza many years before, so I assumed that it would be contained to its present limits, but sneaking through the back side of Esperanza from its fence borders with Arveja came the ceaseless march of death.

Daniel and I discovered new threats to Esperanza, which was ironic since we were the ones who first discovered *El Paraiso*-- The Paradise. My station that night was to observe *La Chinga Ceiba*, while Daniel walked toward Arveja to observe the nest *El Macho*. I quickly made my own nest in the center of the field, shielding my presence with my ever-present camouflage tarps and mesh. Although I was sweating, the heat felt good and I was happy that I was in for an evening's view of parrot wonder. As I cracked my field notebook to begin recording observations, Daniel ran towards me. "Shit," I whispered. Whatever was happening was bad. I was out of my blind and ready to run when Daniel yelled breathlessly, *"Kim, Kim, ellos estan destruyendo El Macho. Venga ahorita!"*-- "Kim, they are destroying El Macho! Hurry-come now!" Throwing my gear into my backpack I ran with him. Between gasps I asked, "Who's trying to destroy El Macho?" *"Los tractores, Kim, los tractores de caña*-- "the tractors, the sugar cane tractors. " Fences had been ripped away and a cleared road led to the back side of the *finca*. "Fuck, fuck, fuck," was all I could say, a word Daniel didn't like, but which he knew now summed up the situation.

I heard the tractor and the scrape of metal against live wood and I sprinted, heavy pack and all. Breaking through the last fence row, I felt like a hand had grabbed my heart and was trying to make me hurt as much as possible when I saw a bulldozer retreating and then advancing upon the now-exposed roots of *El Macho*, pushing the living elder into an early grave. I ran panting and stood between the tractor and the tree. This was going to stop now! Once we had the tractor driver's attention, Daniel ran to speak to the driver. He wasn't getting anywhere, so I joined the *fracas*-- dispute- and said he couldn't remove this tree that contained a *loro* nest and a laughing falcon nest. Besides, we were the protectors of this sanctuary and no trees could be harvested. It was all bluff and bravado, but somehow we convinced him to retreat.

He left and we examined *El Macho*. He was badly damaged, and probably would not survive the next year. But if we had our way, he would live long enough for the current nestlings to fledge. We left the tree, our hopes for a normal watch abandoned. We ran in different directions in hopes of finding the manager's truck so we could talk to whoever was in charge. We didn't have to go far because the tractor driver had alerted his *jefe*, who was speeding towards us in his official, impersonal, white vehicle. I tried to sound sane when the conversation began, but that was hard to do given the rush and urgency of what had almost happened. My vague threats about alerting newspapers and the international conservation community might have slipped out amongst the other, more politically correct and typical standoff phrases I employed. He engaged me according to the usual rules of a passionate but controlled confrontation, and eventually he agreed to halt all tree removal until he talked to his *jefes* and the owner of the *finca*. In the meantime I told him that we would mark all trees to be saved with a "No." The deal struck, we turned down his offer for a ride back to *El Gavilan* because I couldn't even touch the perpetrator's truck.

We rushed to Escuintla to buy paint and return before dark to mark the trees. That evening I made an emergency call to Sebastián for help in contacting the *Don* of Esperanza. Word came back through Sebastián and the *caña* engineers that only roost trees would be spared. All others would be felled unless they currently contained nests, and once the chicks fledged, they too would meet the fate of millions of others.

Into these trees we had watched our few fledged young be led by their parents, first, for protection, then for socialization, then for easy sources of food, and finally to join the juvenile flocks that would one day rule the roost. Training our appreciative eyes on the heavens we beheld birds with life spans similar to ours, and as we became more fluent in bird behavior, we realized that these birds had a society and a language with an incredible complexity and originality. How a fragile egg could grow into a miraculous being, surviving snakes, iguanas, bees, falcons, eagles, and humans, and then complete the species' ancient cycle of birth, death, and then rebirth into future generations, was beyond our meager understanding. It was impossible not to admire these birds, and when they gathered in numbers known in prehistoric times, we worshipped them and the ground they flew over.

Technically we cheated by marking *La Chinga* as a roost tree. It was close to the roost trees, and we thought no would notice. So they left *La Chinga* and the other trees we marked, but they took everything else. The small food trees in the fence rows where *loros* had played and foraged before coming in for the night, the numerous palm trees whose fronds *loros* had slipped and slid over with nuts nearly the size of their heads in their beaks, the corrals, the grass, the cattle, the horses, almost all was taken. Nothing was left but dirt and resting machinery beneath the remaining trees, which were the lone inhabitants of a now stark landscape. Of the eight active nests in Esperanza, seven would be destroyed to plant *caña*, and none produced chicks to fledging.

In late April we were down to one last nest in Tecanal, *La Caja*-- The Box. *La Caja* was so named because a pair of *loros* had elected to build their nest in one of the artificial nest boxes along the Muro road. In this nest, three eggs were laid, three chicks were hatched, and three chicks made it to fledging age. We were so desperate for data and for these last three birds to make it that we had placed a night-time guard at the site for the last month. Being close to the center of the *finca* we felt that with *El Gavilan* parked near the tree and the guards assigned in pairs that no harm would come. We were wrong. A knock late one night at my door was by a flustered Isaac, the oldest child of Alejandra who had been raised by his grandparents. He had worked with us this season

157

and ended up taking a lot of the night watches with Ian, both of whom needed the double pay we offered for the extreme hours.

"*Que paso?*" was about all I could muster, hoping that no one had been injured in the call of duty. "*Kim, disculpe, pero la guerilla esta cerca a La Caja*," "Kim, excuse me, but the guerillas are close to *La Caja*." The guerillas had come across Isaac and Ian and told them to get lost, this was their turf. At an emergency meeting with the others we decided to discontinue guarding the nest as long as the guerillas were running maneuvers in the area. Daniel left my house that night in a funk because there was no way he was going to let the guerillas poach the chicks. Unbeknownst to us, Daniel guarded the nest anyway, but from a distance. Hiding behind a nearby live fence line he kept an eye on the guerillas, who left about 3 a.m. What he'd have done if he'd seen the night-time revolutionaries climb our tree I don't know.

Unwilling to let the chicks go so easily, we placed guards again at the nest the following night. To support the guards, we took turns throughout the night driving down the Muro Road in another car, blowing the horn and flashing the lights. The guerillas were given fair warning to stay away, and we never saw them again. The drama, however, continued when the mother didn't show up one day when the chicks were about a month old. Their weights plummeted until the father figured out how to forage enough for three chicks. Within the week the chicks were thriving once again, but now another *loro* was with the father. We couldn't be sure if it was the lost mother, because the only way we had to identify the adults was by the shape and size of their nape, and this bird's nape couldn't be distinguished from the mother's. But if she was the original female, she no longer entered the nest to feed the chicks. So we were suspicious, like with the family of conures where an adult bird showed up after the mother died, that adult parrots had relationships outside of their primary pair bond.

Whoever this mystery female was she turned against the chicks. As soon as the oldest one was at the stage to peek out of the cavity, she would swoop to the entrance and lunge at the chick. This aggression cowered the chick but didn't significantly delay its fledgling, so strong were its urges it burst forth from the nest to dare the world to do its worse to him, which it did. The chick on his first flight made it to a tree near the Muro Road, where the father fed it. Unfortunately, the female was with him and attacked the chick that tumbled to a lower perch and then took off to another tree. The pair followed, and the biologist reported a great deal of squawking. After things quieted down, Daniel and I took off for Escuintla for a rare dinner out, but we had to return to do a night guard together. When we relieved the previous guard, he said they had found the chick on the ground and Joaquin had placed the chick up as high as possible into a tree. Since it was dark, we could do nothing but hope that the chick would survive the night, the female, and the unseasonably fierce thunderstorm that came through the area that evening.

The next morning, long before sunrise, Ian knocked on the windows of *El Gavilan* with the radio telemetry equipment. He was anxious to see if the chick, who had a radio collar, had survived the night. It took us a while to locate the chick, or at least what was left of her. Her broken right wing was the least of the damage; her entire skull had been pitted and consumed, along with one of her eyes. Some night predator had discovered the low perching bird or had come across it on the ground. This was nature, but it seemed so cruel that the chick had come so close to freedom, only to be driven to death by one of its own kind. After this, we saw the heads of the two remaining chicks only a few times. Perhaps they had sensed the fate of their older sister and there was no way they were budging. They stayed so long that the father eventually abandoned them. In our data books, we counted them for dead, and then took them into captivity.

We toyed with reintroducing them into the wild, but while we caged them in training facilities awaiting their conversion to solid wild foods, several predators tried to get at them, including a spectacled owl and a forest falcon. Knowing that without their parents they would stand little to no chance in the wild, we moved them to RESCAVES where they might live a life that was long and safe, even if it did pale in comparison to the richness of freedom. Their conversion to captivity depressed us all, especially our volunteer Yvonne who had tried so hard to wean the birds and prepare them for release. We had tried, the parents had tried, and the chicks certainly had tried, but it wasn't enough for this nest. All our efforts at protection had resulted in three nests fledging of the 12 in Tecanal, the only three of all 31 nests in the three *fincas*.

With the breeding season over, our quarterly roost count at Esperanza was due. Usually the end of the season was a celebration, as were the roost counts, but gone was the reason to rejoice, laugh, and play because what fun is an artificial desert? We took up an approximation of our old positions and hid as best we could, but the routine was broken. Not only was our scientific methodology disrupted, but so was that which was wild and had existed for innumerable generations. The sun slipped away with our hopes. This roost site was forever altered. Only half of the usual number of birds flew in, and when they did they were silent mourners. Gone were the rowdy interchanges of parrot society and the chaotic element of infinite possibility. Those braving the disturbed area came in without a protest and slinked into the trees, after which we crept away, as beaten as they.

This was my last field excursion of the season. I had accepted the position at the North Carolina State University School of Veterinary medicine as a clinical instructor in the Nondomestic Avian Clinic. I would be on duty while my friend Andrew was on sabbatical. By May, I had made all the arrangements and had shipped most of my belongings to North Carolina. The hardest part was saying goodbye to Moses. He couldn't legally come with me, nor should he. His home was in Guatemala, even though he'd spend the rest of his life in a cage at the aviaries. But I was leaving behind my love for him and many others. As painful as it was to leave, it would have been worse to stay. I simply couldn't take any more. I was plain worn out from attempting to control the fate of so many creatures, humans included. I had nothing left to give, especially when my efforts weren't working anyway. It was time to quit playing the naïve role of some kind of savior and go home.

Chapter 13
BACK IN THE USA
Raleigh, North Carolina, 1995-1997

1996

Peace Accords brokered by the UN are signed in 1996 between the Guatemalan National Revolutionary Unity (the guerillas) and the government. This ended the 36-year civil war, one of the longest and bloodiest in Latin America. Banners at the celebration read, "Let us build peace; Guatemala deserves it" and "Peace is your chance to spread happiness."

Mother Teresa is granted honorary USA citizenship.

Osama bin Laden writes "The Declaration of Jihad on the Americans Occupying the Country of the Two Sacred Places," a call for the removal of American military forces from Saudi Arabia.

Exodor and I flew into New Bern where my mother lived at midnight, after a problem at the Miami airport. It wasn't that Exodor didn't have all his proper papers, or that the veterinarian inspector didn't know he was coming. It was just that sometime during the years in Guatemala I had misplaced Exodor's leg band, which he had never worn, but which I kept. It had completely slipped my mind when returning. The U.S. inspector wasn't going to let Exodor into the country without being quarantined because he couldn't be sure it was the same bird that had left the country three years earlier. I told him that before I would let Exodor be quarantined, he'd have to put me back on a plane to Guatemala. No bird of mine was going to leave my sight (after I'd just left Moses and others behind). The poor guy had no chance because I'd become an expert in bluff and bravado, although from his accent I could tell he originated from a country of standoffs. We attracted quite a crowd with our shouting and refusals, but finally he acquiesced saying, "Since I talked with your mother to arrange this inspection, I guess you and the bird must be okay. Go on through."

Through we went, happy to be safe and sound at last. Mom met us at the airport with a friend's truck for all my luggage. Most of my belongings had already been shipped to my mother's. Using New Bern as a base, I was able to find a house for Daniel and me in Raleigh. Mom helped me move in, tromping up and down the stairs in her delicate footwear of golden sparkly sandals. Not the most sensible choice for moving, but regardless, she was a big help. That first night in the small, two-bedroom duplex in Raleigh, Mom and I set out our sleeping bags and lawn chairs, ready for an evening of cards, drinking, food, and TV.

Daniel called after I had two beers. I had faxed Fabiana in the city the new address and phone number, which she then relayed to him over the radio phone to Tecanal. It was strange to speak to him over a phone. Or maybe it was the numbing of two beers. I hadn't drunk much in Guatemala after Tragedy Struck (Chapter 10), and so I was reeling. Perhaps I felt guilty for drinking because Daniel was dead set against alcohol, having given it up at age 12 after passing out in a ditch and waking up to a dog chewing his leg. I promised him those would be my last beers. I didn't need any conflict with him, and I wanted to find a way to be present to my feelings, and quit running away from pain.

By the time Daniel flew up two months later, the house was nearly complete, and I had been working at the exotic bird clinic at North Carolina State University for over a month. Our first week together didn't go as smoothly as hoped, and it was all downhill from there. He wasn't a happy man, and in his confusion at being dislocated he grew distant. A phone call from an ex-boyfriend put him over the edge. We had a quiet, but intense fight, not unlike many others we'd had before. The following morning, he apologized, admitting that his jealousy was wrong, but he couldn't control it. He said he was going away for several days to work in the tobacco fields. I begged him not to go because he didn't need to leave our home to work. We had plenty of cash for the moment. But off he went, me never being able to stop him from doing anything.

I couldn't tell if he really had a job or just needed distance after our fight. Whatever his motivation, he didn't return as promised and I began to worry. Hispanic field workers labored in uncontrolled conditions and anything could have happened to him. Finally, I called his nephew Lucas in Oregon to see if he had heard from him, thinking perhaps Daniel had gone to visit them before he settled into work here. They hadn't heard a word, and Lucas wished me luck with his *tio loco*--crazy uncle. Next, I called his sister Fabiana in Guatemala to tell her I'd lost him. "Not to worry," she said, "Daniel is here in Guatemala. He came in two nights ago in the middle of the night with no luggage. He said hardly a word but said you were impossible to live with and were interested in other men." He'd left me, really left me, just like I always knew he would, and after only three weeks in the USA.

I kept going to work every day but like a zombie. I simply didn't understand how people could calmly talk of television shows or retirement and spend thousands of dollars on their pets while children and birds were dying and trees were being ripped out of the earth so we could have cheap candy bars. Having lost hope, then Guatemala, and now Daniel, I shut down to the world and escaped to the comfort of my couch.

I kept in touch with *finca* and project business because I was still managing the ongoing work there. Fabiana wrote that she was having words with Daniel. After two months, he still hadn't spoken to me when Hilda and Camila called. The only way that they could have called was for Daniel to make the call from one of the *finca* telephones, or perhaps Chema, but it meant that Daniel was communicating with me through his children. I told them I was coaching a girls' soccer team in Raleigh and that I missed them and their papa immensely. With this shred of hope and slight connection to Daniel I was ecstatic. Perhaps I'd see him again, at least to say goodbye.

The next few weeks passed tolerably enough when one night Hilda called and asked if I wanted to speak with Daniel, the moment I'd been waiting for. I wanted him to come back to the U.S., and I was willing to say anything to make that happen. Daniel spoke as if with a great weight on his chest, telling me how hard the last months had been in Guatemala. He'd been robbed of all his belongings on a bus trip to visit Mateo, our guitar player, and then he told me what made him reevaluate his entire life. Little Esteban had died. He had been a sickly child, and Daniel and I had taken the little boy and his mother Miranda, Daniel's niece and occasional goalie for our women's team, to the hospital and visited them when he had emergency treatment to fight intestinal infections. This last time he didn't make it. "Kim, I had really gotten close to him since I've been back and he was like one of my own. I thought I might help raise him, as I helped raise Miranda. His death has made me think about what is important in life." My breathing stopped, and I waited to hear his declaration of love. He said, "Do you need some help coaching *futbol?* I would like to help you do this." Not much of a love call, but it would do.

We made plans to buy another plane ticket and for me to send money to help Alejandra and the kids. They were being forced to move from the *finca* because neither Alejandra nor Daniel worked there anymore. I was fearful that a move to Taxisco would doom them to the violence and corruption of the cities and that there would be no way to keep Camila and Hilda safe. On the other hand, to get away from the *finca* might be best to expand their horizons. This would also give them a chance for education beyond the sixth grade, which was the highest level that Tecanal offered.

Once again, I went to the Raleigh airport to greet Daniel and his sullen face. He was sad, withdrawn, and embarrassed, as well as apologetic as he gave me bad news. RESCAVES had been torn down, and the last roost count had yielded only twenty-six birds. Even worse was that *caña* had come to Tecanal, taking out the *Campo Santo* trees and hundreds more. With a kicked gut feeling, I foresaw that my beautiful paradise would soon be dead. How would the birds ever survive if there was no stopping the madness?

Snow and ice came to Raleigh that winter, and we frolicked in its newness and novelty. Family came at Christmas, and my brother and Daniel did the male bonding thing while barbecuing our traditional New Year's Eve steaks. We took road trips up to my sister Linda's mountain home in Virginia, enjoying the Burger King stops and piled up snow. Through the spring Daniel and I visited my mother regularly in New Bern, surprising her with an Easter Egg hunt. In addition, we were busy with the soccer team, Daniel's Latin flare and passion for soccer, a bonus for the girls.

1997

The Hoover Institution releases an optimistic report that global warming will probably reduce mortality in the USA and provide Americans with valuable benefits.

When summer came, New Bern was hit by two hurricanes. After the first, we cleaned up at Mom's, and we drove through the next one to get to her house before the eye passed over. Except Hurricane Fran veered and went not to New Bern, but to Raleigh. We returned to Raleigh where five trees were on our house, and one nearly in the kitchen. Daniel had to machete a path to the front door, where we entered our little nest amid pine trees for a glorious three weeks of no electricity or phone. It was like being back in Guatemala, as well as like camping out. In our forest-like seclusion we hid from the world, enjoying each other and not much else.

Most of that year Daniel controlled his jealousy, but before his fortieth birthday in the spring his rage earned over a lifetime erupted into our otherwise uneventful life. I don't remember what set him off that time, but as usual his accusations and cool withdrawal finally made me mad, and when that happened he always walked away. And this time he kept going and didn't come back. Shouting to his retreating form that he disgraced Mother Mary and called her a whore every time he said the same of me, I bid him good riddance. He didn't come back that night, or the next, or the following week. I knew he didn't return to Guatemala because he didn't have the money, so I'd just wait him out. As the week progressed I became more fearful that he really would never contact me. He gave up so easily.

Coming back from a movie, which I cried through, not so much for their story but for mine, I saw a car in front of my house. They were friends of Daniel's that he'd worked with in Raleigh. Hispanic workers in Raleigh were a close-knit group for support in this distant, often unfriendly land. I hoped that they had news of Daniel, but why wasn't he with them? They had gotten a phone call from Javier in Durham that Daniel had been hurt in an accident. Javier, originally from Salvador and a friend of ours who had helped Daniel get work, hadn't said if Daniel was alive or dead, just that I should come. I thanked them for their kindness and jumped in my car for the half-hour drive to Javier's house in Durham.

In this time I did not know if I was coming to claim a body. Daniel's pride and jealousy had caused all this, and maybe had kept us from saying goodbye to each other. I would never forgive him or the world that had caused such tragedy. I knocked on the door, and silently Javier pushed a barely walking Daniel out to talk to me. I felt relief, but not overwhelmingly so. I had no idea what to do with this man. Helping him into my car, we talked, me asking the questions and Daniel wincing with every move and thought. He had a two-story fall from a construction site and had a concussion and messed up his knee again. His co-workers, and not the American construction boss, had taken him to a "doctor" that had placed him in a bed and given him some kind of medicine. He remained unconscious for three days, and when he woke Jose took him into his home for the last week. Daniel had nearly died and he still hadn't called me, despite our mutual need for each other.

What else could I do but take him to our home and care for him until he was better. There was no way I was going to leave him by himself when his boss wouldn't even pay for his emergency hospital care. Sure, they suspected that he working without proper documents and that he didn't have insurance, but why spend the money when there were hundreds willing to work for $6 an hour with no benefits. It was cheap labor compared to what they had to pay

American citizens, and the undocumented Hispanic community was a slave class because they couldn't complain. Of course, this is a much more complicated issue, but there is incredible injustice when men have to leave their families behind so they can work under harsh conditions so their family can move a little beyond the poverty and oppression of their homelands. How could it be wrong for Camila and Hilda to be protected from constant health threats and to finish school?

He stayed that night and several more. His body healed. The jealousy remained, this time an incident with one of the soccer dads. The usual standoff ensued and Daniel began packing his bags once again. I followed him around the house as he did so, incredulous at his childish attempts to run away. He finished rounding up his belongings and said, "I'll be back for them this afternoon after work when I can get someone with a car to come pick them up." I calmly replied, "If you go and leave your belongings behind, I will burn them. If you really mean to go, go now and make a clean break of it." This stopped him in his tracks and he met my eyes, which he never did when he was mad. "*Que?*" was all he said. "You heard me, your stuff will be *quemado* -- burned-- when you come back." With that I burst out laughing and so did he. It wasn't easy to come down from our impassioned state, but the laughter broke the spell and we retreated to the bed to smooth away the hurt.

After that, there were no more incidents for several months. I actually thought that we were going to make it, although sacrifices were needed to maintain equilibrium. There was really no way that we could associate with anyone outside of my family, for Daniel's jealousy was too unpredictable. At the time it didn't seem to be a big deal because I didn't want to do anything but be with Daniel. Back in the USA for over a year and I still didn't get American society or my place in it. Daniel wasn't having an easy time of it either. Everywhere he looked he saw only the *haves* and thought of his family, history, and people, the *have nots*. Our only refuge against the senseless world was to cling to each other, and even though mutual mistrust haunted our relationship, it was more a reflection of how we felt about the world.

We were lying around in bed on a Sunday morning reading the paper when I came across an article about Mother Teresa. I had always been intrigued by her story because I didn't know how she maintained the stamina, love, or faith to work with the desolate. What fed her had broken me. I mentioned to Daniel how I wished to travel to India to meet her before she died, and Daniel looked at me, a look that always brightened my day when he came into a room. After a few moments I responded, "Okay, okay, I know that I don't need to go and spend all that money and Earth's resources to meet someone that in part exists within me." Again that look. "That wasn't what I was thinking. True, I did think it was a waste for you to go there, but for a different reason. I've met *Madre* Teresa."

Just when you thought you had someone figured out. This man, poverty born and largely uneducated, had once again proven his uniqueness. He had surprised me recently when he, my brother, my mother, and I were sitting around my mother's kitchen table playing cards. Daniel had never played cards growing up, and we had all played before we could read. His antics to keep up with us kept him and us rolling on the floor because he couldn't keep track not only of suits but the point of the game. What was the point, really? He nicknamed the suits and when we said clubs, not spades, he said, "Oh, club booboos," a joke about his constant mistakes.

That night he separated his cards into different piles, face down on the table. I didn't know what he was doing because he made five piles, which in no way corresponded to the four suits, or to anything else for that matter. Soon Daniel played his last card, while we all held cards. "Daniel, *que paso*, how are you already out of cards?" We looked under the table for the cards Daniel must have dropped. We thought he'd screwed up again until we realized that one of us had two cards left, another one card, and another three. One of us had misdealt.. We laughed that Daniel was no more clueless than we were. Red-faced, I wondered at the irony that it took a card game to show how complicit I still was with racism and classicism, even with those I loved.

Having learned to be skeptical of Guatemalan stories, I asked, "Are you making it up that you met *Madre* Teresa? When was this?" "When I was twenty years old I was friends with the *padre* at the church in Escuintla. One day he asked me if I wanted to meet *Madre* Teresa. I said yes, and he told me to be at the *Iglesia* the next day. When I arrived, the police escorts were already there, but I was allowed through the barriers. Inside the church I saw her talking with children. Then she talked to me for about five minutes. When she left she gave me a big hug. I was happy to have met the *Santa*."

"Incredible, Daniel! There is still so much I don't know about you." Once again came that look, which invited me into his arms and my fingers stroked the scars on his chest and abdomen. All I saw was brown perfection and had forgotten about his promise to one day tell me the story of how he got the scars and the one across his nose. He said, "The time has come for me to tell you of these scars."

"I was young, about the same age when I meet *Madre* Teresa and lost my thumb. Going out to cut *leña*-- wood-- one day I walked across the grass air strip, which was shorter than walking around. Someone saw me do this, and it was forbidden." "We walked across it all the time," I reminded him. "Those were different times and besides you're a *gringa*, you were allowed," he eyes moving farther from me. "Anyway, I was warned not to do it again, but later I did it anyway. That is when they came after me, the *vigilantes*-- guards-- of the ranch and some of their *amigos*. I could do nothing when they dragged me to a corral post, tied me up, and started beating me. Then one of them came after me with a knife, meaning to take out my eye. I jerked my face at the last minute and he cut my nose instead. My chest scars are from that same knife. They took me to the *Rio*, threw me into the water, and held me under the water no matter how hard I fought them. I was about to stop struggling when a friend scared them off. He picked me up and took me to my mother's house, where I lay in bed healing for weeks. I blew blood-soaked bubbles through the slice in my nose until it healed. "Was it just because you crossed the air strip?" "I don't know, but the *finca* had rules and I broke one too many."

Slowly I began to understand his anger, and his jealousy seemed the natural fruit of a man trying desperately to claim something as his own, to control some small aspect of his life, and to ensure self-respect and dignity that he knew existed within, but which hadn't been accorded to him. Just when our relationship knew peace that seemed to be replacing hopelessness and rage, his year's temporary visa was up. His mother had been ill and was recovering from surgery. His plan was to be gone for two weeks, after which he'd return easily enough on his ten-year permanent visa. I wished him a sweet goodbye at the airport, and returned to Raleigh to take my first theology class and write in this journal. It would be good to have the house alone, although all I did was wait patiently for him to return.

Delighted when the day arrived, I went to the airport, and as each succeeding passenger walked off the ramp my tension mounted when Daniel didn't appear. This had happened once before because of *migracion*-- immigration-- problems in Guatemala, so I was disappointed, but hopeful. I called the airlines and they said that he had boarded the plane leaving Guatemala, but had not boarded in Miami. I went home, went to our bedroom to check the answering machine, but there was no red flashing light. Confused and worried, I went to bed, hoping to hear from him in the night. Miami wasn't exactly the friendliest airport, but how much it could be my enemy I had no idea.

The phone rang at two a.m. and it was Daniel, although there was no life in his voice. "Kim, I'm in prison. I don't know where, but I begged a guard to let me call you. They are going to take me in front of a judge tomorrow. I don't know what's happening," he said, though reluctant to talk. Frantically asking questions I gathered that he was at some jail in Miami where the U.S. Immigration Service had taken him for having a false passport, the same passport that he'd used to travel to Mexico two times and to the U.S. three times. He wasn't allowed to talk any longer and then he was gone.

With only the clue that the name of his prison started with a "C" I made phone calls and was able to find him and talk to him and the arresting officers. I talked to them at length, and tried to present a professional demeanor, though I was in tears most of the time. They backed down from their aggressive stance that he was illegally entering the country when they realized they'd made several mistakes. Daniel hadn't understood his right to legal counsel and his passport was valid. He had done nothing against the law by flying back into the USA. The detention was unjust, if not also illegal. They let hundreds of people come through to stay for extended time in the U.S., but probably not if they are uneducated and easily intimidated, and sport a *campesino's* flare of poverty mixed with radical anger. He didn't stand a chance in Miami because they didn't want anyone coming in the country to work without documents, though millions did to the benefit of USA citizens. The protective nature of this country's borders is just another way of enslaving the masses to either come to this country as second-rate servants or stay in their countries of origin and live without dignity so that we have our cellular phones and perfect lawns.

The officers decided that they wouldn't take Daniel in front of the judge if Daniel would voluntarily return to Guatemala and if I wouldn't bring in a lawyer, which I threatened to do. He could return in less than a week under this plan. This was a great relief, but not trusting this system I called Daniel and filled him in the plan. He sounded a little better, especially after I said I'd talk to him in a few hours when the next shift of *migración* came on. I was fretfully awake until the time Daniel would be taken from jail to the arraignment area, and I called the officer handling the affairs. He concurred with the plan that had been discussed with the officers he'd replaced. I was allowed to talk to Daniel, but only after a barrage of questions and lectures that were dehumanizing to me as well as to those who thought the solution to the world's problems was law enforcement, and nothing else.

Daniel promised to call me as soon as he got back to Guatemala, which he did with no problem, except for one. The immigration service lied. They cancelled Daniel's ten-year visa, and there would be no returning to the U.S. with a big, fat, red "Cancelled" stamped over a page of his passport. I went to an immigration lawyer. She said our best hope, and probably only hope, was to get him back in on a fiancée visa, which would take six months and a lot of money. In the meantime, we could try to get another visa, leaving it up to us whether we'd lie about this incident. Taking her advice, I made plans to return to Guatemala to help him start the fiancée visa paperwork. I was in battle mode, and once together I was sure that we could face whatever the world threw at us.

Stepping through the customs doors and into Daniel's arms I had returned home. The past year-and-half melted into oblivion. The plan was to stay in the city overnight and go to *migracion* at dawn. We had to talk about how our story would go and what we would do if we weren't successful, but first we had to rent a car. Our choice was a deep blue VW bug. Although not as fierce and strong as *El Gavilan*, it was now our chariot. We named it *La Cuca*,-- short for cockroach. We drove to Tony's, our favorite hotel in *Guate*.

We talked until morning when it was time to get in line with the other pawns in the game of kings and countries at the USAconsulate. We were nervous, still debating whether we should lie that this was Daniel's first attempt to get a visa since he now had a new blank passport. We opted not to lie, perhaps not the best choice. They confiscated his old passport and said they would talk to Miami or wait for the information to arrive before they could issue him a visa. It would take months for the paperwork to come through for a fiancée visa, and we were in for the long haul.

There was nothing left to do but to drive to Tecanal. Winding through the volcanoes, we dropped down to the ever enlarging sea of *caña*, and I felt like I could breathe for the first time in over a year. The smell was of trees burning and the burnt offal of *caña* fields was like an elixir clearing the mind. Escuintla had some new stores and a new modern movie theater had opened. Bravo, Las Rosas, and Micaela Linda hadn't changed a bit, and we saw and honked at a few soccer players walking along the road. Driving up over the bridge of Micaela Linda, Tecanal spread out before me. Where there had been fields and trees to the left going up the Reforma road there was now a sprawl of *caña*, but to the right everything looked intact and *loro* welcoming.

Instead of pulling into my old house now occupied by the manager of the zoo, we went to *El Porton* to talk to Sargento, who asked if I'd gained weight. I had, but as no one in the politically correct U.S. would comment on such a thing, I knew now for sure I was back in a culture that resonated more with me than did my own. Onward we went to Daniel's mother's house where he'd been staying and where I would as well. I saw strangers living in Daniel's old house, and I felt the pain of Hilda and Camila's absence. But taking their place was a swarm of younger cousins who ran to the La Cuca to jump in my arms, and onto the seats of the new toy. It was the same scene that occurred with Daniel's own children years before, and the cycle continued.

Daniel's mother Micaelana's was our base camp, and indeed it was like camping out. We slept on the common room floor, the only privacy a drawn curtain that separated us from Micaelana and the closed shutters that kept out roving eyes in the night. Micaelana, however, rose before dawn and shortly afterwards the children peeped into the room giggling until we woke. I stumbled to the outdoor toilet, showered, and brushed my teeth with scattering chickens and children, never alone for a moment. Every move I made was watched by the children, and when I sat still they crowded and fought to be by my side or in my lap. I thought I'd be bored or uncomfortable with Daniel gone for the morning, but I was back in paradise with the heat, close living, and simple lifestyle.

Daniel went with Ian to track down an official set of his annulment papers since he'd lost the others. We had to have a copy for the fiancée visa to work. Officials expected bribes and it had taken some courting to wring out documents from these small-town bureaucrats. To make matters worse, the mayor of Taxisco had fled with the town's funds, and he'd helped Daniel before. So Daniel had to begin anew, which took time and money. He also had to drive to another town to process paperwork there, because Alejandra was born in another Department. There he and Ian survived a gun battle in the main plaza, and the government officials were in no mood to talk to Daniel. He returned in the early afternoon to Tecanal, the task before us increasingly difficult.

Right before lunch, Hilda arrived on a bus from Taxisco. She bounded up, athletic and self-assured. Gone was the long black braid and gone was the child. But she was still Hilda, and soon we were joking and teasing as before. Lunch was a celebratory affair, as were all our meals at Micaelana's that week. Daniel and I had bought a carful of food for the family, and that was our first meal. We took a car load of children to Senieda's for cold drinks, where I was greeted by the blind grandmother that I knew before. Laying in the *hamaca* -- hammock-- with discharge exuding from her closed eyelids, she held out her hand for me to grasp. As soon as she felt my hand she said, "*Ella esta gordita,*"-- 'She is chubby.' Just from a handhold she had discovered the outward expression of my past year's depression. I had forgotten that there was no hiding in this land.

After lunch we went to the cemetery in Bravo to pay respects to little Esteban. His grandmother, Lucas's mother, Constanza, hadn't been to his grave site for a while and knew it needed cleaning up. Daniel hadn't been since the funeral over a year ago. Hilda came with us, as did some of Lucas's children who were staying with Constanza. As usual, wherever we went the vehicle was overloaded, and this was no exception. Although the Bravo cemetery was right across from the soccer field, I had never been down its long dirt road because it seemed private, not for tourists. This time I was family and just one of the many bodies crammed into the back seat. The road ended abruptly in a tight space with no warning. This cemetery wasn't serving those with cars, but those that walked and rode buses, or were carried in by a grieving community.

Into what looked more like a garbage dump, where shreds of colored plastic hung in a chaos of thorned vines, we stepped gingerly over depressions and mounds that marked the older, less cared-for, and perhaps even forgotten graves. Constanza led us to a far corner of the cemetery that had many short graves, those of her children that had not survived past infancy. In the center of these lay little Lucas, his grave already covered by the hungry tropical growth.

But Lucas and his long-deceased uncles and aunts weren't the only small graves. Others were the youth and hope of the people I'd lived and worked with for years. I'd left them to go where I would, but they could go no further than childhood and cheaply adorned graves. My heart felt crushed, tears stole my breath while Constanza's wails and sobs broke free to mix with what might have been. Daniel grabbed a *machete* and began to clear away the foliage, but he stopped, knelt, bowed his head towards Lucas and prayed. Then a miracle happened. He wept. Choking gasps came from this man who'd told me he had never shed tears; not when he was five when his father died and was buried in some unknown pauper's grave, not when he saw other children get Christmas presents and he didn't, not when he finished his first day of work at the age of twelve with feet blistered from his first pair of shoes and hands bloodied from digging fence-post holes. His deep grief rose and shook the ground and me. Always lamenting that he couldn't unburden his sorrow as easily as I did through tears, he wasn't holding back the torment that swept down on us all.

Together we cried for what we'd lost and perhaps for what we knew we would lose. Hilda looked for guidance from the three adults who were laying bare the weakness and tragedy of humanity, and perhaps out of confusion, shock, or survival instinct, she didn't cry but cleared away the overgrowth. Constanza was the first to let her memories and fears recede enough to help Hilda. Releasing Daniel from my grip, I picked up another *machete* and helped them finish the job. Daniel remained quiet while Hilda and Constanza on the way back to La Cuca pointed out the graves of others I'd known and those I wished I'd known.

After such trauma and emotion there was a silent but unanimous vote to play *futbol*. We found a kid's plastic ball, not much different from Camila's that had been the inaugural ball all those years ago. Going no farther than the bare earth in between the *casas*, we decided that the boundaries of the field would be the sides of the houses, *la toma*, and a bush. Into this small space crowded Ian, Daniel, Hilda, a dozen children, and me. Sides were drawn up with a lot of arguing and the game began. The ball bounced off of walls, porches, banana trees, electrical wires, and not a few bruised and bloody noses. The fast pace, ricocheting ball, and risk of injury were like playing indoor soccer, but with a Guatemala twist. With sweat pouring off our bodies and mixing with the mud and laughter, we had one hell of a game that could have gone on forever. We called it quits when Daniel kicked a tree and broke his toe.

It was time to shower and head onto our next stop, a roost count at Esperanza. With Hilda and Ian we had the "four biologists" needed to do the count. With Daniel in Guatemala for the next six months this was an excellent opportunity to do some follow-up evaluations of the birds since we left. Daniel could also earn a "good" salary while waiting to return to the USA. I had travelled with all the tree climbing and field equipment, leaving it to Daniel to manage a field season alone, which at one time supported up to fifteen biologists. Grabbing our binoculars, we arrived just as the *loros* flew in. The scene was depressing with a wasteland surrounding the remaining trees, but we'd seen this before. What came as a surprise were the numbers of birds that flew in. On that night and during other censuses after I left, totals were as high as or higher than before. Without follow-up counts in the months since I moved, there was no way to know what the numbers meant, but we were joyful to have the roost site not only intact, but still in use.

Other developments I saw that trip were also hopeful. The trees we'd planted around the Tecanal soccer field were nearly large enough for children to climb. They would perhaps one day offer refuge, food, and homes for the many, and not just for the humans that already were enjoying the shade that these future giants offered. Isabel came to visit us and shared other good news. The women and girls were still playing soccer, including Alejandra and Hilda in the Taxisco leagues. A trip to the aviary and to Perry's house confirmed that both were thriving.

Typical of Guatemala, the up times were always counterbalanced with the down. I had gone to the aviary not so much to check the progress of this project or to greet the workers and friends (one of whom commented on my weight gain, again), but to see the maturing Moses that had graced my life during his early years. Perry insisted that Moses remembered me, but what I saw was a nervous bird whose past year had been a tough one. He hadn't adapted well and didn't have many parrot social skills. Although he ignored the tame friend that shared his cage, at least he had another bird to pass the long hours with and to perhaps one day become intimate with. Along with Moses, I regretted the many RESCAVES birds that had come to the aviaries when RESCAVES had been closed. They seemed to be doing fine, even if their original home had been stripped of its cages, wood, and vision. All that was left was the overgrown grass choking out what had been planted with hope.

Crime had increased since I had left. During that week, three robberies occurred within a mile of Tecanal, two in broad daylight, and one in front of Micaelana's house. Speaking of crime, the Serengeti nest cavity was full of bees, eliminating the only nest likely to fledge young in our *finca*. We didn't know what happened in other *fincas* because of lack of transportation and staff. In the brief time I was there, it wasn't worth the pain of seeing *caña* growing where there once had been trees to see if any parrots remained. But we didn't have to go far to see the destruction caused by *caña*–it had come to Tecanal. Gone were so many of our nest trees, including the ancient *amate* in *Campo Santo* 4.

On our last day at Tecanal, we took Hilda and Camila to the movies in Escuintla, and just like many times before, I held their hands during the movie and stroked their hair. Both relenting to be children with me again by allowing me into their space was one of the greatest gifts I was given during this trip. I was also generously supported by the rest of Daniel's family. Treated as one of their own, it was a tearful and emotional goodbye when Daniel and I left for a night in Antigua and one in *Guate* before my flight out. Micaelana wouldn't let go of my hand and little Tippi, wouldn't get out of *La Cuca*. He demanded that I take him with me and ran screaming from us when he was finally dislodged from the car. I don't know how I managed it, but I left those I loved once again.

Before flying out of Guatemala City I stopped by to see Anita. As always, she was most gracious. I could count on her to be the only one not to comment on my weight gain. We spoke briefly of my letter and my plans to apply to Divinity School. I wanted to let her know how much she meant to me, though we both could be judgmental of one another. I was grateful to her for bringing me to Guatemala. I was also indebted to her intensity and dreams that changed my life.

The next day at the airport, I felt a strong foreboding. I nearly fled the line through *migración* to return to Daniel, this time forever. Holding my ground and trusting in life, I turned to see Daniel waving goodbye, and then he was gone. Over the next months we talked on the phone, arranging for his visa, but he seemed angry with me. When I asked him what the problem was, he said *"Nada, mi hombrecita,"'* "Nothing, my little man." His letters and field reports dropped off and I lost contact with him for over a month. I called Fabiana and asked her where Daniel was. I had imagined he was on his way to me, unable to wait the six months and willing to risk crossing the border illegally. Instead of coming to me, he had in fact drifted further away. When he called the next night, surely in response to Fabiana's goading, I was angry and hurt. Why hadn't he called, written, or worked on getting his annulment papers? He told me it was impossible to get it straightened out, and I exploded with an ultimatum. If he was so easily willing to give up, then perhaps he should rethink what he wanted. I was tired of being the one with all the energy for our relationship, and if he didn't want to be with me, I was through trying to hold us together. From then on he'd call the shots on getting us together. He said he'd think about it and call back in a few days.

He never called. A week slipped agonizingly by, and again I entertained the thought that Daniel would show up unannounced on my doorstep. Beside myself with worry and the uncertainty of my future, I tried calling Daniel at Tecanal. A guard told me that *Don* Daniel had moved from Tecanal and he didn't know where he'd gone. Certain that this was the end, I mustered the strength to call Fabiana who confirmed my fears. Daniel had gone to live with Alejandra and the girls in Taxisco. Daniel's scars ran deeper than I'd ever imagined. I thought I knew about his anger and brokenness, but I was a temporary traveler in his world, a land of spilled blood and scars that dug deep and marred beauty. Wounds may heal, but the scars don't disappear.

Sobbing became my hourly routine. I found bathrooms at work where I could cry so I could manage to deal with sick pet birds and share knowledge with hungry veterinary students. I wore sun glasses wherever I went to hide my swollen eyes. I couldn't say the words Guatemala or trees without getting squeaky voiced and choked up. I was afraid to go out at night, and with no energy anyway, I cried so hard my gut ached. I let myself feel the grief, and thought there must be a reason for the pain, and for its cause, love and beauty. If I could embody it all, I could give back what the parrots and people of Guatemala had given me.

My searching led me to audit a theology class at North Carolina State University in the fall of 1996. I was looking for tools on how to live with a heart cracked wide open. After a week I knew what I needed to do. Here, within religion, was my path. If I could learn the language of healing the human heart, my own could mend and I could give my all to Earth and her beings. By November I had applied to several divinity schools and by spring I was accepted to Vanderbilt Divinity and given a full scholarship and a stipend. I could go to school and continue to send money to Hilda and Camila, and would one day return, if not to them then to other children of Latin America.

Chapter 14
ATTAINING THE GOOD YOU WILL NOT ATTAIN
Nashville, Tennessee, to Rochester, Minnesota, to Raleigh, North Carolina, to El Paso,
Texas, to Gainesville, Florida, 1997- 2010

Once again I picked up my brother in my Chevy van with all my gear, and we drove west so he could help me move to Nashville, Tennessee. My home was a one-fourth of a rundown house near Vanderbilt University, close enough to bike throughout the year to classes. The apartment was one large room with a booth for a kitchen table, a toy shower, and an extra bed disguised as a couch for visitors. I was still crying every day and waking up from Guatemala stress dreams that made me sob in my sleep. Yet I felt excitement about finding meaning in my suffering.

That excitement carried over into my first day of class. However, upon arriving, no one was in the classroom. I rechecked my schedule and was roaming the halls looking a little bit confused when the Dean of Admissions came up to me and asked if something was wrong. I handed her my schedule she said it was Wednesday, not Thursday. I slunk into my first class, 30 minutes late and humbled.

Humility was my constant companion those first months at Divinity School. I had a science education and when people dropped names like Derrida and Foucault, I was completely lost. My writing was either scientific and analytic, or poetic, and neither was suited to the liberal arts approach taught at Vanderbilt. I did thrive with a sense of the holy, and took every class I could from Sally McFague, who wrote about ecotheology. She asked us in our classes and writing, "How could we love the world as our own body enough so that we would not destroy it?" One way I wanted to show my love for the world was to

177

change my name so I'd never forget the beauty of the birds I left behind in Guatemala. I took part of my middle name, Lorraine, and moved it to the front part of my first name, Kim, and I introduced myself as LoraKim (Parrot Kim). I would always carry the *loras* with me whenever I heard my name. I wanted to connect to beauty every day, even though it was so far away.

One of the first books I read in Divinity school was Thich Nhat Hahn's *The Heart of Understanding,* in which he comments on the Heart Sutra, a foundational Buddhist text. His interpretation of the Prajnaparamita Heart Sutra offers a particularly poignant understanding of enlightenment by using an example of a rose, garbage, and a prostitute. He asks the reader to imagine a perfectly formed rose and then think of garbage. They appear to be opposites. One is pure, the other dirty. One is immaculate, the other defiled. If you look more deeply, writes Hahn, you see the rose will within several days fade and then decompose. It will be thrown into the trash, no longer a thing of beauty. And if you look in your garbage can, you'll see that in a few months' time, through composting, that the contents will give life to plants, vegetables, and even a rose. With the eyes of an enlightened one, when you look at a rose you see garbage, and when you look at the garbage, you see a rose. Thich Nhat Hanh says that humans are made of roses and garbage and many other things, and because all people are part of the whole, we all are holy, and should treat others and ourselves accordingly. He specifically used the example of a prostitute in Manila and a wealthy global businessperson to make his point, and my world rocked when I got to that point, for I had known both.

It happened when I was consulting in the Philippines as an avian veterinarian and commuting between there, Alaska, and Guatemala. One evening I was asked to join a group of wealthy and important men, one of whom was a rich Filipino businessman. After several night clubs, we ended up in a noisy, smoky strip joint, where barely clad women served us drinks, and those even barer served fantasies. The strippers strutted onto the dance floor, not one of them smiling, not one of them over 16. They took off their clothes but never unveiled their eyes. It was as if they weren't there, as if they accepted their role in a garbage society. But they didn't want to be prostitutes. Their families were poor and they came to the big city to make money to send home. People are clever and cruel, and it's not difficult to see how a child can be convinced they can make big money if they will dance a little and flirt a little, but they'll suffer because they'll carry impurity and defilement. They become trash, or so they think.

The true nature of our outing surfaced when a male bartender escorted a girl to each of the five men in our group, after which our party decided it was time to leave. Out walked the eleven of us, the men busily hailing a taxi that were scarce that late. The girls remained quiet, unsmiling. Eventually two taxis appeared. As I was guided into one of them with half the group, a businessman asked if I minded if one of the girls sat on my lap. What could I do? When we arrived at the hotel, we headed to our rooms. As one man guided a girl into his room, he whispered to me he wanted some of the cash that he'd asked me to carry in my purse. What could I do? From his fat wad of brightly colored bills, I counted out the amount he requested as the young girl stared at me over his shoulder.

As I read Hanh's book I could see her eyes. She would always be connected to me in ways that are always uncomfortable and sometimes painful. Suffering would never leave me or anyone because it's always in the world, as the first of Buddha's Noble Truths states. But what could I do with this suffering? Thich Nhat Hanh suggested we look deeply into the lives of soldiers and terrorists, as I'd looked into the mournful eyes of that girl on my lap, and there we'd see garbage and roses. Each beautiful life is connected to her through the global economy that continues the oppression of colonialism, and through the denial that sexual abuse and gender oppression exist in all communities.

With radical interconnection, there need not be oppression anywhere in the world. Moving from Hahn's example of the prostitute, I thought of poachers and conservationists. If a poacher knows that he's a rose and not garbage, he might find a way to elevate his situation, and if we know that he's not garbage but a rose, we'd never allow him and others to exist in sorrowful dead ends. If we find in ourselves the poacher and others like him, we bear his pain, and the pain of the world, and then we can emancipate every one of us.

With such understandings from my classes and with the loving and welcoming community of divinity school, I began to edge slowly out of my cloister in my apartment to attend school and church events. One evening, I attended an immigration event at a local Methodist church, and drove myself there, in the dark. When I got home I realized it was the first time in years I'd been out at night by myself. After that, I attended more activities during my three years at Divinity School. Each class, assignment, and field placement was therapy to help me learn to hold both beauty and tragedy.

My first summer break I served as a student chaplain at a hospital in Wilmington, North Carolina, which continued my self-awareness and acceptance. One afternoon I saw a new movie "The Thin Red Line" that used beautiful bird images and metaphors to tell the story of World War II in the Pacific on Guadalcanal. The hero of the story was walking along a recently bombed hillside when he came upon a baby parrot that had fallen to the ground when its nest tree had exploded and burned. The man said, "One man looks at a dying bird and thinks there's nothing but unanswered pain. That death's got the final word, it's laughing at him. Another man sees that same bird, feels the glory, feels something smiling through it." My tears that evening were tinged with hope, even though the hero died even as he loved the enemy surrounding him.

My first year in divinity school ended with a dream. Tossing and turning, moving in and out of sleep I dreamed I was wondering through a misty terrain looking for the answer of how to save the world. This went on for hours and hours and near dawn I dreamt the answer, "Paracletes for Parakeets." This happened at the subconscious level because I had no idea what a paraclete was and what it had to do with parakeets. Nevertheless, an immense relief flooded my sleep, and I woke feeling euphoric.

The next day I researched paraclete, a Greek word used several times in the Christian scriptures, particularly in John. It means *advocate, counselor, helper, encourager* or *comforter*. It might also mean *summoner* or *the one who makes free*. What stayed with me for weeks was the knowledge that we are here to love one another and to give witness to love's power, and advocate for others based on our call to love. A few weeks later I saw the film, *Paulie*, about a captive, abused parakeet who gives up and becomes silent, as did a silenced migrant from Russia. In a dark basement, in desperation they share their stories, they gain comfort and courage, and both learn to speak out about love, beauty, and the right to freedom and liberation for all. I had to find a way to brave the suffering so I could speak to the reality of the people and parrots in Guatemala.

1998

The Assistant Archbishop to Guatemala City Juan Jose Geradi was murdered two days after publishing a report on the suspected involvement of the military in past atrocities.

Hurricane Mitch hit Honduras and Nicaragua, devastating both economies. The storm killed 10,000 people and left three million people homeless. The USA offered 150,000 immigration temporary work visas as humanitarian aid to both countries.

Needing more time, I opted out of a two-year Master's program for a three-year degree. I began my second year at Vanderbilt by accepting a field placement at the First Unitarian Church of Nashville. It was a bit rocky at first because Unitarianism is a far stretch from my Christian upbringing and nature experiences, but I stayed because it offered the best theological hope for seeing beauty and possibility in life. The minister took me under her wing and opened her ministry so I could work there part-time for a year. One of my first assignments was to lead the Wednesday evening vesper services with Meredith the chair of the Adult Religious Education Committee and former philosophy professor at the historically black Fisk University. We had met earlier in the year when I had attended a class he was co-teaching on medical ethics. I respected his leadership because no matter how far flung my comments were about needing to care for the "least of these," including animals, and questioning the elites, he listened and incorporated my politics into the group. Eventually we made a date for lunch and, frankly, I wasn't impressed. He suggested another date and I had an excuse for everything: I don't spend money on restaurants because I send it to Guatemala. I don't go to movies because I'm busy finishing my memoir on the Guatemala years, *Sugar Cane Scars*. We can't go out because I am a ministerial intern and you are a lay person, and the Nashville congregation suffered clergy sexual abuse in the past.

Eventually we hit on a compromise. He'd ask the minister if we could date, and then we'd play soccer in the park. On the Monday of our soccer date, I finished my memoir, and had it printed and bound. I thought, how ironic the timing was of laying down a chapter of my life as I took up another, for the soccer date with Meredith was a resounding success. We continued to see each other and, early on, I helped him move in, tempting our new and fragile relationship with disaster. But then grace stepped in. We were getting ready to lift his long, five-drawer, metal file cabinet into a truck when he paused to show me the mementos he'd taped to it over the years. That's the first time I heard Zbigniew Herbert's poem "The Envoy of Mr. Cogito" that speaks of how we will fail, and only in that knowing do we attain the good we will not attain. As he read it I stared over his shoulder and cried. He did too. We got each other at a level no other had as of yet. We continued to court over the summer when I served as a chaplain at the Veterinary School in Raleigh, where I'd been a professor. Soon, after returning to Nashville, we were engaged, and happily I called my mother to say that her advice was correct: Church IS a great place to meet people. My mother, a lifelong Methodist replied, "But I didn't mean that church."

We married a week after I graduated Vanderbilt Divinity School, and soon we were on our way to Rochester, Minnesota, where I had a 10-month church parish internship as a minister. After that we moved to Raleigh, North Carolina, where I split my time as a community minister and a congregation minister. I was a chaplain and community advocate at the North Carolina State University School of Veterinary Medicine and a pastoral assistant minister at the Unitarian Universalist Fellowship of Raleigh. I wanted to be with animals, but the veterinary school atmosphere of money and pets didn't jive with my politics, given my time in Central America. After a year I left to become the minister of the Unitarian Universalist Community of El Paso. I wanted to be as close to

Central America as I could, and the border bilingual town of El Paso suited us both fine.

2001

September 11, 2001 - Terrorists of al-Qaeda, led by Osama bin Laden, diverted planes that destroyed both New York's Twin Towers, plowed into the Pentagon, and caused a crash into a rural field in Pennsylvania. There were 2,996 people killed and more than 6,000 wounded.

2003

On November 9, 2003, Óscar Berger, a former mayor of Guatemala City, won the presidential election with 38.8% of the vote. As he failed to achieve a 50% majority, he had to go through a runoff election on December 28, which he also won. He defeated the center-left candidate Álvaro Colom. Allowed to run, Ríos Montt trailed a distant third with 11% of the vote.

The Second Gulf War begins, marshaled by the USA and based on false evidence, leading to the invasion of Iraq.

To satisfy my need to give back to the people of Latin America, I volunteered to lead services at the detention facility for undocumented migrant minors. With my broken Spanish and electric bass playing, we rocked during the services and heard the plaintive prayers of the young people. They were in this detention center because as minors from Central America they couldn't be dumped back over the nearby border in Juarez, Mexico. Instead, family members had to be found where they could travel to safely, either in the USA or back home. During these services, I brought an extra guitar, and a teen from Honduras, Patricio, led the hymns. After one service he asked, *"Quiero hablar con usted, Hermana"*-- [I want to talk to you, Sister.[

He told me his story of domestic abuse in Honduras, of how his father, a drunk, repeatedly beat him and his mother. The night before he left to come to the USA, his father had hung him from a tree branch by a rope around his neck. He barely managed to keep his toes touching the ground so he wouldn't choke. After friends cut him down, he packed his bags and made his way to the

Guatemala border, then through Guatemala, and into Mexico. He didn't even say goodbye to his mother *"por tanto dolor"'* because of so much pain. At the border in Chiapas he took the *Tren de Muerte*-- death train,-- a freight train that migrants hop to make their way to northern Mexico. It is so named because many die along the way, falling under the wheels, resulting in death or in loss of a limb. He was robbed several times and nearly raped, but he made it to the USA border. There his family sent money so he could hire a *coyote*-- a middle-man and guide-- to get him to Tucson and then to North Carolina where he had cousins and friends. The *coyote's* car broke down in Texas and he abandoned his trafficked people along the roadside. After three days without food and water, Patricio said, he couldn't even run from the police. *"Pues, aqui estoy, no puedo regresar a Honduras,"*-- 'Well, here I am, I can't return to Honduras." "Can I live with you, Hermana?"

I told him that I'd look for someone who could sponsor him while he awaited his court case. I made several phone calls, all to no avail, except to get me kicked out of the detention center. "As long as I can't help Central American kids, we might as well take Patricio in," I explained to Meredith. He barely blinked an eye, always loving my politics, and within a week the paperwork was started to have Patricio come live with us. A year later, another joined our household, Axel. Both were nearly 18 when they became our family. I thought they'd take off as soon as they could to join their family and friends, but they called us "Ma" and "Pa" and showed no signs of running away. In fact, they settled in, and within weeks acted like typical teenagers, blaming us for everything that had gone wrong in their lives. We too were triggered, and the judgment flowed both ways.

Then grace stepped in. I had taken up training in Nonviolent Communication, founded by Marshall Rosenberg. I wanted to know how I could contribute to peace because protesting and working on the border didn't stop the Iraq war, or the racism and systematic violence I witnessed every day, and that was within me. I desired to work on building peace within, and could do this with immediate relationships. One evening after another tense discussion with Patricio, and how could there not be given his different ethnicity, culture, country, language, diet, and religion. We were liberal vegetarians, and he was conservative evangelical Christian. That evening, out came the Bible and both my spouse and Patricio flipped through it to prove each other wrong. That night I said, "Meredith, we teach Nonviolent Communication, why we don't try it at home?" And so we did, shifting from trying to change and teach him, to empathizing.

Our home life settled down somewhat, although between the two teens there were plenty of car, girlfriend, police, drug, and prison challenges to last a lifetime. Both sons moved with us to Gainesville, Florida, where we became co-ministers of the Unitarian Universalist Fellowship of Gainesville. Other

Honduran young men lived with us intermittently, and often it was me and four men, three with hormones and energy beyond my ken. Axel was eventually deported for drug charges, but Patricio worked for a year learning English, then got his GRE, and then a BS. We were mostly just witnesses to his hard work that was leading him towards success.

I was able to spend some time caring for him and Axel, for as a co-minister I worked technically only half-time. I still desired to do more, so in my free time I built a nature, multispecies, Latin America ministry. I caught the attention of the Unitarian Universalist Service Committee President Charlie Clements, and he asked me to join him in Guatemala as election witnesses to the 2009 presidential runoff election. I thought that I could manage to return with a group of ministers and seminarians, if it wasn't connected to parrot conservation. This would be my first time back in Guatemala in 13 years and I was anxious. A few months before I flew out, I dared to look on Google Earth to see if the Esperanza roost site was there. Closer and closer I zoomed in on the scorched earth, and there indeed was one clump of trees—the two *ceibas* and the *castaña*. I couldn't see the *Chinga Ceiba* or the other next largest *Ceiba*, but the short, broad-crowned *Ceiba* was still there. I contacted Joaquin and Adrian and suggested we go see what the birds were doing before I had to report to the elections group. Right before I left, however, my mother was in a serious car accident and I delayed my departure. I could meet Joaquin and Adrian only in Antigua, where we had dinner before they dropped me off at the hotel where the election witnesses were lodging. They told me they had both become parents. During my week's stay, I found the phone numbers of a few people, Perry, Sofia, and Fabiana, and called them.

With that trip deemed a success, with only sweet sorrowful tears and no heart wrenching trauma, I decided to take bigger steps to see if I could return to avian conservation. I attended the Association of Avian Veterinarian's annual conference, delivering a paper on the flock of free flying Amazon parrots breeding in El Paso, Texas, outside of their range. There I made the acquaintance of Donald Brightsmith, a parrot biologist, who suggested that I assist Wildlife Conservation Society's project in northern Guatemala in the Maya Biosphere Reserve. They accepted my offer as a veterinary, conservation consultant, and I spent two weeks with them in 2009. The project was struggling because nearly 70% of the reserve had been either illegally settled or deforested, and the macaw population had taken a huge dive because of poaching. The leaders of the projects received death threats because of their testimony about the habitat loss, and a biologist had been kidnapped the year before, but later released. I kicked myself for not relocating my parrot conservation energies from the southern coast of Guatemala to the northern forest in El Petén in the 1990s. Maybe I could have staved off this inglorious end. But I had been in no condition in those years to do anything, suffering from what now I could name post-traumatic stress disorder.

After training them to conduct health exams on wild scarlet macaw chicks, I arranged again to visit southern Guatemala to find out what was going on with the parrots in the area. I worked up the nerve to call Fabiana and ask for Daniel's number, whom I called. His first words were (after asking how I got his phone number) were *"Lo siento"*-- 'I'm sorry." "What for?" I asked? "For how I treated you, and also because of how we have treated the parrots. There are so few left and we should have done more." I apologized too for all that I had done, and not done, and asked him how he was. *"Estoy triste, porque mi Hermano Chema fue matado ,"*-- "I am sad because my brother Chema was killed." I told him I had heard how Chema had been found murdered in a ditch on the road from Escuintla and Tecanal, and that I grieved too, for many things. I then invited him to join Joaquin, Adrian, and me for a reunion at the Esperanza roost site and Tecanal. He met us at Tecanal where I got to spend time with Fabiana, his mother, his sister's family, and his new family, a wife, her two teenage children, and their new son. I looked deep into Daniel's eyes, and saw that unanswerable beauty was still within him, but now I could also see it in me, in those around us. I had been anxious to see how it would go with Daniel, and now with that over with, my anxiety turned to wondering about the parrots at the roost site. Tension mounted as we delayed even longer to inspect the soccer field to see how our planted trees were faring. They were towering, now large enough to be offer seeds and nest cavities for the parrots.

As we traveled down the long, dirt road to the roost site, we kept stopping to look at birds. Joaquin had become quite the birder and taught ornithology at the university. *"Vamos, rapido, es hora de observer a los loros!*-- "Let's go quickly, it's time to observe the parrots." As we drove closer, I saw that the corral edged with trees was still intact. In the distance were a few lines of fence row trees crisscrossing this lunar landscape that was a sugar cane field. Finally, we arrived. We saw, beyond the corral trees, the cluster of three roost trees. Looking in one direction, there was no *Chinga Ceiba*. In the other direction, we saw smoke and the remnants of a tree, and as we approached, the trunk of a once mighty *ceiba* was ashen and smoldering on the ground. I bent down and rubbed my hand along the truck, and smeared my forehead with the ashes. If the birds could see this, perhaps they'd know that I was repentant and yearned for forgiveness for leaving them. If they'd just come, perhaps I could erase that black mark that went deeper than my skin.

We broke into two groups to count parrots, not the four groups that we needed back when there were more trees. Joaquin and I had a spot in the middle of the field where burnt remains of the cane crop lingered. As we waited for the parrots to come in, sugar cane trucks roared through the fields on new roads, throwing up a racket and dust clouds. We waited longer, and then even longer. Finally, around dusk, a few pairs came in calling, no families. We counted 12. Down from 250. We left, with ashes on us all, and also in us as I recalled how we humans are ashes of long dead stars and shine brightly.

2009

A coup occurred in Honduras, sending President Manuel Zelaya into exile. International reaction to the coup was widespread condemnation. USA Secretary of State Hillary Clinton actively sought to prevent Zelaya's reinstatement and backed the new government, which many countries considered illegal and undemocratic. This began a downward spiral into the armed aggression, repression, and high murder rates that continue today.

Back home in Florida, I began working with Dr. Ted Lafeber ifLafeber Company, a well known pet food company. He had seen my grief at one Association of Avian Veterinarian's conference and had taken me under his wing to help heal my heart. We had started with the loss and grief website "Wings of Compassion," and now Ted was helping me with conservation. He knew I had my own grief to work with, and he collaborated with the Puerto Rican Parrot Recovery Project and asked me to visit them. I had consulted with this group in the mid-1990s when I had been a professor at the North Carolina State University School of Veterinary Medicine, and had written their reintroduction protocols. We first practiced with releasing Hispanolian parrots in the Dominican Republic, and, after I left, they hadn't only improved their captive breeding programs of the much endangered Puerto Rican Parrot, but they began releasing them. I was invited to a release of young captive birds at the Rio Bravo conservation site. I toured their aviaries and medical units and saw firsthand how our earlier efforts in the project still influenced management of the species. Though the birds were still endangered, the biologists' efforts were succeeding and the captive population was reproducing enough healthy chicks for continued releases of parrots into the wilds. The aviary manager, Jafet, kindly credited me with some of their success.

With tears in my eyes I listened, and wondered. When I had worked in Puerto Rico I had swung between crying and numbing depression because of Guatemala. But what had happened in Guatemala, had given me the experience to help make Puerto Rico a success, even as Guatemala was failing. In turn, Puerto Rico, now a leader in parrot conservation, was healing me and was a leader, guiding many other parrot conservation projects around the world. Even in the midst of failure, we are giving and receiving. With this healing, I could now once again focus on Guatemala and Central America, vowing to never leave them again, to attain the good I would not attain.

LORAKIM JOYNER

Chapter 15
CONSERVATION IN TIME OF PEACE
Gainesville, Florida; White Plains, New York; many countries in Latin America, 2009-2016

I returned to Guatemala intending to restart our *Proyecto de Loros* in 2010. I visited the south coast and looked for partners and people crazy enough to start a project again when in all likelihood the bird situation was worse than before. Indeed, the south coast was sometimes referred to as *desaparecido*- it has been disappeared. There were still a few patches of forest left, but the cattle fields were steadily losing ground to sugar cane. Sugar refineries belched out smoke and large cane trucks littered the roads with cane offal everywhere we went. Fernando Aldana, *el preservador*-- the preserver-- got the project going along with his sons, Dani and David. They conducted a mini-monitoring project at the roost site. Over the next two years they confirmed our fears, Esperanza was no longer a roost site, with 1-2 pairs at most spending the night in the trees. We didn't know if this population crash was the case for all of Guatemala, so we slowly expanded our project to look for "hot spots," places where the parrots were, and where we could protect them. Colum Muccio of the nonprofit ARCAS joined us, and then others, including many *finca* and private reserve owners, together forming COLORES (Corridor of *Loros*, Reserves, and Sanctuaries).

During one of those trips I wanted to see Alejandra, Hilda, and Camila. I had lost touch with them for several years. I finally got a working phone number and called them to see if they would be open to seeing me. Alejandra answered the phone, and following Daniel's modeling a few years ago, the first thing I said to Alejandra was "I am sorry for my behavior." She said, "No worry, we were all doing the best we could and that is long past. I always knew you loved me and the girls." Whew. That out of the way, I then asked about Hilda, Camila, and Daniel. "We do not hear from Daniel. He is with his new family, and he disowned Hilda because she likes women. Also, we have not heard from Camila in several years. She left one day to Mexico, leaving her two children with me, whom I am raising. Would you like to meet them?" I said I would.

The next week I was in Guatemala City taking a taxi to meet Alejandra, Hilda, and Camila's two children at a park. We had lunch over awkward conversation, though it had moments much like old times with bantering and bawdry comments. They had financial struggles, with Hilda as the main wage earner, but had found new relationships and forged family out of disruptive times. That same trip I visited Daniel's mother at Tecanal. She was living with Fabiana and her daughter Yolanda. Barely able to walk, she greeted me as always with *Seña* and I held her hand as we talked. There wasn't much left of her body, and all of us seemed smaller and older. The trees we planted around the soccer field were also older, but fatter. Looking down on Google Earth, one can see a rectangle of tall trees on the *finca*, our work.

I didn't know how much work we could still do in that *finca*. There were hardly any parrots left on Tecanal or Esperanza, or any of the *fincas* we had visited. I wasn't giving up on Guatemala, but wanted to find where I could help. I went again to my parrot conservation friend Donald Brightsmith, "Okay, it's great helping out the scarlet macaws and yellow-naped Amazons in Guatemala, but I want to help more. Where do I go?" He spoke about La Moskitia in eastern Honduras. No one was doing any parrot conservation there, and no one knew what was going on there. He gave me the name of Héctor Portillo Reyes, a biologist in Tegucigalpa who might be interested in working with me.

Héctor was interested, and so was his friend Maria Eugenia Mondragon Hung. Over the next months we arranged for a trip during the breeding season in the spring of 2010. I thought arrangements were fairly well set when Héctor called one day and said he had news that might change my desire to work in Honduras. My heart sank to hear a conversation start off like that, because I wanted to work in Honduras, the home of Patricio and Axel.

Héctor told me about the instability since the coup in 2009 and how Tomás Manzanares, an indigenous leader of Rus Rus, and had been nearly killed by assassins. Drug traffickers and corrupt government officials were all part of the chaos that allowed invaders to take the land from the indigenous, and Tomás had had enough. He'd reported the names of the land grabbers and illegal loggers to the authorities who did nothing. But the men he reported did do something. Four men waited for him at the river where he took his daily bath, and each shot him. His brother was nearby and scared off the men and called for help. Tomás nearly died of his wounds, but after many surgeries, he lived. "But LoraKim, the danger is still there. The villagers of Rus Rus where he lived had to flee, and his parents' home was burned. Other nearby villages have been abandoned and leaders murdered. I hate to tell you this, but I think you should know. We can still cancel the trip." "It makes me want to go even more. How can we get there and work as safely as possible?"

I flew to Tegucigalpa, and then took a small plane with Héctor and Maria to Puerto Lempira. There we hired a military escort to the four-hour dirt-road drive to the village of Rus Rus. Tomás accompanied us, against everyone's advice. It had only been five months since the shooting, he was still in pain, and the area was dangerous. With Tomás, some forestry officials, four soldiers, Alicia, Tomás' spouse, and our driver, we pulled into Rus Rus in the evening, and had to break open the doors that had been nailed shut to keep out intruders. We slept on floors and in tents, unable to go to the outhouse without a soldier escorting us.

The next morning, we packed into the truck, with pistols bulging from day packs and pockets, and went to Mabita, Alicia's home village. Tomás took us for a walk to the Rus Rus River, where I asked him to share what had happened. He took off his shirt to show us the still-pink scars where bullets had torn his flesh, and where some remained. "Tomás, why are you willing to risk your life to save the parrots?" I asked. "*Doctora*, everything is at risk. I am willing to risk everything. If the parrots don't make it, neither do my people."

Though I was only there for four days in the field, La Moskitia had my heart. I planned to return the next year, in 2011, for a longer time to study the scarlet macaws. We flew into Pt. Lempira, picked up a military escort, and with a packed truck of supplies and people, headed to Rus Rus for a ten-day study. Our headquarters was Rus Rus, but our co-workers were the brothers of Alicia in Mabita, Santiago and Pascacio. The next morning we meet with the villagers and began our nest survey. I asked everyone to gather around and share our hopes for safety and compassion before we began the field work. This being a Catholic village and the leaders being lay pastors, the prayers began around the circle in the middle of the village. When it came my turn, I recited my favorite poem, "Wild Geese" by Mary Oliver. As they didn't have geese in Mabita I substituted macaws for geese (Please forgive me, Mary). I spoke in English, and then it was translated into Spanish, and then into Miskito.

I told of how one doesn't have to be good, or ravage oneself with repentance, but that, as Mary Oliver said, "You only have to let the soft animal of your body love what it loves." We each have despair to share with one another, and while we do that, the world doesn't stop for us. Storm and rainclouds move over the savannahs, the deep pines, the jungles, and the bean fields. Macaws, high over the trees, go home to their nests.

Then we heard the calls of macaws, five of them, a rare sighting when most chicks never fly free because of poachers. They flew towards us as I continued, saying how we each have loneliness, but a world of beauty is offered to us, given to us by the macaws whose harsh calls tell us repeatedly how we all belong in the "family of things."

At that point, the birds were directly overhead. We wept, those of us of many nations and ethnicities. The birds told us we belong, and in that knowing we committed ourselves to the life around us, in us, even if it meant until our own death. As a symbol of the friendships formed on that trip and shared passion, I gave Maria, whom we called Maru, my bird and human skull bracelet that I had made years before to help me remember how tragedy and beauty, and death and life cannot be separated. Micaela looked at the gift, raised her arm, and we said together *hasta la muerte* "--until death." We would work for parrot and people in her land until we died.

After our work in the field, we returned to Tegucigalpa for a few days of meeting and presentations. During that time, I called Axel, who had returned to his stepmother's house after being deported. He agreed to meet me the next day with his stepsister. They met me at the hotel. He looked older and more tired than a year ago. Meredith and I had asked him to move out of our house because his drug affiliations and dishonesty harmed the family. Just when he seemed to be making better decisions, he was caught with felonious amounts of drugs, and he was deported. We had only spoken a few times on the phone since then.

We embraced and at lunch he told me of his life. He was making $2 a day shoveling gravel from a river bottom into trucks, and not one day didn't go by that he regretted his actions in the USA. He admitted that he'd been using drugs, when always before he had denied this, and said, *"Lo siento, Ma"*-- "I'm sorry." I told him we were sorry too that we hadn't found a way to connect with him that would have helped him make different choices. "That's okay, Ma, I always knew you loved me." We cried and hugged each other goodbye, and I suspected I'd never see him again. Love was all there was and all that I had to give, but it wasn't enough to ensure his safety. I never heard from him again, hopefully only lost to me and not to this world.

For years, I worked in Honduras and Guatemala and then began projects in Belize, Nicaragua, Guyana, and Paraguay. I had left parish ministry and became a full-time community minister, working beyond a congregation's walls. I called my work Multispecies Ministry, and founded One Earth Conservation to empower the people who were saving the planet. If ever Earth needed this, it was now. The news was bad everywhere; no one could escape the effects of climate change, terrorism, mass migrations of the displaced, and loss of diversity. The poaching rates continued to be extreme, habitat were in crisis, and increased drug trafficking and lack of rule of law made conservation challenging even in the least violent regions. Wendell Berry wrote, "It is the impeded stream which sings," and so with deep gratitude I followed my joy to work more and more in Latin America.

Meeting the world's needs was almost derailed in 2011-2012. My left knee, initially injured in a biking accident when I was 12, was by then causing too much pain for field work. I had a knee replacement before the 2012 field season, but it didn't go well postoperatively. My knee was swollen and painful, and fibrous material kept me from extending or bending the knee. After several months, the orthopedist performed a "manipulation" and forcibly bent the knee, tearing the internal scar, thankfully under anesthesia. It wasn't successful, and I went for a second manipulation. This time the doctors accidentally broke my femur, and I had to have that fracture pinned as well as a second knee replacement. On my back or on the couch for most of six months, I was told I might not walk again. Wishing I was more enlightened didn't stop the depression from the constant pain and fear that I wouldn't return to the parrots and people of Latin America.

Slowly, though, over the next two years the pain lessened and strength returned, but not flexibility. I was okay on flat terrain, which almost doesn't exist in volcano-ridden Central America. I bought a monopod for my field camera, and it served as my walking stick. When the walking got tricky, I used someone's shoulder to navigate the hills, tall grass, or rough waves in a beach landing. I missed the 2012 field season, and some of the 2013, but it didn't slow me down much after that.

During my down time and the following years, the La Moskitia project remained one of the most compelling projects, and the most devastating. In 2014, not one chick escaped the illegal wildlife trade in our conservation area. Though we had been working with the village for four years, some of the villagers still poached macaws, as well as smaller parrots. One man had died stealing parrots the week before we arrived in April. He had grown up in Mabita, and defied the decision of the village to quit poaching. He had climbed a towering macaw nest tree where he made a mistake and fell. He crashed to the ground, killing one of the macaw chicks he'd stolen. The other survived, but was emaciated and ailing when I examined her a few weeks later. The villagers were distraught that poaching was going on, that the poacher's family wouldn't give up the macaw chick to be released, and that they had lost a community member.

Leaving the village to return to Pt. Lempira, our truck convoy passed the nest tree where the man died. At its base was a memorial of stones, a cross, and flowers. The villagers who rode with us piled out of the trucks and began wailing and crying. The elderly leader of the village, Mamatara, nearly blind, was guided to the tree base, where she moved her body in a mournful dance as she cried and chanted. I looked out at these people, up at the top of the tree where

193

a family of scarlet macaws should have been flying free, and wept myself. I couldn't hate this man, or any of the poachers who steal beauty and cause so much suffering. I imagined one day that this man's grandchildren would come to the base of this tree, and play, safely, while overhead, macaw children could also play, safely. Dreaming beyond knowing, I began to sing:

I add my breath
To your breath
That our days on this earth may be long
That the days of all beings may be long. (Adapted from Zuni Pueblo Prayer)

After each trip to Latin America to help the parrots and people, I became more convinced that now was the time to stop the pain in both humans and parrots, and it was a time for mending. I had been a poacher of birds. As a child I had an Australian parakeet, whose parents generations before had been taken from the wild. I also had a chevron-winged parakeet, a white-eyed conure, and a black-hooded parakeet, all three from Paraguay. I had made money and a career out of working with wild parrots torn from their native lands, including taking care of orange-winged Amazon parrots at a research center at the University of California at Davis and my sister's turquoise-fronted Amazon, both species also from Paraguay. It was time to lay that burden down. Taking the feathers from some of the birds I had long guarded, I traveled to Paraguay in the fall of 2014. There, in a small patch of forest, I placed the feathers in a circle around the ashes of my sister who died a few weeks before. My fellow conservationists helped me read a poem she wrote, "Fly Home." I ended our brief ceremony with words adapted from William Blake:

They who bind to themselves a joy
Do the winged life destroy
But they who kiss the joy as it flies
Live in eternity's sunrise.

Joyful is not how I would describe my growing conservation work, and it was with trepidation that I returned to La Moskitia, Honduras, in 2015. The year before we had lost everything to poaching. This year we set out earlier than usual to stave off the poaching. There had been some macaw chicks that were not poached when we left. We upped our ante in commitment by hiring community members to protect the nests, and by supporting a Rescue and Liberation Center in Mabita so the confiscated parrots could be released to the wild. The villagers had been caring for a liberated flock of parrots since 2011, but with very little support.

Upping the commitment, I stayed for two months in 2016. Every day bad news came like a kick in the gut. Corruption, bribes by drug traffickers, and the pressure of poaching were destroying lives all around me. Then grace stepped in, again. Not a single scarlet macaw chick entered the wildlife trade in our core conservation area in 2016, and no one was hurt in the process of protection and conservation in our area.

This wasn't true for all Honduras, or Latin America in general, the most dangerous region on the planet for environmentalists. Berta Caceres, an indigenous activist, was assassinated in March 2016 when I was in Honduras working with the yellow-headed parrot in another part of the country. Her death had sparked global outrage, which faded by the middle of the nest season when I was in Mabita. I still heard her words, though in my daily confrontation with those that would harm life, I adapted her words to our situation: "Arise my people, that the parrots might catch the wind of our indignation and always fly free, all of us."

After two months in Honduras I was pleased that ordinary people under extraordinary conditions could produce extraordinary results. Indignation mixed with reverence and commitment could go a long way, though this recipe couldn't save everything, and everyone.

After I returned, Santiago called a few months later with news about our beloved Rosa. Rosa came into this world weighing maybe 20 grams, all pink with unruly yellowish down. I imagined her parents loved and cared for her. They stroked her body with their beaks, pulling at the sheath of her new feathers so they could sprout rainbow colors and rise over us. But men found her nest, and pulled Rosa screaming from the warm comfort of the place where she'd been safe and loved. At least that's my version of her early life. Another telling is that the men hacked her pine tree, and felled it to get to Rosa on the ground. She became a prisoner of human desire and ended up with broken legs and wings. Her parents swooped, calling until they couldn't anymore, but to no avail. They'd never see Rosa again.

Men bound her in a burlap sack so she could be easily moved from the fields to a nearby town. She was given little water, and no attention was given to her brokenness, even though she cried in pain as she was moved clandestinely from house to house. New men with a different vision, found her in squalor, reclaimed her. Her legs were swollen, scabbed over from where the bones had once protruded. Tomás Manzanares, with his own deep scars from fractured limbs, took care of Rosa, nursing her to a semblance of health, enough to grow out her feathers, though dull and damaged. I saw her pictures from afar and wondered if she would ever fly, let alone live.

Live she did, finding her way to Anayda. Anayda and her spouse Santiago, and other villagers, had cared for rescued scarlet macaws and yellow-naped parrots for the past few years in the village of Mabita in La Moskitia, Honduras.

Rosa joined the liberated flock, though she had to be hand-carried from branch to feeding platform to porch. I met her when she was 18 months old, sad and pain-ridden. She cried constantly, her lungs were congested, she was desperately thin, her ears leaked fluid from a mite infestation, and her legs were bowed, one side from a break, the other, dislocated at the hip. She couldn't extend her wings, both bound with internal scar tissues and contracted joints, early fractures that hadn't been allowed a chance to heal. I thought she'd die, and said to Anayda, "Without you, Rosa won't live." Anayda heard that as a challenge and didn't let Rosa die. She continued my treatments, and never let Rosa out of her sight. When she went to Nicaragua to tend fields, Rosa rode in her shirt, both of them behind Santiago on a motorcycle.

I next saw Rosa when she was two, and she was transformed. Still fearfully thin, she had regained her health, her feathers had grown in shiny and shockingly red, the disease was gone and replaced with feistiness. By age three she attempted short flights, abrupt in their landing but able to get her closer to Anayda, and the other macaws. Macaws, being macaws, would often pick on her, but some were her friends, such as Lempira who preened her feathers and kept her company at night. Then Lempira healed enough to fly off with all the other macaws, leaving Rosa alone in *Casa Ara*-- Macaw House,-- the center of the rescue efforts in Mabita. That didn't stop Rosa from engaging the world, using her beak for balance to walk, taking hobbling steps with her bowed legs and curled feet to get to food and companionship.

When I was in Mabita for two months, I spent time with her near her fourth birthday. I wondered about her future, all broken, so un-macaw-like with her diminished ability (Earth, please forgive me for such thoughts). I'm now a hobbler too, with legs in declining function, so it's perhaps myself I judge for being less than my species can be, just as I have judged others. I watched Rosa closely, and found a fierce friend who taught me that even the broken can shine and serve.

Just past her fourth birthday, Mocorón was brought to the Rescue Center. He was weak, timid, and beaten down with captivity. We were afraid to introduce him into *Casa Ara*, knowing there could be fights. Anayda said, "Rosa will take care of him. That is what she does with newcomers." It took all of five minutes before Rosa zeroed in on him. Beak advancing to grab wood or wire, she pulled herself slowly to him. Within ten minutes they were preening each other, thereafter rarely leaving each other's side, Mocorón safe in the company and protection of Rosa.

Some visitors from the USA came to the village one day and stopped at *Casa Ara*. They had been led to believe that the birds could be handled, and only one was "brave" enough to grab a macaw, the only one he could get, Rosa. I saw this from afar and ran running, "*No toque las guaras, no toque Rosa*"--

"Don't touch the macaws, don't touch Rosa." The man quickly let Rosa go, apologizing to me, "I just didn't know it wasn't okay."

Not long after that was when Santiago told me on the phone that Rosa had died. She had developed a cough and was taken into Anayda's home. There was no clinic, no veterinarian, inadequate medicine, and no diagnostic ability to know why she was so sick. She died two days later. I didn't feel much then, couldn't, because I had to work with Eduardo on diagnosing her illness and who else might have it. Eduardo performed a necropsy, cutting up little Rosa so her tissues could tell us something of the mysterious illness that threatened the liberated flock.

Rosa was in bits and pieces, and a month later I finally let myself break into pieces. I couldn't write about her any earlier, I couldn't risk the grief. Now on my way to Paraguay, yet another country where macaws are trashed and broken for the illegal wildlife trade, on the long flight I saw the movie, *Me Before You*. It's about a woman who tries to love a paraplegic enough so he won't choose to die. She failed, but she gave him companionship and love before he left his life of pain. They were both changed by knowing each other, despite their wounds.

Our love and care wasn't enough for Rosa. We all failed her, and her kind. But Rosa didn't falter. She lived in pain during her unique and precious life; she gave us and the macaws companionship. She taught us with the kind of love that tasks us to bone-deep rending and mending that never ceases. I wish my love was enough to keep Rosa alive. But I don't have the power to end pain, anyone's.

I'd like to go back to the days before I met Rosa, before Moses, before Guatemala when I wasn't responsible for all those crippled and tortured birds in the illegal wildlife trade. I have no idea what I'm doing, or how to move forward, while living in love, beauty, and pain, but I don't suppose Rosa did either. She shone and she served. Anayda said when I asked her why she dedicated her life to caring for macaws, "Once I saw Rosa, I couldn't let it happen anymore."

I can't let it happen anymore either. So, dear Rosa, and all the parrots I feel I failed, I promise you now my devotion. Though you're gone, you're still visible and ever with me. Your beauty flies ahead of me, leading me.

Rosa, *Pree Palisa* (Miskito for Rosa, Fly Free).

And to all humans, *no los toque*! Don't touch them. Let them fly free.

2010

An international body passes the 2010 Universal Declaration of Rights of Mother Earth and campaigned for it to be adopted by the UN.

Ríos Montt was convicted of genocide and crimes against humanity. On 20 May 2013, his conviction was overturned by the Constitutional Court of Guatemala. A retrial began January 2015, and a Guatemalan court stated he can stand trial for genocide and crimes against humanity, but he cannot be sentenced because of his age and deteriorating health.

2012

The yellow-naped amazon status changes from "least concern" to "vulnerable" on the International Union for Conservation of Nature and Natural Resources Red List of Endangered Species.

2013

This year marks 80-year anniversary of the end of the USA occupation of Nicaragua, which began in order to stabilize the financial and business interests of the USA.

2014

The USA experiences an immigration crisis of unaccompanied children from Central America seeking entrance to the USA. Most are children from El Salvador, Guatemala, and Honduras, fleeing economic hardship, political instability, and drug- and gang-related violence. Records show that 52,000 children were apprehended, challenging immigration services to adequately care for these children.

Epilogue
WE WILL NOT GO
South Coast Guatemala, Los Esperanza, January 2017

2017

Newly elected USA President Trump threatens to withhold federal funding to sanctuary cities protecting immigrants and has taken steps to reduce entry into the USA of both undocumented and documented immigrants.

According to a recent scientific study, capture for the domestic pet trade is currently the threat most closely associated to decreasing population trends in neotropical parrots. (In Press, "Current threats faced by neotropical parrot populations" – Ivan Berkunsky et al).

I ride to the site of the Esperanza roost site where at least half the trees had still been standing the last time I was here in 2013, and two birds had roosted. That long road once again elicits anxiety, for I have been away from here too long. Apparently last year the ownership of the *finca* had turned over, and perhaps the promises to keep the trees standing had not been honored. As Manuel Galindo, our new Project Coordinator drives up to the location where once we had counted hundreds of parrots, now we only see trunks severed and piled as if they were bones thrown upon a trash heap. "Oh my god," I gasped, "they are gone!" The solitary, broken and burned *castaña* leans like a skeleton hung up as a warning to who might dare to hope. Not only were the roost trees gone, but so were the few remaining food trees. The creek bottoms had been cemented in, making the whole area look like an industrial agri-cemetary.

We drive around, a little nervous because of recent murders on Tecanal, but we must document the devastation by making videos to spread the word. One the way out I ask the manager of the *finca* why the trees had been felled, and he said they needed room to put in irrigation equipment and that there weren't any parrots left anyway. On the way back to Escuintla I wonder about the logic of the manager, or his overseers, and of perhaps a large swath of humanity; If it's all gone to crap anyway, why worry about making it even worse, let alone, fixing it? What good would it do, even if one could stand to be in the thick of such ugliness and monetarily directed values? I had left this area over 20 years earlier, seeing wonder and beauty slipping away. I had gone to where life might be easier, but not more meaningful.

Lost in Escuintla trying to find our hotel in the dark, I think of the film *Virunga* which has a song with this refrain, "We will not go." The movie is about the park guards in the Congo protecting the mountain gorillas. Over 150 guards have been killed in the history of the park, yet it's still there. Corruption, powerful international corporate interests, war, and poverty bring violence into the heart of the park, but still the conservationists will not go. The park is one of the most stable institutions in the Congo, but it has come at a cost. One tag line for the movie is, "Conservation is War." During the film, the director interviews several guards and this is what two of them say:

"You must justify why you are here on this earth. Gorillas justify why I am here. They are my life. So if it is about dying, I will die for the gorillas." – Andre

"I have accepted to give the best of myself so that wildlife can be safeguarded. Beyond all pressure. Beyond all spirit of greediness about money. Beyond all things. All that could happen to me I will accept. I am not special." – Katembo

Their words are mine, parrots justify my life, and they and their world are beyond all things. I am not special. I am simply one of many conservationists who will fail to make a difference in most places. But in other places, love shines and reveals the scars that bind us together in life, and for one moment, bright hope scatters ashes and uncovers deeper and deeper truths that each of us as individuals can only dimly see, let alone document and explain. Together though we can nurture one another to hold the mystery and contradictions in life, and in that journey, become different ourselves. As we change, so might too the future. The change may only last one breath, or reach to only the next relationship, individual parrot saved, or community cheered. Time tells a better story than what we know. All we can do is love and open ourselves to the future, whatever it may bring.

My first years working in the Maya biosphere seemed desperate, as Roan McNab, Director of Wildlife Conservation Society in Guatemala told me about the threats against his life and the willful disregard of life by the *Guatemaltecos* and internationals around him. The story could have ended there, but he did not go. Now, after more than twenty years working in that country, he and others are taking the forest back. They have made significant gains in recovering land from invaders, stabilizing the area, and reducing the poaching of parrots. I asked him how he had come to stay throughout all those hard years and what his motivation was. He wrote back to me:

I believe it has to do with a combination of a number of things, including a strongly held collective belief that saving these areas is the right thing to do. But one interesting question is how do some of us get to that point, and why do others never get there (or perhaps never "leave that point behind"!)? Many of us have observed the beauty of nature, wildlife, and realized that it has intrinsic value—value beyond the utilitarian importance to humans which is often used to convince the world to conserve "for future generations." That beauty is part of an equilibrium that goes way beyond mundane anthropocentric arguments. It's something where each life, each animal soul, is recognized as having value—even if they can't add to a country's GDP or vote for a politician. We've seen animals in their element, not as an impediment to our element. Animals having fun. Animals in families. Animals teaching. Animals in pain. Animals bathing, and preening, and eating. And to the observer, all of that pushes towards an inevitable conclusion that animals are really no different than us, that is to say, that we too are animals.

There are also scars, etched indelibly on our grey matter, from seeing the results of areas abandoned by the guardians of nature. We have walked through ravaged parts of the landscape where deforestation and fire have wreaked havoc. We've discovered the twisted carcasses of deer unable to escape, turtles charred, and turkey eggs cooked by the advancing flames. We've found scarlet macaws shot dead and left at their nesting trees in an effort to intimidate. We've tasted the noxious smoke of a forest converted into ash, and felt the heat radiating from the earth during the fires—and after—as cool forests are replaced by sere pastures. And we've seen how greater and greater amounts of the land end up in the hands of wealthy ranchers, without providing any real relief to the landless poor. No doubt, there must be a more spiritual element behind all our folk do, the risks they take. Something far beyond their monthly salaries or their adventures in the field—because, after all, there is fun and excitement, energy and adrenaline in this calling. There too must be something of the unseen architecture that binds us all. An unseen hand; the unspoken word which simply is.

When I think of these words by the guards in the Congo and Roan in Guatemala, I don't see conservation as war, but as the practice of peace. Somehow, in each of us, we must find places where we can see the beauty and the tragedy that binds us. An existence that simply is. In that acceptance, we move past existing only to protect ourselves, but rejoice in connecting to all of life, no matter what it brings. We find a way to drop our solitary ego to love, cherish, and protect Earth. That peace within that comes with the death of the separate self, and with even tender welcoming of physical death, is connected to the peace without. Conservation may manifest, at times, as war around us, but it's the war within us that must shift from combat to embracing. In that fiery embrace of all that is, we forge not a sword or a gun, but communities of solidarity and hope that resist the systemic violence and oppression that is no longer acceptable. We take back, we give back, and from this path we will not go.

Acknowledgments

This story is possible because of the richness of the lives of the people and parrots of Latin America. You are too numerous to name, but know that you are in my heart forever, and I will give back all that I can, for you have given me much, and continue to do so.

I have special adoration for the conservationists, whose dedication continues to save me. There are so many of you, and yet, not enough. I am grateful to Roan for sharing his words describing what so many of us experience.

Many donors, foundations, and grants continue to make this work possible. You too are many, and you are deeply appreciated.

I give a huge thanks to Jane, author, editor, and playwright, who read, reread, edited, encouraged, advised, and adapted this memoir to a screen play. This book would not exist without you and your steady companionship and gracious gift of time and talent to this endeavor.

Thank you to Cynthia whose love of Spanish and Spanish speaking people brought life and accuracy to the bilingual conversations. Joyce, you journeyed to Guatemala those many years ago, and you continue to travel with me, and support this conservation work – thank you for powering out proofreading! Robin Weisz gave beauty to this work through the cover design, a gift from someone I hope to meet soon to thank in person.

Thank you Gail, my dearest partner in One Earth Conservation, who read, edited, designed, nurtured, and supported the production of this book. Because of you, I am nurtured and emboldened.

A deep bow of gratitude to Meredith, my beloved spouse, who read an earlier edition of this memoir while we were just beginning to know each other, and who stayed with me anyway. Your loyalty and deep abiding love is my foundation for the work I do.

To the others who read early editions of this, including Susan, and Dori, thank you for this and telling me that it was an important story to get out, and encouraging me to keep reworking it so others could share the journey.

To the readers who are just now sharing my journey, thank you for embarking on this path through the wilderness, fraught with tragedy, infused with beauty, and full of love and promise.

Further Insights, Inspiration, Information

www.oneearthconservation.org

"Conservation in Time of War" is a conversation and a community project. Accordingly we invite your comments, questions, suggestions, and edits for future publications and for the work of One Earth Conservation (info@oneearthconservation.org).

For discussion, sharing, and study, such as in a book club, we offer discussion and reflection questions to guide you: www.oneearthconservation.org/book-conservation-in-time-of-war.

This memoir is a story about how humans can be nurtured, and nurture, against all odds. If you desire to increase the amount of nurturing and naturing in the world, please share this book and following resources with others.

To find out more about LoraKim's projects in Latin America, visit this website blog for weekly updates: www.oneearthconservation.org/blog.

To learn more about the tools and practices that LoraKim uses to gain resilience for her work, visit her organization One Earth Conservation's Nurture Nature Program: www.oneearthconservation.org/nurture-nature.

To grow your own resilience, joy, empathy and power, visit the Nurture Nature Academy and enroll in one of the classes there: www.nurture-nature.thinkific.com/.

To build community and grow inspiration and motivation, consider joining or starting a Nurture Nature Community in your area: www.oneearthconservation.org/calendar.

To request a presentation or workshop by LoraKim, contact her at: info@oneearthconservation.org. To see where she is scheduled to speak, go here: www.onearthconservation.org.

To donate time or resources to support the people and parrots of Latin America, please visit our website: www.oneearthconservation.org. The world needs you to witness to and be in solidarity with these communities of life.

About the Author

Birds have always called to LoraKim. Since an early age she always had birds in the home, out in the pigeon coop, or eating at the yard feeder. Her hope for avian flourishing led her to a B.S. in Avian Sciences and then to a D.V.M. where she specialized in birds. A later Masters in Preventive Veterinary Medicine emphasized avian research. Hearing birds call to her heart, she worked in other countries as a consultant in avian medicine and conservation, with an emphasis on parrot conservation. Her hopes for the birds led her to the Philippines, Panama, Costa Rica, Mexico, Dominican Republic, Puerto Rico, and Guatemala where she lived for several years. Her work with birds has also included working as a Clinical Instructor and Research Assistant Professor at the Nondomestic Avian Clinic at the College of Veterinary Medicine, North Carolina State University. There she later served as the Community Advocate, where she taught ethics and grief management as well as assisted staff, faculty, and clients in dealing with grief and ethical issues. Seeing the need to address human well-being, LoraKim obtained a M.Div degree, was ordained a Unitarian Universalist minister, and became a Certified Trainer in Nonviolent Communication. She served in parish ministry for 10 years and now is a community minister emphasizing Multispecies Ministry and Nonviolent Communication. She celebrates with joy her position as Co-Director of One Earth Conservation, a nonprofit organization, where she can support birds and people around the world make life-giving connections. Her approach is that of "Nurturing Nature" where the inherent worth, dignity, and needs of all individuals are incorporated into conservation strategies, organizational processes, and workshops and retreats she regularly leads. Recently her conservation work has taken her to Belize, Guatemala, Nicaragua, Honduras, Guyana, and Paraguay.